D0936808

CLASS STRUCTURE AND
INCOME DETERMINATION

This is a volume in the

Institute for Research on Poverty Monograph Series

A complete list of titles in this series appears at the end of this volume.

CLASS STRUCTURE AND INCOME DETERMINATION

ERIK OLIN WRIGHT
Department of Sociology
Institute for Research on Poverty
University of Wisconsin—Madison

ACADEMIC PRESS
New York   London   Toronto   Sydney   San Francisco
A Subsidiary of Harcourt Brace Jovanovich, Publishers

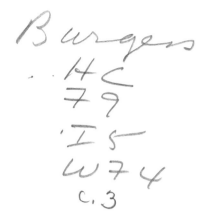

This book is one of a series sponsored by the Institute for Research on Poverty of the University of Wisconsin pursuant to the provisions of the Economic Opportunity Act of 1964.

Copyright © 1979 by the Board of Regents of the University of Wisconsin System behalf of the Institute for Research on Poverty
All Rights Reserved
No portion of this book may be reproduced in any form by print, microfilm, or any other means without permission from Academic Press

ACADEMIC PRESS, INC.
111 Fifth Avenue, New York, New York 10003

United Kingdom Edition published by
ACADEMIC PRESS, INC. (LONDON) LTD.
24/28 Oval Road, London NW1 7DX

Library of Congress Cataloging in Publication Data

Wright, Erik Olin.
    Class structure and income determination.

    (Institute for Research on Poverty monograph series)
    Bibliography: p.
    Includes index.
    1. Income distribution. 2. Social classes.
3. Marxian economics. I. Title. II. Series: Wis—
consin. University––Madison. Institute for Research
on Poverty. Institute for Research on Poverty monograph
series.
HC79.I5W74   301.44   79−9500
ISBN 0−12−764950−6

PRINTED IN THE UNITED STATES OF AMERICA

82   9 8 7 6 5 4 3 2

To my parents

871081318
8

125271139y

The Institute for Research on Poverty is a national center for research established at the University of Wisconsin in 1966 by a grant from the Office of Economic Opportunity. Its primary objective is to foster basic, multidisciplinary research into the nature and causes of poverty and means to combat it.

In addition to increasing the basic knowledge from which policies aimed at the elimination of poverty can be shaped, the Institute strives to carry analysis beyond the formulation and testing of fundamental generalizations to the development and assessment of relevant policy alternatives.

The Institute endeavors to bring together scholars of the highest caliber whose primary research efforts are focused on the problem of poverty, the distribution of income, and the analysis and evaluation of social policy, offering staff members wide opportunity for interchange of ideas, maximum freedom for research into basic questions about poverty and social policy, and dissemination of their findings.

Contents

I   THEORETICAL PERSPECTIVE

1   What Is Class?   3

Appendix C   Statistical Procedures   **255**

List of Tables

List of Figures

Foreword

Staff members of the Institute for Research on Poverty have contributed a great deal to our understanding of inequality in the United States. For example, in *Public Expenditures, Taxes, and the Distribution of Income: The United States, 1950, 1961, 1970* (Academic Press, 1977) Morgan Reynolds and Eugene Smolensky trace the post-World War II trend in inequality. Similarly, David L. Featherman and Robert M. Hauser in *Opportunity and Change* (Academic Press, 1978) dissect the intergenerational transmission of inequality in the U.S. and how that has changed in our time. Erik Olin Wright's *Class Structure and Income Determination* is a part of this growing body of research. But there is a difference: Wright is the first scholar at the Institute to approach this topic from a Marxist perspective. As a consequence, his book is likely to be even more controversial than others on the ever-controversial topic of inequality.

Whereas most sociologists and economists who have studied inequality emphasize occupation and education, respectively, Marxist theory leads Wright to emphasize class. Furthermore, since class is defined in terms of positions within the social relations of production, Wright focuses on the way in which different kinds of jobs—particularly whether the job entails being supervised, supervising someone else, or working as one's own boss—affect individual economic outcomes. Calling attention to, and then demonstrating, the significance of jobs in determining income is one of the important contributions of this work.

Perhaps the book's most important contribution, however, is that it attempts for the first time to test Marxist theory empirically, with modern econometric techniques. As Wright notes in his acknowledgments, few Marxist social scientists have the statistical training and skills to undertake such a task. But Wright does. He finds, for example, that even a crude measure of class explains at least as much of the variance in income as the more elaborate Duncan occupational status scale. Similarly, he finds that when class position is held constant, the commonly reported differential returns to education between blacks and whites and between men and women virtually disappear.

No doubt these and other findings in the book will stimulate criticism and new research. Wright is already pursuing the research, because the empirical data used for this study were not ideally suited to his purpose. Currently he is engaged in a major new data collection and analysis project funded by the National Science Foundation. The data will be gathered in four countries (the United States, Italy, Sweden, and Great Britain), thereby making possible a comparative approach. This book, therefore, may be viewed as the opening shot in the lively intellectual battle that it is likely to stimulate.

Irwin Garfinkel
Director, Institute for
Research on Poverty

Preface

This study began as an attempt to demonstrate to non-Marxist social scientists that Marxist categories mattered, that class was consequential for understanding American society. In many ways, the quantitative investigation of income inequality is an ideal empirical problem for this purpose. Quantitative studies of the causes and consequences of inequality have almost totally ignored Marxist categories, even though social inequality probably plays a more central role in the Marxist perspective than in any other theoretical tradition in social science. Marxists have been suspicious of quantitative, multivariate approaches to the study of social reality, and the practitioners of multivariate statistics have generally dismissed Marxist theory as offering little of interest for empirical research. The result has been that class, defined in terms of common positions within the social relations of production, has never been systematically included in quantitative research on income inequality.

The present research is a first step in bridging this gap between the Marxist theoretical perspective and the growing body of quantitative studies of social inequality. As such, it will, I hope, have something to say to both Marxist and non-Marxist social scientists. For Marxists, the research represents a theoretical and empirical investigation of the link between social relations of production and social relations of exchange in advanced capitalist society. Of particular importance is the analysis of various "intermediary" positions within the social relations of production, and the relationship of such positions to income inequality. For non-Marxists, the research demonstrates that class position has a significant and consistent impact on income. Thus, even if the overall Marxist framework is not adopted, any thorough empirical investigation of income inequality must still include position within social relations of production as an independent variable in the analysis.

The basic theme of this study is that *class, defined as positions within the social relations of production, plays a central role in mediating income inequality in capitalist society*. This does not mean that class by itself is sufficient to explain all income variation. Indeed, much income inequality occurs within class positions. Rather, the argument is that class organizes the structure of income inequality, in the sense that class position shapes other causes of income. The heart of the empirical investigation will therefore be an analysis of the interactions between class position and various other causes of income, in particular education.

Before we can explore such interactions, however, it is necessary to have a more precise understanding of what "class" really means. Chapter 1 will briefly discuss the range of meanings attached to the concept of class in the social science literature. The purpose of this chapter is less to provide a comprehensive analysis and critique of alternative perspectives than to highlight the distinctive character of the Marxist conception of class.

Chapter 2 will then attempt to develop a coherent set of criteria for class position within advanced capitalist societies. The heart of the chapter is a fairly detailed discussion of capitalist social relations of production and how these have been transformed in the course of capitalist development. This analysis forms the basis for a rigorous definition of classes, particularly of those social categories that are often loosely described as "middle classes." Although most of this chapter does not directly touch on the problem of income determination as such, it provides the general conceptual framework for the analysis of income in subsequent chapters.

Once this groundwork is laid, we will turn in chapter 3 to a specific comparison of the logic of analyzing income determination within Marxist and non-Marxist frameworks. The central purpose of this chapter is to make it as clear as possible precisely how Marxists pose the problem of income determination and how this strategy of analysis differs from both conventional sociological and economics approaches. I hope this chapter will make the empirical analyses that follow more accessible to readers relatively unfamiliar with the logic of Marxist theory.

Chapter 4 will then use the general analysis of class structure in chapter 2 and the approach to analyzing income inequality presented in chapter 3 in order to develop a series of concrete, testable hypotheses about the relationship between class and income determination. The general strategy will be to show how positions within the social relations of production influence the ways in which factors such as education are likely to affect income. This general analysis will then be extended to form a series of hypotheses about the interrelationship between class and race and class and sex in the income determination process.

Chapter 4 will be followed by five empirical chapters. Chapter 5 presents a direct comparison between class position and occupational status as predictors of income. The basic conclusion is that a very simple operationalization of Marxist class categories is at least as powerful a variable in predicting income variation as is the elaborate Duncan occupational status scale. Chapter 6 explores the basic class interactions with the income determination process. It is found that the returns to education vary considerably between classes and that these interactions cannot be considered "artifacts" of the characteristics of the individuals occupying class positions. Chapter 7 then looks in detail at the relationship between specific positions within managerial hierarchies and income. Much of the general interpretation of the link between class relations and income inequality developed in chapter 4 revolves around an analysis of the logic of hierarchy within the capitalist production process. The analysis in chapter 7 allows for a partial direct test of this interpretation.

Finally, chapters 8 and 9 apply the general categories developed in earlier chapters to an analysis of race and sex effects on income. If class really does play a fundamental mediating role in the structure of income inequality, then it would be expected that class position would be important for understanding income inequality between races and sexes. One of the most significant findings in the study is that the differential returns to education between blacks and whites and between men and women, which have been found in virtually every study of race and sex effects on income, disappear almost entirely when class position is held constant.

This empirical investigation will not "prove" that the overall Marxist theory of capitalist society is correct. But it does demonstrate that class has a systematic and pervasive impact on income inequality. We trust the book will show that to ignore social relations of production in stratification research is thus to ignore one of the fundamental dimensions of social inequality in capitalist society.

Acknowledgments

Acknowledgments usually end with a caveat: Although the author is deeply indebted to friends and colleagues for valuable suggestions and criticisms, all of the errors in the work are his or her own responsibility. If the production of knowledge is a genuinely social process, then both the strengths and weaknesses of a work must be understood as being influenced by its collective setting. This book should be evaluated in such terms. Just as the new insights and findings cannot be seen simply as the fruits of my own reflection, so the limitations of the study should not be seen simply as a failure of my own imagination. This work is the product of an historically specific intersection of academic sociology and Marxism; its strengths, and its weaknesses, reflect that setting.

More concretely, the strengths have grown out of a period of intense debate over fundamental questions of Marxist theory. The various

ideas in this study have been subjected to many rounds of criticism in
various study groups, seminars, and conferences, and at the end of such
a process it is impossible to identify those ideas that are my own and
those that grew out of the discussions themselves. The weaknesses of
the study, on the other hand, reflect the relative underdevelopment of
quantitative research and sophistication among Marxists. This has
hampered the quality of the response that I have received on the more
empirical parts of the work from people committed to its theoretical
framework. Many Marxists still regard quantitative research as intrinsically "undialectical" and thus an inappropriate strategy for advancing
Marxist social science, and those Marxists who are more sympathetic to
the endeavor generally lack the statistical skills to get inside the empirical argument. This study would undoubtedly have been better if its
empirical strategies, and the links between the theory and the data, had
been subjected to discussions as intense as was the theoretical
framework itself.

The original research in this study was conducted for my doctoral
dissertation in the Sociology Department at the University of California, Berkeley. From the start, Arthur Stinchcombe was especially supportive of my work, and more than anyone else has taught me how to
link quantitative methods to theoretical substance. His insistence that
"what is interesting about Marxist theory is whether or not it is true"
has constantly pushed me to clarify the connections between the
theoretical argument and the statistical investigation. Barbara Heyns's
good-natured skepticism about the importance of social relations of
production and exploitation in understanding income inequality has
forced me to make explicit many of the assumptions underlying the
analysis. Michael Reich's comments and criticisms have also been extremely valuable. More than anyone else, he has pushed me to elaborate
the political implications of the research and avoid getting bogged
down in purely scholastic issues. And Tom Rothenberg's endless
capacity to solve econometric problems encountered at each stage of
the research and to explain the solutions in ways I could understand
facilitated the technical part of the research immensely.

Many of the core ideas in the study, especially those in chapters 2
and 4, were formed through my participation in the editorial collective
of the journal *Kapitalistate* between 1973 and 1976. I would also like to
thank the many people who have given me written comments on various papers that served as the basis for several of the chapters in this
study: Marcia Kahn Wright, Ron Aminzade, Sam Bowles, Wini Breines,
Michael Burawoy, Roger Friedland, David Gold, Alex Hicks, Bob
Jackson, Robert Kahn, Rebecca Kharkov, Andrew Levine, Ruth

Milkman, Jim O'Connor, Claus Offe, Nicos Poulantzas, Aage Sørenson, Ann Steuve, Al Szymanski, Maurice Zeitlin, and Rob Mayer.

All of the data in this study were gathered by the Institute for Social Research at the University of Michigan. Without the cooperation of the Institute it would have been impossible to conduct this empirical investigation of class relations and income inequality. In particular, I am especially grateful to Arnie Tannenbaum for letting me use the Hierarchy in Organizations Study data, and to James N. Morgan, project director of the Panel Study of Income Dynamics, for his interest in the problem of authority relations on the job and his willingness to include a number of questions that tapped class position on the 1975 panel of the study. I would also like to thank Greg Duncan, Robert Quinn, Linda Shepherd, and Graham Staines for their assistance at various stages of the research.

Parents are always part of their children's accomplishments. But I feel that I owe both of my parents an especially deep debt for encouraging my intellectual development for three decades and giving me the self-confidence necessary to make my own way and discover my own truths. In particular, I am grateful for whatever it was they did that made me enjoy writing.

Finally, I would like to express my gratitude to a former fellow graduate student, Luca Perrone. During our first three years in graduate school, we coauthored most of the papers we wrote. This book is the direct descendant of one of those efforts (Wright and Perrone, 1975). At one point, we fantasized writing a joint dissertation, each of us submitting the same document for his doctorate degree. In the end, however, we were spared the trauma of trying to convince the university to accept a joint thesis, since Luca returned to Italy to teach sociology at the University of Calabria. Nevertheless, the basic strategy of the analysis and the core ideas of this study come equally from both of us. In order to be embodied more immediately in the final product, Luca has sent me the graphic illustration on page xxv of the fundamental conclusions of the research. Although this drawing may seem somewhat cryptic at this point, I hope that by the end of the study its meaning will be apparent.

I

THEORETICAL PERSPECTIVE

1

What Is Class?

Sociology has only one independent variable, class.

—ARTHUR STINCHCOMBE, 1973

Sociology's one independent variable is a chameleon which blends into virtually every sociological tradition. To some sociologists, *class* refers to categories of people occupying common positions within status hierarchies (Warner, 1949; Parsons, 1970; Williams, 1960). To others, classes are defined as conflict groups determined by their position within authority or power structures (Dahrendorf, 1959; Lenski, 1966). Sociologists within the Weberian tradition see classes as groups of people with common economic "life chances" (Weber, 1922; Giddens, 1973; Parkin, 1971). And Marxists have defined classes primarily in terms of common structural positions within the social organization of production (Bukharin, 1921; Lenin, 1914).

As Stanislaw Ossowski (1963) has emphasized, these diverse interpretations of class do not simply reflect differing claims about the causes and consequences of a particular phenomenon; they also represent different claims about the way inequality should be conceptualized in the first place. The concept of class is not simply a contested concept; it is an essentially confused concept (see Plant, 1978). The debate is over the very object of investigation—what the concept of class denotes—and not simply over the formal definition of an agreed-upon subject.

This chapter will try to sort out the salient theoretical underpinnings of these differences in the definition of class. The purpose of the chapter is less to adjudicate between the competing definitions than it is to clarify rigorously the distinctiveness of the Marxist definition of class. The validation of such a Marxist concept of class must come through a demonstration of its capacity to reveal the underlying dynamics of social processes (i.e., to explain the world), and not simply through a conceptual argument. The empirical investigation of income inequality in the second half of this book will attempt to accomplish such a demonstration. For the moment, the task is simply to specify the difference between the meaning of *class* within Marxist theory and the various meanings adopted in other traditions of social science.

At the risk of some oversimplification, the diverse definitions of *class* can be analyzed in terms of three nested theoretical dimensions: (1) Whether class is fundamentally understood in gradational or in relational terms; (2) if class is understood in relational terms, whether the pivotal aspect of class relations is seen as located in the market or in production; (3) if class relations are primarily located within production, whether production is analyzed above all in terms of the technical division of labor, authority relations, or exploitation.[1] These three theoretical dimensions generate five basic types of definitions of class, as illustrated in Figure 1.1.

---

[1]There are other reasonable ways to categorize definitions of class. Various sociologists have stressed the contrast between unidimensional and multidimensional perspectives on class and stratification (e.g., Lipset, 1968, p. 310), the distinction between realist and nominalist conceptions (e.g., Lenski, 1966, p. 23), the distinction between continuous and discontinuous gradations (e.g., Landecker, 1960), the distinction between classes defined at the superstructural level in terms of political or ideological relations or at the economic level (Wright, 1976a), or the distinction between structural, historicist, and economistic conceptions of class (Poulantzas, 1973b, pp. 58–70). I have chosen to focus on these three dimensions because I believe that they are substantively the most important for grasping the relationship of Marxist understanding of class to non-Marxist approaches.

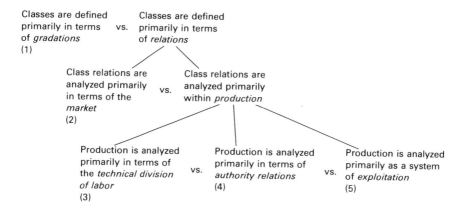

Figure 1.1. A typology of definitions of class.

GRADATIONAL VERSUS RELATIONAL THEORIES OF CLASS

The distinction between gradational and relational views of class is a familiar one in sociology. Using slightly different terms, Ossowski (1963) emphasized this distinction in his important study of conceptions of class structure. Theories of class, Ossowski argued, could be divided into those based on "ordering relations" (gradational views of class) and those based on "relations of dependence" (relational views). In the first interpretation, "the class division is conceived as a division into groups differentiated according to the degree in which they possess the characteristic which constitutes the criterion of division, as for instance income-level [p. 145]." In the second interpretation, on the other hand: "social classes form a system according to their one-sided or mutual dependence, dependence being understood in both cases as a dependence based on causal relations [p. 146]."

The hallmark of the gradational view is that classes are always characterized as being "above" or "below" other classes. The very names given to different classes reflect this quantitative, spatial image: upper class, upper middle class, middle class, lower middle class, lower class, and so forth. While there may be debates about the extent to which these divisions are purely conventional or real (the famous problem of continuous versus discontinuous gradations within systems of stratification), the basic conceptualization of classes remains the same: classes, in Barber's (1957) words, are "divisional units within systems of social stratification [p. 73]."

Within contemporary sociology, there have been two basic versions of gradational conceptions of class; one defines class gradations primarily in terms of income, the other primarily in terms of social status. The former is undoubtedly the most common popular definition of class: poor people constitute a lower class; middle-income people constitute the middle class; and rich people constitute the upper class. Mayer and Buckley (1970) essentially adopt this view when they write: "In a class system, the social hierarchy is based primarily on differences in monetary wealth and income [p. 15]." Within such a conception, the shape of the class structure becomes virtually identical to the shape of the income distribution. The frequent claims that the United States is becoming a more or less homogeneous middle-class society moving from a "pyramid-shaped" to a "diamond-shaped" class structure usually adopt, at least implicitly, such a conception of class.

Most sociologists, even those working firmly with a gradational image of class, do not reduce the class structure to income differences. The most common gradational conception is that class distinctions reflect common positions within a status hierarchy. As Parsons (1970) writes, classes should be defined as "an aggregate of such units, individual and/or collective, that in their own estimation and those of others in the society occupy positions of approximately equal status [p. 24]." In somewhat simpler language, Williams (1960) also defines classes in status terms:

> The distribution of privileges ... begins to take on full sociological meaning only when it is related to *prestige rankings, social-interaction groupings* and *beliefs and values held in common.* We shall use the term "social class" to refer to an aggregate of individuals who occupy a broadly similar position in the scale of prestige. [p. 98]

In contrast to these gradational notions of class, relational conceptions define classes by their structured social relationship to other classes. Classes are not defined simply *relative* to other classes, but in a social *relation* to other classes. While classes may differ empirically along a variety of quantitative dimensions, the criteria for class are based on qualitative differences. Again, as in the gradational perspective, the very names of classes within relational views of class reflect this underlying definition. Classes are not labeled along a continuum from lower to upper; instead, they have names such as: capitalist class, working class; lord, serf; ruling class, subordinate class. In a gradational view of classes, lower classes are simply defined as having less of something that upper classes have more of—income, wealth, education, status—but within a relational view, the working class is defined by its qualitative location within a social relation that simultaneously defines the capitalist class. Within Weberian theory, for example, workers are understood as sellers of labor power, capitalists as buyers of labor power. The issue is not that workers have less of something than capitalists, but rather that they occupy a specific qualitative position within a social relationship which defines both the capitalist and the worker: the social relation of exchange on the labor market.

It could be argued that, at least implicitly, there is within gradational views of inequality a notion of social relations. After all, to argue that someone has "more" social status than someone else requires that both people agree on the relative rankings of status positions, and this implies that the two people exist within a social relation: the person in the lower status acknowledges the person in the higher status as having greater status, and vice versa. Even for a dimension of inequality as seemingly gradational as income, it can be argued that a person's income is lower only in relation to someone else's higher income; thus there is an implicit relational aspect of inequality within income gradations.

All concepts of inequality must, by definition, capture some aspect of relative position. The key issue is whether the operative criteria for class are based on the qualitative social relations which define such relative positions, or on the quantitative dimensions which are generated by such positions. Gradational perspectives all organize their definitions of class around these quantitative dimensions; relational views, in contrast, all attempt directly to map the social relations themselves.

At one level, it appears that the debate between relational and gradational conceptions of class is a purely semantic one, a disagreement about how the word *class* should be used. At a deeper level, however, as in many apparently semantic debates within social science, the disagreement over the use of a term reflects a more fundamental disagreement over how to study the world. Relational conceptions of class all insist, in one way or another, that the basic structures of inequality in a society are also structures of interests and thus the basis for collective social action. Social relations do not simply *define* classes, they also *determine* classes; classes as social forces are real consequences of social relations.

A class structure defined in gradational terms remains fundamentally a static taxonomy. Such definitions may provide a basis for descriptively labeling people in terms of the distribution of valued rewards, but they are incapable of designating the dynamic social forces which determine and transform that distribution. To give just one simple example, it is hard to see how the French Revolution could be explained in terms of gradational schemes of class. While it might be the case that most of the participants in the storming of the Bastille had status scores of under 40, and most of the French aristocracy had scores above 70, such labels do not capture the underlying dynamics at work in the revolutionary process. The decisive actors in the revolution were people defined by their position within qualitative relations (nobles, peasants, merchant capitalists, professionals, petty bourgeois, and sansculottes) not by their location on a simple, quantitative dimension.

All relational views of class, regardless how they conceive of those relations, see class structures as the potential basis for collective class struggle, class activity. Marx's distinction between a class-in-itself and a class-for-itself, Dahrendorf's definition of classes as conflict groups determined by authority relations, and Weber's conception of classes as the potential bases of communal action all attempt to link the analysis of class structure to a dynamic theory of class struggle. Gradational definitions of class are wholly inadequate to this task.

Knowing that a theory of class is based on a relational understanding of inequality, however, is only the starting point. A wide variety of social relations have laid claim to constituting the relational basis for classes: authority relations, occupational relations, market relations, social relations of production. It is, therefore, necessary to make theoretical distinctions among relational conceptions of class.

CLASSES DEFINED BY MARKET RELATIONS
VERSUS PRODUCTION RELATIONS

In the theoretical debates over relational definitions of class, two spheres of social relations have vied for the role of constituting the foundation of the class structure: market relations and production relations. In the most general terms, market relations are defined by the relations of exchange between the sellers and buyers of various kinds of commodities. Production relations comprise the relations between actors within the production process itself.

The classic formulation of the market conception of class appears in a chapter in Weber's *Economy and Society* (1922) entitled, "The Distribution of Power in the Community: Class, Status and Party." Weber writes:

> In our terminology, "classes" are not communities; they merely represent possible, and frequent, bases for communal action. We may speak of a "class"

when (1) a number of people have in common a specific causal component of their life chances, in so far as (2) this component is represented exclusively by economic interests in the possession of goods and opportunities for income, and (3) is represented under the conditions of the commodity or labor markets. . . .

But always this is the generic connotation of the concept of class; that the kind of chance in the *market* is the decisive moment which presents a common condition for the individual's fate. "Class situation" is, in this sense, ultimately "market situation." [1968 ed., pp. 927–28]

One of the implications of this definition of class is that classes exist only in capitalist societies, that is, only in societies in which there is a genuine market for labor power and capital. While there may be conflict groups in other societies, they cannot, within Weber's formulation, be properly viewed as classes, since the structural basis of their life chances is not ultimately rooted in a market situation.

Weber's basic notion that classes are defined by capitalist exchange relations has been extended by recent theorists in a number of ways. Wiley (1967), for example, has argued that classes in American society are determined by three different, intersecting markets: the market for labor, the market for credit, and the market for commodities. These three markets define six classes: employers (capitalists) and workers, creditors and debtors, and sellers and consumers. The more these three dimensions of class (exchange relations) overlap, Wiley argues, the more intense class conflict is likely to be.

Giddens (1973) emphasizes Weber's argument that "market capacity" is defined not simply by the possession of capital or labor power, but also by the possession of market-relevant skills (see also Parkin, 1971, pp. 18–23).[2] Giddens defines market capacity as "all forms of relevant attributes which individuals may bring to the bargaining encounter [in the market; p. 103]." He then discusses the specific capacities which shape classes in capitalist society:

There are three sorts of market capacity which can be said to be normally of importance [in structuring classes]: ownership of property in the means of

---

[2]When market capacity is extended explicitly to include skills, then the market definitions of class may closely coincide with definitions based on occupational categories, since skill level is one of the basic ways in which occupations are differentiated within the technical division of labor. Frequently, in fact, when sociologists equate blue-collar workers with the working class and white-collar workers with the middle class, they are thinking of occupations in terms of market capacities more than technical conditions per se. Unfortunately, very few discussions of occupation and class attempt to provide a coherent theoretical rationale for the linkage of occupations to class categories, and thus it is often impossible to know exactly what substantive criteria underlie the analysis. For a sustained discussion of class and occupation, see Mok (1978) and Wright (1978b).

production; possession of educational or technical qualifications; and possession of manual labor power. In so far as it is the case that these tend to be tied
to closed patterns of inter- and intragenerational mobility, this yields the
foundation of a *basic three-class system* in capitalist society: an 'upper',
'middle', and 'lower' or 'working' class. [p. 107]

Giddens then extends Weber's analysis by trying to link the concept of classes defined by market capacities to an analysis of social
relations within the production process itself. In particular, he elabo-
rates a number of social processes which he labels as sources of "proximate structuration" of class relationships. Two of these directly tap
aspects of relations of production: the division of labor within the enterprise and the authority relationships within the enterprise. Giddens
argues that in capitalist society such "proximate structuration" over-
laps with the patterns of market capacities and thus tends to reinforce
class divisions defined by market relations.

However, in spite of this reformulation of Weber's conception of
class, Giddens still sees the capitalist social organization of economic
relations as fundamentally defined by exchange relations, and thus,
like Weber, he sees classes as still fundamentally determined at the
level of the market. As a result, class struggles are seen primarily as
market struggles. Weber stresses that the distinctive class struggle
within capitalist society is "wage disputes on the labor market [1968
ed., p. 131]" and Giddens emphasizes that "of predominant importance
in sociological terms are the types of overt conflict which are linked to
oppositions of interest entailed by differing forms of market capacity
[1973, p. 135]." Struggles within the production process might reinforce such market-based conflicts, but the prime arena of class conflict
is clearly outside of production itself.

In contrast to Weberian conceptions of class as market relations, a
number of different theoretical traditions have argued that the heart of a
class analysis must be located within the sphere of production. Although, as we will see below, there is little agreement among such
perspectives about how production itself should be theorized, in all
cases there is a recognition that the relational basis of social conflict,
and thus of classes, should be sought in the structure of production
rather than simply in the structure of exchange. In one way or another,
each of these production-level theories argues that the location within
production defines decisively the command over social resources and
social action.

Within such theories, market relations may still be of theoretical
interest, but that interest is derived from the relationship of markets to
production. Generally speaking, this relationship is conceived in two

ways. First, market relations are seen as important in helping us to understand how actual individuals are sorted into the production positions themselves. Although classes are defined in terms of the structure of positions in production, it is recognized that the structure of the sorting process may influence the ways in which classes become organized collectively. Secondly, markets are seen as one of the important arenas within which classes engage in struggles. Workers are, as Weber emphasized, sellers of a particular kind of commodity, labor power, and since capitalists attempt to buy that commodity for as little as possible, conflicts over wages become an intrinsic feature of capitalism. To say that conflicts take place within the market is not to say, however, that the actors in that struggle are fundamentally defined by market relations per se. In different ways, each of the production-level accounts of the class structure argues that such conflicts are themselves ultimately shaped by the structure of class relations within production.

CLASSES DEFINED BY THE TECHNICAL DIVISION OF LABOR VERSUS AUTHORITY RELATIONS VERSUS EXPLOITATION

In order to put real content on the claim that classes should be defined within production rather than within the market, it is necessary to understand what it is about the organization of production that forms the basis for the determination of class. Three different ways of understanding the structure of production relations have dominated the analysis of classes within production: production is defined primarily as a system of technical divisions of labor; production is analyzed above all as a system of authority relations; and, production, insofar as it determines classes, is seen fundamentally as a system of exploitation. Let us look at each of these in turn.

Classes and the Technical Division of Labor

Perhaps the most common of all definitions of class among sociologists is that based on categories of occupations: blue-collar occupations define the working class; white-collar occupations the middle class; and professional and managerial occupations the upper middle or upper classes (or sometimes even the "professional class"). The precise theoretical status of this occupational typology of classes is generally not very clear. Sometimes occupations are basically viewed as status categories; in that case this conception should rightfully be seen as one variant of the gradational view of class. This is particularly true when occupation is scaled as an occupational status or prestige variable and then treated as a measure of class (or class background). In other situations, occupation is treated as a proxy for market capacity, and thus forms part of the definition of classes in terms of exchange relations (see below). But at least among some theorists, occupational categories are seen as defining classes by virtue of their location within the technical division of labor (or technical relations of production). Since, it is argued, in modern industrial society the technical relations of production determine the conditions of work, the command over resources, and the relative power and status of different positions in the social structure, and since occupations represent similar locations within the technical division of labor, occupations should be considered the structural basis for classes.

Probably the most important contemporary version of this conceptualization of class can be found in certain theories of "postindustrialism." Bell (1973), among others, has argued that in advanced stages of industrial development, experts of various sorts—scientists, engineers, certain categories of technicians—are gradually emerging as a new dominant class. Their position within the technical relations of production gives them a monopoly of scientific knowledge, which, Bell argues, enables them to control the key institutions of the postindustrial society. In a deliberately exaggerated manner, Bell describes the class structure of postindustrial societies as follows:

> In the Scientific City of the future there are already foreshadowed three classes: the creative elite of scientists and the top professional administrator...; the middle class of engineers and the professorate; and the proletariat of technicians, junior faculty and teaching assistants. [pp. 213–14]

Touraine's (1971) analysis of technocracy follows a similar logic, although Touraine tends to be somewhat closer to Ralf Dahrendorf in emphasizing the role of bureaucratic authority in the definition of class. In any event, for both Touraine and Bell, the role of experts and technocrats within the technical division of labor becomes the basis for defining them as a class in postindustrial society.

There are relatively few sustained theoretical reflections on the logic of linking class to positions within the technical division of labor. Perhaps the most influential theoretical rationale for this conception is found in the classic functionalist account of stratification by Davis and Moore (1945), although the authors do not systematically discuss class as such. Davis and Moore attempt to understand the structural basis for distributive inequality in terms of the "functional importance" of positions within the technical division of labor. The logic is that unequal rewards are needed to induce people to fill the functionally most important positions, and that the functional importance of positions is derived from the technical imperatives of production systems. With minimal extension, this can become an argument that the class structure is ultimately based on the functional imperatives of the technical organization of production.

Classes and Authority Relations

In authority definitions of class, the social content of class relations returns to the center of the stage. Classes are understood as based directly on a system of relations of domination and subordination, and while those relations may be shaped significantly by technical constraints, the classes themselves cannot be defined in terms of the technical division of labor.

More than any other sociologist, Dahrendorf (1959) has championed the conceptualization of class in terms of authority relations: "classes are social conflict groups the determinant (or *differentia specifica*) of which can be found in the participation in or exclusion from the exercise of authority within any imperatively coordinated association [p. 138]." Within such imperatively coordinated associations there are always two basic classes—command classes and obey classes. Since in the society at large people generally belong to more than one such association, it is likely that many people will occupy command positions in some associations and obey positions in others. The overall societal class structure, therefore, is likely to be a complex web of cross-cutting class cleavages based on intersecting structures of authority relations in different organizational settings.

Lenski adopts a similar position to Dahrendorf, although he tends to pursue a more eclectic usage of "class," including a variety of other dimensions besides authority. Lenski (1966) first defines class broadly as "an aggregation of persons in a society who stand in a similar position with respect to some form of power, privilege, or prestige [p. 75]." He then goes on to say that "if our goal is to answer the question 'who gets what and why?' ... *power* classes must be our chief concern," where *power class* is defined as "an aggregation of persons in a society who stand in a similar position with respect to force or some specific form of institutionalized power."

Several general characteristics of authority definitions of class are worth noting. First, authority definitions of class tend to treat all organizations as conceptually equivalent. Dahrendorf in particular sees classes as being defined by authority relations in *any* imperatively coordinated association, and provides no criteria for ordering those associations into those which are central to a class structure and those which are peripheral.[3]

Secondly, authority definitions of class tend to see authority itself as a unidimensional relation of domination/subordination within a given organization. No systematic theoretical distinctions are made concerning the object of authority. What matters is having authority or power; little is said about how it is used. Conceptions of class in terms of authority relations thus tend to emphasize the form of class relations over the content of those relations.

Finally, because of this formal character of the conception of class, authority definitions generally do not provide a sustained account of *why* social conflict should be structured around authority relations. Implicitly, one of two arguments is usually made. Either it is assumed that human beings somehow have an intrinsic drive for power for its own sake, and thus the division between the powerful and the power-less intrinsically constitutes the basis for social cleavage; or it is argued that power and authority enable the powerful to appropriate various kinds of resources, and that as a result the powerless will attempt to gain power for instrumental reasons. The evidence for the first of these assumptions is particularly weak. People may have an intrinsic drive to control their own lives, but there is little evidence that most people have a basic need or drive to control other people's lives. In any event, empirically most struggles over power are struggles over the use of power, not simply the fact of power. The second assumption is thus more plausible. But in order for it to provide a sound basis for an explanation of the relationship of authority to social conflict, it is necessary to develop a systematic theory of the relationship between authority and the appropriation of resources. Most discussions of authority lack such an account. This is precisely what the theory of exploitation is meant to accomplish.

Class and Exploitation

The hallmark of Marxist discussions of class is the emphasis on the concept of exploitation. In later chapters we will discuss exploitation

---

[3]Because of this it is perhaps inaccurate to consider Dahrendorf's theory of class as strictly a variety of production-level conceptions, since he explicitly rejects the notion that classes can be viewed as simply economic categories. Nevertheless, since his analysis is so bound up with a specific way of understanding the social organization of production (i.e., as a system of authority relations) it is useful to discuss his work in comparison with other more narrowly production-based theories of class.

in much greater depth; here it is sufficient to define it in very general terms. Exploitation within Marxist theory denotes a relation of domination within which the people in the dominant position are able to appropriate the surplus labor of people within the subordinate position. Such labor is generally appropriated in the form of products produced by that labor, and thus in many instances the expression "surplus product" is used as an equivalent to "surplus labor." Surplus labor or surplus product, in this context, refer to labor above and beyond that which is required simply to reproduce the individuals who perform that labor.[4]

Why is the capacity to appropriate surplus labor of such significance that it can be considered the core of the definition of class relations? Several reasons can be given. First, the capacity of a dominant class to control the surplus makes it possible for members of that class to consume without producing (or at least to consume far in excess of anything that they produce). The control over the surplus product, as we shall see in later discussions, is thus one critical basis for the distribution of income across classes. Secondly, the control over the surplus product gives the dominant class substantial social and political power beyond purely economic concerns, both because it provides material resources for political activity and because it shapes the economic framework within which social practices take place. Ultimately this implies that control over the social surplus product gives the dominant class the capacity to shape the direction of social change, social development. This is most obvious in the case of material development, since such development comes directly out of the use of the surplus (i.e., investments). But it is also true for political and cultural development, since the use of the social surplus directly and indirectly constrains their possible directions of development as well.

When class is understood in terms of relations of exploitation, the initial task of an analysis of class structure is to understand the social mechanisms by which surplus labor is appropriated. The Marxist theory of modes of production is designed to accomplish this task. Modes of production are differentiated fundamentally in terms of the central mechanisms through which dominant classes appropriate the surplus labor of subordinate classes. For example, in classical feudal societies this labor is appropriated through forced labor dues; in capitalist societies it is appropriated through the difference in the labor

---

[4]"Reproduction" in this context does not primarily refer to biological reproduction, but to the day-to-day reproduction of the capacity of individuals to work. This is usually referred to as the "reproduction of labor power" within Marxist discussions.

time embodied in the wages of workers and the labor time embodied in the products produced by workers. (The logic of this claim will be discussed more thoroughly in chapters 3 and 4.)[5]

Once such mechanisms of exploitation are adequately identified, then the analysis of class structure itself can begin. Lenin (1914) provides an extended definition of classes based on this conceptualization:

> Classes are large groups of people which differ from each other by the place they occupy in a historically determined system of social production, by their relation (in most cases fixed and formulated in law) to the means of production, by their role in the social organization of labour and, consequently, by the dimensions and method of acquiring the share of social wealth of which they dispose. Classes are groups of people one of which can appropriate the labour of another owing to the different places they occupy in a definite system of social economy. [1947 ed., p. 492]

The heart of an analysis of class structure, then, revolves around defining, for every class, the content of the "different places they occupy in a definite system of social economy."

Within such an account of class relations, a discussion of both the technical division of labor and the authority relations within production will also play a role. The technical division of labor enters the story since, as we will see in chapter 2, one of the critical aspects of the "places" within the system of social economy is their capacity or incapacity to control the technical organization of production. To say that workers do not "possess" their means of production in part at least means that they do not have the capacity to shape the basic contours of the technical division of labor itself.

Authority relations enter the account of class structures since within the capitalist mode of production the capacity to command labor (i.e., to tell workers what to do and be able to impose sanctions if they do not do it) is an essential requirement for being able to ensure that surplus labor is actually performed within production. A capitalist

---

[5]Because different class systems are seen as rooted in qualitatively different mechanisms of exploitation, Marxist theory cannot rest on a purely technological typology of macrohistorical development. Instead, history is understood as marked off by epochs stamped with different dominant modes of production. The names of different historical periods, therefore, are not such things as "agrarian society" or "industrial society," but feudalism, capitalism, socialism. In a sense, this distinction between typologies can be considered the macrostructural analogue to the gradational-relational conceptions of class structure. Typologies of society based on the technical organization of production can be viewed as gradational conceptions of whole societies; typologies based on modes of production, in contrast, reflect relational or qualitative views of the structure of societies.

may hire workers for eight hours, but unless the labor of those workers is controlled within the production process (i.e., unless they are subordinated within authority relations), there is no way of ensuring that they will perform anything near eight hours of actual labor.

Exploitation views of the class structure therefore incorporate both technical and authority definitions, but subordinate them to the dynamics of control over the surplus product. Classes, in these terms, are most pivotally defined by the relations of appropriation of the surplus product and secondarily defined by the relations of control over the technical division of labor and relations of authority.

This chapter has tried to establish the distinctive character of Marxist definitions of class. To recapitulate:

1. The Marxist concept of class defines classes in relational rather than gradational terms. Although classes do differ along various quantitative dimensions, the fundamental theoretical criteria for classes are based on an analysis of their qualitative location within social relations.

2. Within the Marxist concept of class, the central axis of class relations is located within the social organization of production rather than within the market.

3. Within the analysis of the social organization of production, Marxist theory roots the analysis of class relations in an examination of the process of exploitation rather than either the technical division of labor or authority relations (although both of these play a role in the theory as well).

Classes within Marxist theory, in short, are defined as *common positions within the social relations of production*, where production is analyzed above all as a system of exploitation.

As should be clear from the discussion of alternative definitions of class, the Marxist definition rests on a number of pivotal assumptions: in particular, that economic relations play a basic role in structuring (setting limits upon) other relations, and that within economic relations, the social relations of production structure both technical relations of production and social relations of exchange. If these assumptions are accepted, then the Marxist definition of class is very compelling; if they are not, then this definition has no privileged claim over other possible definitions.

There is, of course, no simple way of empirically "proving" these assumptions. While it is possible to establish their plausibility and to illustrate them by recourse to historical examples, it is hard to imagine a critical social or historical "experiment" which would directly validate them to a skeptic. These assumptions thus constitute paradigmatic premises, to use Kuhn's (1970) formulation, and as such they are not subject to immediate validation or refutation. Instead, they should be judged on the basis of the coherence and power of the substantive theory of class relations which is built upon them. The central objective of this study is to take one particular theoretical problem, income determination, and demonstrate this coherence and power through a systematic empirical investigation.

Before we can do this, however, it is necessary to develop more rigorously the Marxist conception of class relations. Although the definition above may adequately differentiate the Marxist concept of class from other definitions, it is not yet precise enough to be used in empirical study. How should the specific social relations of production of capitalist society be defined? Once defined, how can they be operationalized for research purposes? What concrete criteria define the various positions within the social relations of production? These and other related questions will be discussed in the following chapter.

2

Classes in Advanced Capitalist Societies

> We must of course not be surprised to find classes differing
> from each other along various lines: in production as well as
> in distribution, in politics, in psychology, in ideology. For all
> these things are interdependent; you cannot crown a proletar-
> ian tree with bourgeois twigs; this would be worse than placing
> a saddle on a cow. But this connection is determined, in the
> last analysis, by the position of the classes in the process of
> production. Therefore, we must define the classes according to
> a production criterion.
>
> —BUKHARIN, Historical Materialism

The previous chapter focused on the differences between Marxist and other conceptions of class. In this chapter* we will look more deeply at the Marxist conception; in particular, I shall try to elaborate a

*Parts of this chapter have appeared in Erik O. Wright, Class, Crisis and the State (London: NLB, 1978), ch. 2.

19

rigorous understanding of the class location of various positions in the social structure commonly called "middle class." The vague and often inconsistent discussions of such positions by both Marxist and non-Marxist theorists have been a source of endless confusion. In order to develop a proper class map of advanced capitalist societies it is essential that a precise definition of these positions be developed.

The chapter will begin by elaborating in some detail the general definition of classes that I presented in the previous chapter. I shall then give an overview of the substantive analysis of capitalist class relations, and discuss the historical transformations of their basic dimensions. This will be followed by a detailed discussion of three different categories of positions within those class relations that are generally designated "middle class." Finally, I shall present some very rough estimates of the distribution of people in the class structure of the contemporary United States.

Readers who are not interested in the nuances of the definitions of classes will be able to get a general understanding of the categories which underlie the theoretical and empirical investigation of income determination in this research by reading the first two sections and skipping the rest of the chapter.

CLASS AS A SOCIAL RELATION

What does it really mean to define classes in terms of capitalist social relations of production? One thing is very important to clarify from the outset: classes defined in this way are not *things*. They are not concrete social groups or statistical aggregations of individuals; nor are they social organizations. Class relations may give rise to class organizations, but classes per se are not organizations. Classes *constitute common positions within a special kind of contradictory social relationship, social relations of production*. There are four important parts of this definition: classes constitute common *positions*, those positions are *relational*, those relations are *contradictory*, and those contradictory relations are located within *production*. I shall discuss each in turn.

Classes Constitute Positions

To say that classes constitute "positions" implies, to use Przeworski's (1977) apt expression, that there are "empty places" in the social structure which are filled by individuals. The analysis of class must be understood as the analysis primarily of such empty places, and only secondarily of the actual individuals who fill the slots. While questions of social mobility are important in a class analysis, there is a logical priority to understanding the empty places into which individuals are sorted. Poulantzas (1973a) has emphasized this point: "the question of who occupies a given position, i.e., who is, or becomes a bourgeois, proletarian, petty bourgeois, poor peasant, etc., and how and when he does, *is subordinate to the first aspect*—the reproduction of the actual positions occupied by the social classes [pp. 49–50]." This view is quite in keeping with Marx's own usage. In the preface to the 1867 German edition of *Capital* Marx wrote: "Individuals are dealt with only in so far as they are the personifications of economic categories, embodiments òf particular class-relations and class-interests [1967 ed., p. 10]."

Positions Exist Within Relations

Classes are not, however, just any "empty places" in the social structure which can be ordered in a hierarchical fashion. As we argued in the previous chapter, classes constitute common positions within social *relations* of production, and this means that classes must always be understood in terms of their relationship to other classes.

The notion of "positions within relations" is a complex one. On the one hand, the relationship itself is definable only in terms of the positions which are in a relation with each other; on the other hand, the positions are determined by the relations of which they are elements. It is incorrect to see classes as positions which exist independently and only then enter into relations with other classes; but it is also incorrect to see those relations themselves as in any sense existing prior to the classes which they determine. Classes are positions within relations; the analysis of the positions and relations must occur simultaneously.

Relations Are Contradictory

Classes within Marxist theory are more than just positions within social relations; they are positions within contradictory social relations. To say that a relationship is contradictory implies that there is an *intrinsic* antagonism between the elements (positions) determined by that relation. "Contradiction," in this sense, must be distinguished from "conflict." To say that two groups are in conflict with each other is simply to describe them as pursuing opposing objectives; it is not to make the theoretical claim that such an opposition is an intrinsic part of the very definition of the two groups. In contrast, when we say that two classes are in a contradictory relationship to each other, such opposition is viewed as a necessary consequence of the very relationship which defines the classes. For example, the bourgeoisie and the proletariat are definable only in terms of their relationship to each other; the existence of one class presupposes the existence of the other, and they are thus *necessary* conditions for each other. But, at the same time, the relationship which determines the bourgeoisie and the proletariat is a relation of exploitation and domination: the bourgeoisie exists only because it is in a position to dominate and exploit the proletariat. Thus, the class interests defined by this class relation are fundamentally opposed to each other. It is in this sense that there is an intrinsic—as opposed to purely contingent—contradiction between classes.

This claim about the intrinsically antagonistic character of class relations is ultimately a claim about class struggle, not simply the nature of class structure. If manifest class behavior is fundamentally determined by class structure (a premise of all relational views of class), and if the class relations which define that class structure are intrinsically contradictory, then class struggle itself becomes an intrinsic rather than a contingent consequence of the structure of class relations.[1] While the form and intensity of class struggles may vary historically—indeed, much of the theory of class is devoted precisely to understanding the dynamics of such variation—the fact of class struggle is a constant of class societies.

One very important consequence follows from the proposition that not only class contradictions but class struggle are intrinsic to class societies: class structures themselves can never be totally static. Class struggles are not simply struggles *between* classes; they are struggles *over* class relations. This implies that the class structures themselves are continually transformed by the very class struggles which they determine.[2]

It is for this reason that Marxists insist that an analysis of class structure must always be historical—not in the sense that is necessary

---

[1]Poulantzas (1975) has insisted on the indissoluble link between class structure and class struggle: "Classes involve in one and the same process both class contradictions and class struggle; social classes do not firstly exist as such and only then enter into a class struggle [p. 14]."

[2]As I shall argue more extensively in chapter 3, this relationship between class structure and class struggle implies a notion of atemporal, structural causation. Class structure (the contradictions within class relations) sets limits of variation on class struggle without in any sense being prior to class struggle in time, just as class struggle transforms the class structure itself without existing prior to class structure.

always to return to the origins of class relations, but in the sense that class positions must be viewed as part of a process in which class struggle constantly reshapes the "empty places" which define those positions, and class positions constantly shape the terrain on which class struggle is fought. It is through the historical investigation of this dialectical relationship between class structure and class struggle that the basic logic of the class structure itself can be revealed.

Contradictory Relations Are Located Within Production

The final element in the Marxist definition of classes, as was stressed in chapter 1, is that the contradictory social relations which determine classes are located within the social organization of production itself. "Production," in this context, must not be understood narrowly as the production of physical commodities, but includes the production of services as well.

Given these four elements of the definition of class, the theoretical starting point of a class analysis is to decode the historical transformations of the social relations of production in order to uncover the class positions which these relations determine. This is no simple task, for these social relations are often hidden by the outward form of capitalist institutions. Many theorists have mistaken form for substance and have thus completely mystified the nature of class relations in capitalist society. Dahrendorf, for instance, confuses formal legal title to property—the outward appearance of class relations—with substantive relations of production, and thus insists that the formal separation of legal ownership from actual control in the modern corporation implies the demise of capitalist relations of production altogether. What we must do is go below the level of outward appearances in order to discover the substantive processes that define class relations in capitalist society.

OUTLINE OF THE ARGUMENT

Before plunging into the historical examination of the processes underlying class relations, it might be helpful to anticipate the conclusion of the analysis. I shall argue that capitalist social relations of production can be broken down into three interdependent dimensions or processes:

1. *Social relations of control over money capital*, i.e., control over the flow of investments and the accumulation process, or alternatively, control over *how much* is produced and *what* is produced.

2. *Social relations of control over physical capital*, i.e., control over the use of the physical means of production, or control over *how* things are produced.

3. *Social relations of authority*, i.e., control over supervision and discipline within the labor process.[3]

The first of these is often referred to as "real economic ownership"; the second and third are often grouped together under the rubric "possession."

The term *control* within each of these dimensions of social relations needs some explanation. As I shall use the term, *control* does not primarily refer to an aspect of the relationship of people to things, but rather an aspect of the social relations among people. In everyday language, *control* implies a capacity to make some kind of decision, and thus a capacity to dispose of some kind of resource. A *social relation of control* thus implies that this capacity is an attribute of a relation. Individuals per se, in these terms, do not "have" control over money capital, physical capital, or labor; that control is lodged in the social relation into which the individual enters. To say that "capitalists" control the means of production, for example, is to say that the social relationship between capital and labor simultaneously confers on the capitalist position the capacity to dispose of the means of production and deprives the working-class position of that capacity. In a sense, the social relation between capital and labor defines a relationship between these positions and things and thus between the incumbents of these positions (individuals) and things.

This distinction between "positions" and "individuals" cannot be overemphasized. It becomes clearest when the actual decision-making process is lodged in a collectivity of positions, so that even in behavioral terms individuals qua individuals are not "making" decisions. But even when a single capitalist makes all of the decisions about investments, use of physical capital, deployment of labor, etc., the

[3]This way of breaking down class relations has been developed in different ways by a number of European Marxists, in particular, Balibar (1970), Poulantzas (1973a, 1975), and Bettelheim (1975). A related, but rather different treatment can be found in Carchedi (1977). A discussion of the differences between the approach I am presenting here and a variety of other Marxist approaches to class can be found in Wright (1978e).

control involved in such decisions must be understood as an aspect of the social relation between capital and labor and not simply a characteristic of the capitalist as an individual human being. It is by virtue of being in a particular position within this social relation and not by virtue of being an "individual human being" that capitalists have this control. An individual who leaves a capitalist position within the social relations of production and becomes a worker loses the capacity to dispose of the means of production (i.e., no longer has control over the means of production).

There is a clear logical hierarchy among the three dimensions of control. Control over investments sets limits on the range of possible decisions over the use of the physical means of production, and control over the physical means of production sets limits on control of actual labor within the labor process. In effect, it is impossible to make significant decisions about investments which do not have real effects on the control of physical capital and labor, if only in the sense that future options over the allocation of physical capital and labor become constrained. It is possible, on the other hand, to have control over labor within the labor process which does not have significant direct effects on overall investments. It is thus reasonable to consider a rentier as a member of the capitalist class, whereas a foreman should not be included in that class. The former controls investments (even if in a rather passive way); the latter only controls labor within the labor process.

The fundamental class antagonism between workers and capitalists can be viewed as a polarization of each of these three underlying processes: capitalists control the authority structure as a whole, decide how the physical means of production are to be used, and control the accumulation process. Workers, in contrast, are excluded from control over authority relations, the physical means of production, and the investment process.

When the capitalist system is analyzed at the highest level of abstraction—the level of the pure capitalist mode of production—these are the only class positions defined by capitalist relations of production.[4] When we move to the next lower level of abstraction—what is generally called the level of the "social formation"—other class positions appear. First, real capitalist societies always contain subordinate relations of production other than those of the capitalist mode itself. In

[4]The notion of "levels of abstraction" is central to a Marxist epistemology. Abstraction, as used by Marxists, does not refer to the "unit of analysis" under study (such as society, institution, individual). Rather, it refers to the way in which that unit of analysis is analyzed—in terms of its most *fundamental* contradictions and determinations (high levels of abstraction) or in terms of its most concrete contradictions and determinations

particular, simple commodity production (i.e., production organized for the market by independent, self-employed producers who employ no workers) has always existed within capitalist societies. Within simple commodity production, the petty bourgeoisie is defined as having economic ownership and possession of the means of production, but having no control over labor power (since no labor power is employed). Table 2.1 illustrates the relationship of the petty bourgeoisie to the working class and the capitalist class in terms of the three underlying processes of class relations.

Secondly, the three processes that comprise capitalist social relations of production do not always perfectly coincide. This fact is the key to our understanding the class position of the social categories that are labeled "middle class" (or more exactly "*new* middle classes" to distinguish them from the traditional petty bourgeoisie). The new middle classes can be defined as social categories that occupy *contradictory locations within class relations*. Of course, in a sense all class positions are contradictory, in that class relations are intrinsically antagonistic social relations. The point is that certain "empty places" in the class structure constitute doubly contradictory locations: they represent positions which are torn between the basic contradictory class relations of capitalist society. (That is, they represent positions which deviate from the "pure" patterns illustrated in Table 2.1.) Rather than use such a cumbersome expression as "contradictory positions within the basic contradictory class relations of capitalist society," I shall for convenience simply refer to these positions as "contradictory class locations."

(lower levels of abstraction). A high level of abstraction identifies basic causes; a low level of abstraction identifies secondary causes. It should be noted that this is a rather different notion of "abstraction" from that which prevails in positivist conceptions of science. Within a positivist framework, a more abstract concept or model is a *simpler* concept or model: the mass of details of immediate life are sifted in order to distinguish the contingent from the general. Abstraction, then, is virtually the equivalent of simplification. Within Marxism, on the other hand, abstract concepts are understood as designating the most fundamental *real determinations* within a given process. Their function within the theory is less to simplify reality than to penetrate reality. Abstractions are thus not merely arbitrary, analytical conventions used to formulate generalizations about the world; they are conceptual tools necessary to construct real explanations of the world. In a sense, within Marxism, the most abstract concepts designate the most real determinations of social relations (real = fundamental), whereas within positivism, the most abstract concepts are the least real (real = empirical, and thus complex).

For discussions of abstraction see Carchedi (1977, pp. 18–23), Poulantzas (1973b, pp. 70ff), Sweezy (1942, ch. 1), Dos Santos (1970).

TABLE 2.1
Basic Positions Within Class Relations

	Processes Underlying Class Relations		
	Economic Ownership	Possession	
Class	Control over Investments and the Accumulation Process	Control over Physical Means of Production	Control over Labor Power of Others
Bourgeoisie	+	+	+
Proletariat	−	−	−
Petty bourgeoisie	+	+	−

Source: Wright, 1978a, p. 75.
+ Full control
− No control

Three clusters of such contradictory class locations are especially important (see Figure 2.1, p. 42):

1. *Managers and supervisors* occupy a contradictory location between the bourgeoisie and the proletariat.

2. *Semiautonomous employees* who retain relatively high levels of control over their immediate labor process occupy a contradictory location between the working class and the petty bourgeoisie.

3. *Small employers* occupy a contradictory location between the bourgeoisie and the petty bourgeoisie.[5]

This conception of the middle class will constitute our general conclusion. Now let us turn to the historical analysis which suggests that this is a sensible way to analyze the social world.

THE PROCESSES OF CLASS RELATIONS

A number of critical historical transformations of capitalist production can help us to unravel the various processes which underlie the

[5]Several other contradictory locations could be discussed. For example, the owners of fast food and gas station franchises could be seen as occupying a contradictory location between the petty bourgeoisie or small employers and managers. While they maintain some of the characteristics of self-employed independent producers, they also become much more like functionaries for large capitalist corporations. Professors with large

class relations of advanced capitalism. Since our basic purpose is not to investigate the transformations of class structures as such, and since each of these transformations has been thoroughly studied elsewhere, I shall only briefly review them here.

The Worker's Loss of Control over the Labor Process

The saga of the progressive dispossession of the direct producers in the course of capitalist development has been told many times. The point that needs stressing here is that the loss of control over the labor process is not an all-or-nothing phenomenon, but has occurred gradually over a long period of time and exists in varying degrees even today. In the earliest capitalist production, the direct producers generally maintained considerable control over the labor process. Often, especially in cottage industries, they even owned all or part of their immediate means of production. Thus, although economic conditions certainly acted as a powerful constraint on workers in cottage industries, nevertheless they often retained relatively high levels of control over the pace of their labor, the length of the working day, and other aspects of the labor process. Such a situation made it more difficult for capitalists to raise the rate of exploitation, and this in turn acted as a serious constraint on the accumulation process in early capitalism (see Wright, 1978a, pp. 170–71).

Much of the history of class struggle between capitalists and workers, especially in the nineteenth century, can be seen as a struggle over the terms of the control of the labor process. As Marglin (1974) has argued, one of the major impulses for the creation of factories was the desire to undermine worker control. At a minimum, factory owners had much greater control over the length of the working day, and generally over other aspects of the labor process as well, than capitalists in the putting-out system.

Once workers were gathered within factories, the assault on their remaining control of the labor process continued in the form of technical innovations which fragmented the production process and which progressively "deskilled" the labor force (see Braverman, 1974). Capitalists could force workers to work in the factory for ten hours by the clock, but as long as the worker maintained real autonomy in the labor process it was difficult for the capitalist to be sure of getting

research grants which enable them directly to hire research assistants, secretaries, etc., could be thought of as occupying a contradictory location between the semiautonomous employees and small employers. Other special cases could be described, but the most important contradictory locations are the ones discussed above.

anywhere near ten hours of actual labor from the worker. The close supervision of the labor process is much easier when tasks are simple and routinized and their pace is determined by machinery rather than the worker. Thus, capitalists look for innovations which tend to reduce skill levels and reduce the autonomy of workers on the job. The culmination of this process was the mass-production assembly line regulated by the principles of Taylorism, in which the worker lost almost all autonomy and became virtually a human component of machinery itself.

Many Marxist accounts of transformations of the labor process leave the analysis at this point, concluding that such transformations have produced a monotonic trajectory of proletarianization. Such an account is incomplete; there are at least three important countertendencies to this general process: (a) successful resistance of workers to loss of control over work; (b) changes in technology which generate new skills; (c) changing conditions of accumulation and social organization which may encourage a relaxation of strict control within production.

To say that control over the labor process is a dimension of class relations is simultaneously to say that it is a dimension of class struggles. While in the balance the interests of the bourgeoisie may dominate within this struggle, nevertheless there are innumerable cases where resistance has been successful. Burawoy (1978) argues this point brilliantly in a critique of Braverman. Taylorism itself, Burawoy argues, is a good example of this: it did not universally increase the actual capacity of the capitalist class to control the labor of workers, for their collective resistance to Taylorism in many cases reduced the control of capital. Burawoy suggests that it was only through the technological changes (mechanization) which accelerated in the wake of the failure of Taylorism that such resistance was weakened. Noble (1978), in a careful case study of the machine industry, argues that numerical-control technologies were introduced consciously to reduce highly skilled machinists' control of the labor process, but that workers were able to subvert the effectiveness of the technology to such an extent that the net effect was virtually no degradation of work. The labor process is thus an arena of struggle, not just of domination, and workers have often effectively prevented capital from undermining their control within it.

The introduction of new technologies may also generate new skills and new categories of jobs in which the worker may have greater immediate control over the labor process. Whole new industries have emerged in the past few decades (e.g., computers), and at least some of the jobs within those industries require considerable skill and involve considerable degrees of autonomy.

The question is, then, whether this "counteracting tendency" of the expansion of skilled positions is systemically stronger or weaker than the tendency toward degradation. Little systematic data are available to assess this issue. Anecdotally, it is clear that within the sectors of new technologies there are real pressures to reduce the skill levels of the newly created positions. When computers were first being developed, the actual operators of computer hardware tended to be engineers. Gradually over the last twenty years this job has been "deskilled" until, at present, computer operators are generally technicians with only one or two years of post-high-school training.

Anecdotal evidence, however, can always be countered with opposing anecdotal evidence. What is needed is systematic data which examine the process of proletarianization over time. Two recent studies, one by Browning and Singelmann (1978) and another by Wright and Singelmann (1978), provide some very provisional findings on these issues. Browning and Singelmann decomposed the changes in the occupational structure between 1960 and 1970 into three components: (a) an occupational-shift effect due to the changing occupational structure within industries, (b) an industry-shift effect due to the changing distribution of the population across industries, and (c) an interaction-effect due to the interaction of changes in the occupational and industry structures. This procedure makes it possible to see whether the overall growth of professional occupations (as defined by conventional census categories), for example, is due primarily to an upgrading of jobs within a given industry (occupation-shift effects) or to a more rapid expansion of those industries which employ relatively more professionals (industry-shift effects). The results were striking. The occupational-shift effect indicates an actual *decline* in the proportion of the labor force in professional occupations. That is, if all industrial sectors had grown at the same rate, then there would have been proportionately fewer professionals in 1970 than 1960. All of the net growth of professionals in the society as a whole, therefore, was due to the industry-shift effect (the interaction-shift effect was negligible), and most of this industry-shift effect was due to the rapid expansion of social services during the period.

The study by Wright and Singelmann has extended this analysis, in a very crude way, to examine changes in the class structure. If a rough distinction is made between relatively autonomous and relatively nonautonomous employees (on the basis of data from the 1969 Michigan Survey of Working Conditions), then it can be shown that *within* industrial sectors there was a substantial decrease in autonomous positions between 1960 and 1970. Again, all of the net increase in autonomy in the society as a whole was due to the relatively more rapid expansion of those industrial sectors with a relatively less proletarianized labor force.

These data suggest that the process of degradation of labor, of the reduction of workers' autonomy, is a systematic tendency within capitalism that may to a greater or lesser extent be counteracted by changes in the industrial structure. In the most recent period, this has above all involved the rapid expansion of social services. If the fiscal crisis of the state limits future expansion of such services, then this counteracting tendency would itself be expected to decline.

The third counteracting tendency to an intensification of proletarianization is the emergence in recent decades of various "human relations" approaches to the problem of worker productivity which have replaced, at least partially, the principles of strict discipline and crude scientific management as the ideology of labor control. One part of such new approaches is, in principle, the "enrichment" of jobs and the enlargement of the sphere of decision-making under the control of the worker.

Such shifts in the ideology of control have often been taken as indicating a transformation in the real relations of control within production. Without suggesting that these changes are of no consequence, let us note that generally the enlarged autonomy embodied in job enrichment schemes is confined within very narrow limits and subordinated to the imperatives of increasing worker productivity (see Zimbalist, 1975). That is, control is relaxed—and generally peripheral control at that—only when it is more than compensated for by increased production. Thus, in a report to the Conference Board[6] Rush (1971) writes:

> the current emphasis [in job design] is on gaining internal motivation from the employee so that he performs his tasks with more dedication and commitment, as contrasted with coercion, robot-style control, and machine-like pacing. . . . The design and redesign of jobs may be said to have a single purpose, though it is a purpose with a double edge: to increase both employee motivation and productivity. [pp. 10–11]

Greater worker control of the labor process, or what is often called "worker participation," is one important form of this redesigning of

---

[6]The Conference Board is a nonprofit business research organization which is, in its own words, "an institution for scientific research in the fields of business economics and business management. Its sole purpose is to promote prosperity and security by assisting in the effective operation and sound development of voluntary productive enterprise." Members of the Conference Board are drawn from among the top executives of the largest corporations in the United States; generally the Board's views can be interpreted as reflecting the "vanguard" position of the American capitalist class.

jobs to increase productivity. In a second Conference Board report on worker participation in management, Roach (1973) writes:

> A Conference Board survey of top level executives in 50 countries indicates that participation concepts are winning increased acceptance as approaches to improving productivity, motivating job satisfaction, and resolving labor-management problems both within and outside traditional collective bargaining processes. Indeed, responses from the international panel suggest that a widening emphasis on participation is adding a broad new dimension to the operation of free enterprise in the Western World.
>
> That is not to say that management has decided it should share any of its board-room prerogatives with unions, works councils, or other worker representatives. On the contrary, the general mood of the 143 executives cooperating in the Board's survey is that management must resist attempts to usurp its ultimate authority to make the big decisions. [p. 1]

The occasional trends toward increased worker participation do not contradict the importance of control of the labor process as a dimension of class relations; rather, they reveal its underlying logic. Capital tries to extract as much actual labor out of the worker during the work day as possible (this would hardly be denied by any capitalist). Control over the labor process is a basic means of accomplishing this. Under certain historical conditions, for example, when a large proportion of the industrial work force are newly proletarianized petty bourgeois (artisans, peasants, etc.) with little experience of factory discipline and without proper work habits, strict and despotic control of the labor process may be the most effective structure of control from the capitalist point of view. Under contemporary conditions, a partial relaxation of direct control may accomplish the same end.

The loss of control over the labor process by workers is thus not a simple, homogeneous process of proletarianization. Workers resist their own degradation, at times successfully; technological change expands relatively autonomous job positions, even if that autonomy is simultaneously being eroded; and changing social conditions of accumulation make possible less rigidly authoritarian forms of control within the labor process. Nevertheless, for our present purposes, all of these countertendencies still demonstrate our central point: the social relations of control over the labor process constitute a basic dimension of class relations.

The Differentiation of the Functions of Capital

No development in capitalist social relations has been used more often as "proof" that Marx's image of class structure is outmoded than the so-called "separation of ownership and control" in the modern corporation. Of course, no one can deny the considerable growth of managerial hierarchies in the modern corporation and the general decline of the traditional family-owned firm in favor of the joint-stock company (although, as Zeitlin [1974] forcefully argues, there are considerable data to indicate that the proponents of the "managerial revolution" have grossly exaggerated these changes). The issue is not whether professional managers play a bigger role in running corporations today than a hundred years ago, but how such positions should be structurally interpreted in terms of a theory of class relations.

The apparent separation of ownership and control in the large corporation hides a whole series of structural transformations and differentiations. Two such transformations are of particular importance here: the functional differentiation between economic ownership and possession, and the dissociation between legal and economic ownership. In the nineteenth century, all three of these were embodied in the entrepreneurial capitalist. As capital became more concentrated and centralized, these three dimensions of ownership tended to become at least partially differentiated.

Before we proceed further, these terms need to be defined somewhat more precisely. *Legal ownership* is simple enough. It constitutes the various forms of legal title to property in the means of production. The usual form of such ownership in advanced capitalism is stock ownership. *Possession* is a bit more complicated. It designates, in de Vroey's words (1975), "the ability to put the means of production to work. It thus pertains to the management of capitalist factories [p. 3]." As we will see below, possession, in turn, can be divided into authority relations (control over labor power in the labor process) and control over the actual physical means of production. Finally, *economic ownership* is the most complex of all three dimensions. Bettelheim (1975) defines it as "the power to assign the objects on which it bears (especially the means of production) to specific uses and to dispose of the products obtained through these means of production [p. 58]." Less abstractly, this means control over the flow of resources into production (i.e., investment and accumulation).

Marx was one of the first writers to recognize the dual quality of the capitalist as both the owner and the manager of capital. In *Capital*, he writes:

> the employer of capital, even when working with his own capital, splits into two personalities—the owner of capital and the employer of capital; with reference to the categories of profit which it yields, his capital also splits into

capital-*property*, capital *outside* the production process, and yielding interest
of itself, and capital *in* the production process, which yields a profit of enterprise through its function. [1967 ed., p. 375]

In our terms, the *owner of capital* refers to the dimension of economic
ownership while the *employer of capital* refers to that of possession.

In the course of capitalist development, this distinction between
functions of capital begins to correspond to a distinction between actual positions. Again, Marx writes:

> Stock companies in general—developed with the credit system—have an in-
> creasing tendency to separate this work of management as a function from the
> ownership of capital, be it self-owned or borrowed. . . . The mere manager who
> has no title whatever to the capital, whether through borrowing it or oth-
> erwise, performs all the real functions pertaining to the functioning capitalist
> as such, only the functionary remains and the capitalist disappears as super-
> fluous from the production process. [1967 ed., pp. 387–88]

This partial separation of economic ownership from possession is a
consequence of the concentration and centralization of capital growing
out of the accumulation process. (*Concentration* refers to the increasing absolute magnitude of capital units; *centralization* to the increasing relative magnitude.)[7] Increasing concentration and centralization
have encouraged the differentiation of economic ownership and possession, for two reasons: first, and most obviously, as the scale of both
ownership and production increases, it becomes less and less practical
for the same individuals to be equally involved in both functions.
Competitive pressures will tend to push capitalists to hire professional
managers to deal with specific aspects of production and eventually to
help coordinate production as a whole. Secondly, there has been a
general tendency in the development of monopoly capitalism for the
concentration and centralization of economic ownership to develop
more rapidly than the concentration and centralization of possession.
(Concentration and centralization of *possession* refer to the absolute
and relative growth in the scale of production under unified manage-

[7]The use of the expression *concentration* within Marxist theory should not be confused with its usage in neoclassical economics. In economics, concentration refers to the
degree of competition within the market; in Marxist theory, concentration refers to the
absolute size of the unit of capital. *Centralization* in Marxist theory is much closer to
concentration in neoclassical theory, since it designates the relative size of accumulating
units; it should be noted, however, that centralization directly refers to the relative
magnitude of assets rather than to the portion of the market controlled (although this
would generally correspond closely to the relative size of capital).

ment rather than simply under unified ownership.) Poulantzas (1975) discusses this pattern in some detail:

> These forms of the expansion of monopoly capitalism, historically accomplished by the advancing concentration of economic intervention, themselves involve a dissociation, this time between economic ownership and possession. The dominant form that replaces competitive capitalism, i.e., individual economic ownership and individual capitalist possession in a determinate production unit, is that of a single, concentrated economic ownership embracing several separate production units, i.e., an economic ownership subordinating ('subsuming') relatively distinct relationships of possession. The typical form found here is that of the holding company or trust, which, with its concentrated economic ownership, can control extremely diversified production units, extending to the most diverse and distant branches, and whose labour processes exhibit a characteristic autonomy. [p. 124]

Where a diverse collection of production processes is formally united under a single economic ownership it becomes impossible for the two functions of capital—ownership and possession—to be completely united in a single position.

Capitalist development has also been characterized by a gradual dissociation between formal legal ownership and real economic ownership. This is the famous phenomenon of the dispersion of stock ownership in the large corporation. The fact of such dispersion has been the core datum used by supporters of the managerial revolution thesis to argue that the control of the corporation has moved from property owners to professional managers. Marxists have generally drawn quite different conclusions. Building on the arguments of Hilferding, de Vroey (1975) writes, "Rather than seeing the dispersion of stock as an obstacle to concentrated control, Marxism interprets it in exactly the opposite way: as a means for reinforcing the actual control of big stockholders, who thus succeed in commanding an amount of funds out of proportion to their actual ownership. Paradoxically, dispersion of stock thus favors the centralization of capital [pp. 4–5]." For the managerial revolution proponents to prove their case, therefore, it is not enough to show that stock is widely dispersed. They must show that real economic ownership is in the hands of nonowning, professional managers, i.e., that they actually control the accumulation process as a whole.

The emphasis on economic as opposed to formal legal ownership should not be taken to imply that legal title to stocks and other forms of property is irrelevant to understanding class relations. On the contrary: as long as capitalist relations of production are reproduced through the legal superstructure of private capitalism, formal legal ownership is in general a necessary condition for economic ownership. The point of the distinction between economic and legal ownership is that formal title is not a sufficient condition for actual participation in the control of the investment and accumulation process.

The Development of Complex Hierarchies

The same process of concentration and centralization of capital that differentiates economic ownership from possession also generates various forms of differentiations within each of these dimensions of ownership. First, let us look at relations of possession (i.e., the direction and control of the capitalist production process). Such direction involves two analytically separable aspects: (a) direction and control of the physical means of production, and (b) direction and control of labor. Even in the earliest capitalist enterprise, there was some structural differentiation between these two aspects. Foremen typically were excluded from any real control of the means of production and yet played an important role in the supervision of workers. As the capitalist enterprise expanded, additional layers of supervision were added, leading eventually to the complex hierarchy of social control within the monopoly corporation.

Concentration and centralization of capital are not the only factors contributing to the transformations of the authority structures of modern corporations. In particular, technological change itself has undoubtedly also played a role. Dunkerley (1975), discussing the work of Woodward (1965), writes:

> As organizations became more technologically advanced, so the number of levels of authority within the organizations increased. Thus, the longest lines of command were to be found in process industry (the actual median numbers were three levels in small batch; four levels in mass; and six levels in process production).
>
> Parallel to the growth in the number of levels of authority was an increase in the ratio of supervisory staff to nonsupervisory staff. Thus in unit production there was one manager or supervisor to twenty-three employees; one to sixteen employees in mass production and one to eight nonsupervisory employees in process production. [pp. 52–53]

Capitalist development has also produced an elaborate hierarchy within the other aspect of possession, control over the physical means of production. At the highest levels of the hierarchy, top managers control the entire apparatus of production.[8] Below them various middle

---

[8]*Level* refers principally to the *scope of control* attached to a particular position rather than to the formal position within an organizational hierarchy (although the two

levels of management participate in the control of segments of the production process. And at the bottom, certain categories of workers maintain some control over their immediate production process.

A similar line of reasoning can be developed for economic ownership. In the earliest capitalist enterprise, economic ownership was not organized hierarchically. A single figure was essentially responsible for the entire accumulation process. In the modern corporation, however, different levels of economic ownership can be distinguished. Full economic ownership refers to participation in the control of the overall investment and accumulation process. Typically, the highest executives in the corporation and certain members of the board of directors occupy this position. Below this level there are executives and managers who participate in decisions concerning investments in either subunits of the total production process (e.g., branches) or partial aspects of the entire investment process (e.g., marketing). Finally, at the bottom, there are positions which marginally participate in ownership relations by being involved in decision-making over narrow aspects of subunits of production.

These various hierarchical levels within the relations of economic ownership and relations of possession are summarized in Table 2.2.

The purpose of this rather schematic historical discussion of changes in capitalist relations of production was to provide a justification for the three dimensions of class relations used in Table 2.1: social relations of control over investment and accumulation (economic ownership), over the physical means of production, and over labor. Other dimensions have been proposed by some Marxists and there is certainly no reason to regard these three as completely defining class relations within capitalist society, even at the level of production. The claim is simply that these three are essential underlying dimensions of class relations and that they will help us to understand classes in advanced capitalism.

---

would generally tend to coincide). The highest levels have the broadest range of control; the lowest levels the narrowest range. It should be noted that the actual content of the top "level" changes in different stages of capitalist development, especially in the case of levels of economic ownership. In competitive capitalism, the highest level of ownership refers to the control of the overall investment process of a single capitalist enterprise. In monopoly capitalism, on the other hand, the highest level of ownership refers to the finance capitalist who participates in the control of accumulation in a large number of enterprises. Finally, in "state capitalism" (assuming, for the moment, the validity of this concept in the first place), the highest level of ownership refers to control of the entire system of accumulation. See Carchedi (1977) for an extended discussion of these changes.

TABLE 2.2
Levels of Control Within Ownership Relations

Level of Control	Relations of Economic Ownership	Relations of Possession	
		Control of Means of Production	Control of Labor Power
Full	Control over investment and accumulation	Control over the entire apparatus of production	Control over the entire supervisory hierarchy
Partial	Participation in decisions concerning allocation of resources to subunits of production, or partial aspects of investments	Control over one segment of production	Control over one segment of the supervisory hierarchy
Minimal	Participation in decisions about design of products (i.e., control over aspects of what is produced)	Control over one's immediate instruments of production; some control over how production occurs in one's immediate labor process	Control over the direct producers, over immediate subordinates but not part of the hierarchy as such
None	Complete exclusion from participation in investment and accumulation decisions	Negligible control over any aspect of the means of production	No ability to invoke sanctions on other workers

CONTRADICTORY LOCATIONS WITHIN
CLASS RELATIONS

We can now turn to the question of rigorously defining the contradictory locations within class relations. We will explore two different kinds of contradictory class locations:

1. Contradictory locations between the bourgeoisie and the proletariat, i.e., positions defined by contradictory combinations of the three processes underlying class relations within the capitalist mode of production.

2. Contradictory locations between the petty bourgeoisie and both the proletariat and the bourgeoisie, i.e., positions situated between the capitalist mode of production and simple commodity production.[9]

Table 2.3 schematically presents the relationship of these contradictory locations to the three basic processes of class relations, and to the juridical categories often used in identifying classes: legal ownership of property, legal status as the employer of labor power, and legal status as a seller of labor power. It is immediately clear that if only juridical criteria are used to define class, most of the contradictory locations within class relations become indistinguishable from the working class. This is why juridical criteria must be considered of strictly secondary importance to the substantive dimensions of class relations we have discussed.

Several general comments about these contradictory locations might be helpful before we examine each of them in turn. First of all, these contradictory locations do not represent classification problems in an abstract typology. The three dimensions of class relations constitute the real stuff of social relations of production, not simply analytical abstractions; and the contradictory locations constitute objectively contradictory locations within those class relations.

Many critics of the Marxist framework have argued that the fact of such "intermediate categories," such ambiguities in the class structure, negates the value of the Marxist perspective on classes altogether. This is equivalent to saying that because the platypus has webbed feet and a

---

[9]We will not consider contradictory locations that occur because an individual simultaneously occupies two class positions within social relations of production. For example, a craftsman who works in a factory on weekdays may operate as a self-employed petty bourgeois artisan on weekends and evenings. Such dual class membership may be important in certain historical circumstances, but it does not pose the same kind of analytical problems as positions which are themselves located in a contradictory way within class relations.

TABLE 2.3
Formal Criteria for Contradictory Locations Within Class Relations

Class Positions		Dimensions of Social Relations of Production			Juridical Criteria		
		Relations of Economic Ownership	Relations of Possession		Legal Ownership of Property (e.g., Capital, Stocks, Real Estate)	Legal Status of Being the Employer of Labor Power	Seller of One's Own Labor Power for a Wage
		Control over Investments, Resources	Control over Physical Means of Production	Control over Labor Power of Others			
Bourgeoisie	Traditional capitalist	+	+	+	+	+	−
	Top corporate executive	+	+	+	Partial	−	Minimal
Contradictory class location between the bourgeoisie and the proletariat	Top managers	Partial/minimal	+	+	Minimal	−	+
	Middle managers	Minimal	Partial	Partial	−	−	+
	Technocrats	Minimal	Minimal	Minimal	−	−	+
	Foremen/supervisors	−	−	Minimal	−	−	+
Proletariat		−	−	−	−	−	+
Contradictory class location between the proletariat and the petty bourgeoisie	Semiautonomous employees	Minimal	Minimal	−	−	−	+
Petty bourgeoisie		+	+	−	+	−	−
Contradictory class location between the petty bourgeoisie and the bourgeoisie	Small employers	+	+	Minimal	+	Minimal	−

Source: Wright, 1978a, p. 76.
+   Full control
Partial   Attenuated control
Minimal   Residual control
−   No control

bill, the concept of "mammal" is useless. These ambiguities are ambiguities precisely because of their relationship to the basic structural categories. It is clearly important for the Marxist theory of class relations to try to understand them rather than to ignore them, but there is no intrinsic incompatibility between a theory of class antagonisms rooted in the social relations of production and the existence of social positions which occupy contradictory or ambiguous locations with respect to those antagonisms.

Secondly, contradictory locations must not be thought of as midpoints on a scale, the endpoints of which are defined as the "working class" and the "capitalist class." Contradictory locations are locations within class *relations,* and the content of their contradictory character is definable only in relational terms. They are contradictory precisely in the sense that they are simultaneously in more than one class. The class interests of contradictory locations are thus not in any real sense "half-way" between the interests of basic class locations; rather, their class interests are internally incompatible combinations of the interests of different classes.

Each of the "levels" within specific contradictory locations must be understood in precisely these same terms. Different levels are not points on a ladder; rather, they are defined by their social relationship with other levels. To have partial control over the means of production implies a specific social relation with those positions involving full control as well as those involving no control. The spatial metaphor should not obscure the relational character of each of these positions.

Finally, the notion of contradictory positions within class relations has little in common with the concepts of "status crystalization" and "status incongruity." The underlying processes of class relations are not simply independent status rankings with no systematic structure of interrelationships; they represent interconnected dimensions of social relations of production and have a very specific interrelationship determined by the dynamics of capitalist development. In status crystalization studies, the analysis focuses on the statistical congruence between different rank orders. The central methodological problem is how to define statistically what is meant by high and low statuses on each hierarchy and by congruent and incongruent combinations across hierarchies (see Hope, 1975). In our analysis, both contradictory class locations and the basic class categories constitute empty places defined by the social relations of production. The contradictory locations are thus not merely statistical categories, but have a precise theoretical status in their own right.

Let us now look briefly at each of the basic contradictory locations illustrated in Figure 2.1 and Table 2.3.

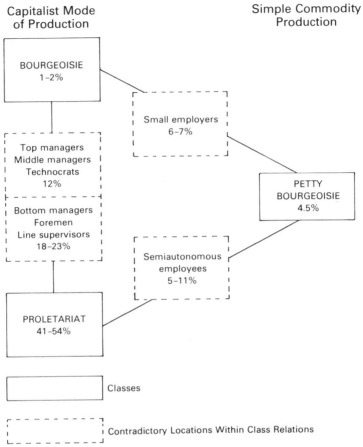

Figure 2.1. The relationship of contradictory class locations to basic classes in capitalist society. Note: The percentage distributions are discussed on pp. 49–52. (*Source:* Wright, 1978a, p. 63.)

Contradictory Locations Between the Proletariat and the Bourgeoisie

One thing is immediately obvious from Table 2.3. The contradictory quality of a particular position within class relations is a variable rather than an all-or-nothing characteristic. Certain positions can be thought of as occupying a contradictory position around the boundary of the proletariat; others as occupying a contradictory position around the boundary of the bourgeoisie. As a general proposition, it would be expected that, all things being equal, the closer a contradictory position is to the working class, the more likely it is that the individuals occupying those positions will side with the working class in class struggles; and conversely, the closer a contradictory position is to the bourgeoisie, the less likely the individual is to side with the working class.

The contradictory position closest to the working class is that of foremen and line supervisors. Foremen typically have little real control over the physical means of production, and while they do exercise control over labor power, this frequently does not extend much beyond being the formal transmission belt for orders from above.

It is difficult to say whether, during the course of capitalist development over the past century, the class location of foremen has moved closer to or further from the working class. On the one hand, the early foreman often participated directly in the production process alongside workers and occasionally defended workers against arbitrary treatment by the boss. On the other hand, the foreman in the nineteenth-century factory often had much greater personal discretion and personal power than today. In the nineteenth century, authority within the capitalist factory was typically organized in much the same way as an army. There was a simple chain of command and the authority at each level was absolute with respect to the level below. Such a system Marx aptly termed "factory despotism," and foremen in such a factory had at least the potential of being petty despots. As the capitalist enterprise grew in scale and complexity, the authority structure gradually became more bureaucratized. As Weber would put it, foremen increasingly became the administrators of impersonal rules rather than the dispensers of personal fiats.

Edwards (1972), in a study of work norms in bureaucratically structured capitalist organizations, describes this shift in authority relations as follows:

> What distinguishes modern enterprises from their earlier and cruder prototypes—and in particular, what distinguishes bureaucratic organization from simple hierarchy—is that in bureaucratically organized enterprises, the exercise of power becomes *institutionalized*. External, arbitrary, personal commands from the boss are replaced by established rules and procedures: "rule of law" replaces "rule of personal command." Work activities become directed by rules. Supervisors at all levels, no longer directing the worker's activities by personal instruction, merely enforce the rules and evaluate (reward or penalize) their subordinates according to pre-established criteria for adequate work performance. More and more, the work structure is designed so that administrative control can replace executive control. [pp. 101–2]

The net effect of these changes in the overall structure of authority on the specific character of the position of foreman is summarized by

Dunkerley (1975) as "a change from a fairly central and important composite managerial role to a more peripheral and less important specialist and dependent role outside the mainstream of management decision [p. 30]." The indications are that at least in the present period the class location of foremen is moving closer to that of workers.

In any event, when the control of supervisors over labor power becomes so attenuated that the supervisor lacks even the capacity to invoke negative sanctions, then the position really merges with the working class proper and should no longer be thought of as a contradictory location. This would be the case, for example, of the chief of a work team who has certain special responsibilities for coordinating activities of others in the team, but lacks any real power over them.

At the other end of the contradictory locations between workers and capitalists, top managers occupy a contradictory position at the boundary of the bourgeoisie. These managers generally have only limited participation in economic ownership, but they differ little from the bourgeoisie in terms of relations of possession. Again, at the very top of the managerial hierarchy, corporate executives essentially merge with the capitalist class itself.

The most intensely contradictory locations between the bourgeoisie and the proletariat are occupied by middle managers and what can loosely be termed "technocrats." Middle managers control various pieces of the labor process, and have control not only over immediate subordinates but over part of the authority hierarchy itself. They may even have some residual participation in actual investment decisions. In this context, technocrats are technicians and professionals within the corporate hierarchy who may have some control over their own work (*minimal* control of the physical means of production) and over subordinates, but who are not in command of pieces of the productive apparatus.

Both middle managers and technocrats have, in Braverman's words, one foot in the bourgeoisie and one foot in the proletariat. In discussing new technical occupations and middle management, Braverman (1974) writes:

> If we are to call this a "new middle class," however, as many have done, we must do so with certain reservations. The old middle class occupied that position by virtue of its place outside the polar class structure; it possessed the attributes of neither capitalist nor worker; it played no direct role in the capital accumulation process, whether on one side or the other. This "new middle class," by contrast, occupies its intermediate position not because it is outside the process of increasing capital, but because, as part of this process, it takes its characteristics from *both sides*. Not only does it receive its petty share of

the prerogatives and rewards of capital, but it also bears the mark of the proletarian condition. [p. 467]

Unlike line supervisors and foremen on the one hand, and top managers on the other, middle managers and technocrats do not have a clear class pole to which they are attached. The contradictory quality of their class location is much more intense than in the other cases we have discussed, and as a result it is much more difficult to assess the general stance they will take within the class struggle.

Contradictory Locations Between the Petty Bourgeoisie and Other Classes

The analysis of these contradictory locations poses a somewhat different problem from that of the contradictory location between the bourgeoisie and the proletariat, because it involves locations between different modes of production rather than within a single mode of production.

The contradictory location between the petty bourgeoisie and the bourgeoisie is conceptually simpler than that between the petty bourgeoisie and the proletariat. The distinctive feature of capitalist production is the appropriation of surplus value through the exploitation of workers in the labor process. In simple commodity production, in contrast, there is no exploitation; whatever surplus is produced is generated by petty bourgeois producers themselves. In general, of course, the surplus is likely to be very small, and thus little if any accumulation is likely to occur.

When a petty bourgeois producer employs a single helper, there is an immediate change in the social relations of production, for the labor of a worker can now be exploited. Still, the surplus value appropriated from a single employee is likely to be very small, and most importantly, it is likely to be less than the surplus product generated by the petty bourgeois producer him- or herself. This is especially likely since in most petty bourgeois production a considerable amount of labor is contributed by unpaid family members.

As additional employees are added, the proportion of the total surplus product that is generated by the petty bourgeois family declines. At some point it becomes less than half of the total surplus product, and eventually becomes a small fraction of the total surplus. At that point, the petty bourgeois producer becomes firmly a small capitalist. There is no a priori basis for deciding how many employees are necessary to reach this point. The number would vary considerably for different technologies and for different historical periods. In any event, between such a small capitalist and the pure petty bourgeois producer lies the contradictory location between the capitalist class and the petty bourgeoisie. Again, as in the contradictory location between the bourgeoisie and the proletariat, the closer such small employers are to true petty bourgeois producers, the more likely they are to side with the petty bourgeoisie in political and economic struggles; the closer the position is to the bourgeoisie, the more likely is it that the class behavior of individuals so placed will resemble that of a full-fledged capitalist.[10]

The contradictory location between the petty bourgeoisie and the proletariat can perhaps best be understood by returning to the historic process of proletarianization of the petty bourgeoisie. The central dynamic underlying this transformation was the need by capital to increase its control over the labor process. Each step of the transformation involved a deeper penetration of capitalist domination into the heart of the laboring activity of direct producers until, in the classic form of scientific management, direct producers have no control whatsoever over their work. This process is constantly being reenacted within capitalism; it is not a development which was somehow completed at the beginning of this century.

Today there are still categories of employees who have a certain degree of real control over their own immediate conditions of work, over their immediate labor process. In such instances the labor process has not been completely proletarianized. Even though such employees

---

[10]Marx himself recognized the character of small employers as a contradictory class location. In *Capital*, he writes: "Of course he [a small capitalist] can, like his laborer, take to work himself, participate directly in the process of production, but he is then only a hybrid between capitalist and laborer, a 'small master.' A certain stage of capitalist production necessitates that the capitalist be able to devote the whole of the time during which he functions as a capitalist, i.e., personified capital, to the appropriation and, therefore, to the control of the labor of others, and to the selling of the products of labor. The guilds in the middle ages, therefore, tried to prevent by force the transformation of the master of a trade into a capitalist, by limiting the number of laborers that could be employed by one master within a very small maximum. The possessor of money or commodities actually turns into a capitalist in such cases only where the minimum sum advanced for production greatly exceeds the maximum of the middle ages. Here, as in natural science, is shown the correctness of the law discovered by Hegel (in his 'Logic') that merely quantitative differences beyond a certain point pass into qualitative changes [1967 ed., pp. 308–9]." This passage clearly designates small employers as contradictory class locations, or as Marx puts it, "hybrid" locations. And Marx also recognizes that as the amount of surplus value increases through increasing the number of employees, this hybrid eventually becomes a proper capitalist.

work for the expansion of capital and have lost the legal status of being self-employed, they can still be viewed as occupying residual islands of petty bourgeois relations of production within the capitalist mode of production itself. In that they are directly dominated by capital in production and do not control the labor of others, such positions are located in the working class; in that they retain significant levels of real control over their immediate labor process, such positions are located in the petty bourgeoisie.

The decisive content of this control over the immediate labor process is the control (within limits) over *what is produced*, not simply control over *how* things are produced. Given the available technologies and the conditions of the market, petty bourgeois producers may not have a great deal of discretion about how to produce a given commodity, but generally speaking they retain considerable control over the choice of what commodities to produce.

At first glance it might seem that virtually no employees have any control whatsoever over what is produced in modern, corporate capitalist production. If we look a bit closer, however, we see that many positions which are involved in the design and planning of production retain limited, but real, capacities to influence what is produced. This may become clearer if we take a concrete example by comparing the work of an engineer with a draughtsman. Engineers typically are responsible for creating aspects of the actual design of the product. While they are told what projects to work on—and thus have only limited control over what they produce—nevertheless, within those limits their activity involves genuinely specifying, refining, and elaborating the actual design of the product. A draughtsman, on the other hand, is responsible for faithfully and precisely translating such design specifications from one medium to another, without changing the content of those designs in any way. Such work of translation may involve tremendous skills (training), but it does not involve control over any aspect of what is produced. Draughtsmen in most cases would, therefore, be fully in the working class; engineers would typically be in semiautonomous employee class locations.[11]

[11]This discussion of semiautonomous class location is closely related to the traditional distinction in Marxist discussions of the labor process between "conception" and "execution." All production, no matter how routinized, involves some degree of cognitive process, so the distinction between conception and execution cannot be read simply as a distinction between thinking and manual labor. The real heart of conception is the choice and design of the object of production, that is, control over what is produced. When Braverman (1974) characterizes the historical transformation of the capitalist labor process as a degradation of work involving the progressive separation of conception from execution, much of what he is talking about is the loss of any design and

Several further points of clarification of the semiautonomous location are needed. First, as should be clear, the notion of semiautonomy is not equivalent to skills, although it is probably the case that semiautonomous employees in modern corporations tend to be skilled. *Skills* refer to the amount of labor time it takes to produce a given type of labor power (i.e., the training necessary to perform the task). Certain extremely skilled positions may have virtually no control over what is produced, as the example of draughtsmen demonstrated. Class locations must always be defined relationally, and thus the issue is the relations of control over the use of skills, and not the existence of skills per se.

Secondly, control over what is produced generally implies a certain degree of broad control over how production takes place as well. It is much more difficult to routinize the work procedures, the pace, the rhythm, the scheduling, of activity which does not involve the execution of established plans. Semiautonomous employees, therefore, will typically have a limited degree of possession of the means of production (control over their immediate physical means of production, or how to produce) as well as limited economic ownership (control over what is produced). As we shall see in chapter 4, this dual control over what is produced and how it is produced gives people in semiautonomous class locations a certain real capacity to control their own productivity, and this in turn has important implications for the ways in which income is determined within such positions.

Third, the notion of semiautonomy refers to *individual* control over the labor process, not *collective* control. When workers collectively control aspects of what they produce and how they produce, through their unions or other devices, they are constituting social relations which prefigure in a limited or primitive way socialist relations of production, rather than reflecting residual forms of petty bourgeois production.

Finally, even though we have given content to the notion of autonomy, it is still somewhat ambiguous how much control is needed for a position to be considered a semiautonomous class location—the contradictory location between the working class and the petty bourgeoisie. If we were to take the notion of design to the extreme, then it could be argued that to the extent workers on a production line can influence the quality of the products, if only in a negative way, then they can affect what is actually produced (cars which have bugs in

---

planning activities by the direct producers. In our terms, this is a destruction of semiautonomous class locations.

them vs. cars which do not). It is unlikely that there are any labor processes in which workers have lost all capacity to influence certain specifications of the product. Conversely, it would be inappropriate to limit the notion of semiautonomy to those very rare positions which have extremely broad ranges of control over what they produce and how they produce it, such as professors in elite universities who can choose (within limits) what courses to teach, what research to do, what books to assign, when to come to work, how many hours to work and how intensely, etc. Clearly, then, a certain amount of ambiguity will inevitably enter into any attempt to define rigorously the boundaries of the class location of semiautonomous employees.

A similar problem exists with the other contradictory locations. How many employees are necessary to transform a small employer (the contradictory location between the petty bourgeoisie and the bourgeoisie) into a capitalist? How residual must the authority of a foreman be before he or she should be considered a worker? How much participation in investment decisions is necessary before a top manager should be thought of as part of the bourgeoisie itself? This suggests that there are certain locations within class relations which are objectively ambiguous, not simply contradictory: they are ambiguous in the sense that it is impossible in terms of a strictly structural analysis of class relations to situate such positions within either contradictory locations or basic class locations. Class structures may therefore differ not simply in terms of the relative magnitudes of contradictory locations, but also in the ambiguous locations that exist at the boundaries of the basic class locations.

The existence of such ambiguous locations indicates the theoretical limits of a purely structural analysis of classes. Classes are not simply slots within a social structure; they are also organized social forces. The decisive question, then, is how these ambiguous class locations (as well as contradictory locations) become formed into classes; this, in turn, depends on class struggle, not just class structure.

THE SIZE OF CONTRADICTORY CLASS LOCATIONS

It is very difficult to obtain plausible estimates of the size of different class locations. Census data are of little help, since labor force data are gathered largely in terms of occupational categories (positions within the technical relations of production). And very few social surveys ask sufficiently precise questions on the objective relations of production to enable estimates of class distributions to be made.

Some very rough estimates can, however, be made on the basis of data from the 1969 Survey of Working Conditions conducted by the University of Michigan Survey Research Center. The results are presented in Figure 2.1, and the criteria used to operationalize the high and low estimates for each category are given in Table 2.4.

The biggest limitation in these data is in the operationalization of the semiautonomous employee category. No objective data on control over the labor process were available in the survey. The survey did ask, however, a number of questions that provide subjective evaluations of job characteristics. Respondents were asked to indicate whether a series of job descriptions characterized their own jobs "a lot," "somewhat," "a little," or "not at all." Two of these descriptions bear on the question of job autonomy:

"A job that allows you a lot of freedom as to how you do your work"

"A job that allows you to make a lot of decisions on your own"

Obviously, it was left up to each respondent to define what is meant by "a lot," "freedom," "decisions," and so on. The fact that 46% of the respondents said that having a lot of freedom characterized their jobs "a lot" and 49% said that making "a lot" of decisions described their jobs "a lot" reflects the subjective quality of the questions. For the purposes of the present analysis, I shall assume that individuals within positions which are genuinely semiautonomous will answer "a lot" to *both* of these subjective job descriptions. The high estimate of the contradictory location between the proletariat and the petty bourgeoisie (11% of the economically active population) includes all nonsupervisory employees who score high on both of these descriptions. The low estimate adds information about the respondent's occupation to this subjective criterion of job autonomy. The U.S. Department of Labor has constructed a *Dictionary of Occupational Titles* (DOT) which codes all occupations in terms of the typical relationship to data, things, and people which characterizes that occupation. The low estimate of the semiautonomous employee category (5% of the economically active population) includes all nonsupervisory employees who scored high on the subjective autonomy questions and whose occupation is classified as having a complex relation to data and things in the DOT (see Table 2.4 for more detailed explanation). Because of the extreme vagueness of the subjective autonomy question, this low estimate is probably closer to the correct proportion.

The figures for the contradictory location between the working class and the bourgeoisie are also only rough estimates. Since all that is known is whether or not the respondent supervises people, some posi-

TABLE 2.4
Criteria Used in High and Low Estimates for Sizes of Classes in Figure 2.1

Class	High Estimate	Low Estimate
Semiautonomous employees	All nonsupervisory employees who score high on both questions concerning subjective autonomy[a]	Those nonsupervisory employees who score high on the subjective autonomy questions and whose occupation is classified as having a complex relation to data and things by DOT classification[b]
Small employers	Fewer than 50 workers	Fewer than 10 workers
Top/middle managers	Professionals, technicians, and managers (by occupational title) who say they supervise people on their job	
Bottom managers/ supervisors	All supervisors not classified as top/middle managers	Excludes operatives and laborers
Workers	All nonsupervisory employees plus semi-autonomous employees whose occupations are classified as noncomplex by the DOT, plus supervisors whose occupations are operatives or laborers	Nonsupervisory employees who score low on either subjective autonomy question

Source: Wright, 1978a, p. 84.

[a]Jobs which the respondent claims are characterized "a lot" by *both* of the following descriptions:

(1) "a job that allows a lot of freedom as to how you do your work"

(2) "a job that allows you to make a lot of decisions on your own"

[b]The *Dictionary of Occupational Titles* codes occupations in terms of their relationship to data and to things in the following way: *relationship to things*: 0. setting up; 1. precision working; 2. operating-controlling; 3. driving-operating; 4. manipulating; 5. tending; 6. feeding-offbearing; 7. handling; 8. no significant relationship to things. *relationship to data*: 0. synthesizing; 1. coordinating; 2. analyzing; 3. compiling; 4. computing; 5. copying; 6. comparing; 7–8. no significant relationship to data. An individual whose occupation scored 0–2 on data and 0–2 on things, or who scored 0–2 on things and 7–8 on data, was classified as having a "complex" job.

tions have certainly been included which involve virtually no real control over labor power and thus should belong to the working class proper. Also included in the contradictory location are some top executives who should really have been placed in the bourgeoisie. In any event, this latter problem involves a very small proportion of the total population, perhaps 1–2% of all managers. No questions were asked in the survey which enable us accurately to distinguish top or middle managers and technocrats from line supervisors and foremen. We can use occupational titles to make some crude estimates. I shall assume that all supervisors who say that they are professionals, managers, or technicians are probably technocrats, middle managers, or top managers. All the rest I shall assume are line supervisors or foremen. The high estimate for this bottom category includes all supervisors who are not classified in the top or middle management position; the low estimate excludes operatives and laborers, most of whom are probably heads of work teams rather than actual foremen. On the basis of these estimates, approximately 12% of the economically active population fall into the contradictory location of middle or top manager, between the working class and the bourgeoisie, while somewhere between 18% and 23% occupy the contradictory location at the boundary of the working class. If we take ten employees as the cut-off point for small capitalists, then the contradictory location between the petty bourgeoisie and the bourgeoisie consists of about 6% of the population. If we take fifty employees as the cut-off, then this increases to 7%.

On the basis of these statistics, the working class (i.e., nonsupervisory, nonautonomous wage laborers) in the United States constitutes between 41% and 54% of the economically active population. If anything, the figure is probably closer to the upper bound. At the boundaries of the working class are another 20–35% of the population, depending upon which estimates are used. These contradictory locations closest to the working class constitute the most likely class allies of the working class in class struggles. The working class and its immediate class allies, therefore, constitute about 60–70% of the population.

Is this large or small? Does this indicate that the United States is becoming a middle-class society? Is the historical trajectory of this class structure one which will lead to the progressive expansion or erosion of contradictory locations? In the absence of time-series and comparative data on class relations, it is impossible to answer these questions. What is clear is that although class structure in the United States is characterized by significant contradictory locations, nevertheless the working class, defined in terms of social relations of production, remains unquestionably the largest class in the United States and that it approaches a majority of the population.

CONCLUSION

Briefly to recapitulate the argument, we analyzed the class relations of capitalist society in terms of three processes underlying social relations of production: control of labor, control of the physical means of production, and control of investments and the accumulation process. The basic classes of capitalist society—the bourgeoisie and the proletariat—can be understood as representing polar class locations within each of these three processes. The petty bourgeoisie, in contrast, is defined by the second and the third of these processes within simple commodity production. We then defined contradictory locations within class relations as situations in which these three processes did not perfectly correspond to the basic classes within the capitalist mode of production or to the petty bourgeoisie in simple commodity production. This led to the analysis of three contradictory positions: managers and supervisors occupy a contradictory position between the bourgeoisie and the proletariat; small employers occupy such a position between the bourgeoisie and the petty bourgeoisie; and semiautonomous employees occupy a contradictory position between the petty bourgeoisie and the proletariat.

No mention has been made thus far of the problem of the class location of positions in the social structure that are not directly defined by the social relations of production.[12] Such positions would include housewives, students, the permanently unemployed and, depending upon how narrowly one defines "production," positions within the administrative and repressive apparatuses of the state. Marxists have suggested two broadly different strategies for dealing with this issue. The first is to argue that certain positions in the social structure have no class position, that they are positions "outside" class relations altogether (see, for example, Cutler et al., 1977). Classes, in this perspective, are strictly defined by the social relations of production, and only positions defined within those relations constitute "class positions."

An alternative approach is to argue that positions in the social structure are determined not only by social relations of production, but also by social relations of reproduction, political relations, ideological relations, etc., and that these other relations can also situate these positions within the class structure. The theoretical problem, then, is to establish the relationship between these other relations and the social relations of production. In these terms, for example, a worker's wife who does not herself work would be considered part of the working class because she occupies a position in the social relations of repro-

[12]For a more thorough discussion of the class location of positions outside of production, see Wright (1978a, pp. 87–97; 1978c).

duction which is tied to working-class positions within the social relations of reproduction. In an analogous way, a top bureaucratic official
in the state would be considered part of the bourgeoisie (or at least part
of the contradictory location near the bourgeoisie) because such an
official occupies a position within political relations which is tied to
the capitalist class position within the social relations of production. A
clerk or janitor within a state bureau, on the other hand, would belong
in the working class, since within the political relations of domination
and subordination, such positions are totally excluded from any control over state activity.[13]

In all such cases, the task of analysis of structural class location is
to understand the specific ways in which such positions are linked to
and determined *by* the social relations of production even if they are
not directly determined *within* those relations.

The overall class structure of capitalist societies thus consists of (a)
those positions within production relations which define the basic
class locations (bourgeoisie, proletariat, petty bourgeoisie); (b) those
positions outside of the sphere of production which are linked to basic
class locations; (c) those positions within production relations which

[13]The analysis of the position of state officials is actually rather more complex than
suggested here. Two problems in particular need emphasizing: (1) Different positions
within the state are tied to the bourgeoisie in different ways, through different
mechanisms, and this determines whether or not they should be considered bourgeois
positions within the state apparatus, or contradictory locations. A full analysis of the
class location of state officials would require a rigorous deciphering of these mechanisms
and their consequences. (2) In situations of structural political crisis, when the capitalist
state ceases to function reproductively for the interests of the capitalist class, political
social relations may no longer effectively tie the top officials of the state to the
bourgeoisie. The class character of those positions is then temporarily indeterminate (not
contradictory); the positions cease to be effectively constrained by their link to the social
relations of production. Such a situation is unlikely to persist for an extended period. It
would be resolved either through a radical transformation of the social relations of production or a restoration of effective ties of the state to the dominant class. (For a discussion
of the possibility of such nonreproductive forms of the state, see Wright, 1978a, ch. 4.)

One further point should be noted. The formal criteria used to define class positions
within the relations of production can also be applied to class positions within the state:
the working-class position in the state is excluded from any control over the labor of
others, the use of the physical means of production in the state, or the basic policy
decisions about state activity (allocation of state resources). The bourgeois position
within the state has control over all three of these, but especially over policymaking (the
exercise of state power). The contradictory class locations within the state apparatus are
excluded from basic policymaking, but have some control over the implementation of
policy and over labor within the state. In practical terms, therefore, it is unnecessary to
distinguish between state employees and private-sector employees in operationalizing
class relations. It is for this reason that in Figure 2.1, state and private employees are
mixed together.

define contradictory locations within class relations (managers, semiautonomous employees, small employers); (d) those positions outside of the sphere of production which are linked to contradictory locations.

Taken together, these positions would define a comprehensive class map of capitalist society. Such a structural map, however, is only the starting point. The central purpose of a class analysis is not to describe class structure but to use a structural analysis of class relations in order to explain some historical or theoretical problem. The rest of this book is devoted to using the class categories developed in this chapter to understand one particular problem: the process of income determination in contemporary American society. In chapter 3, I shall lay out the basic logic of a Marxist approach to income determination and contrast that logic with economic and with sociological theories of income determination. Chapter 4 will then develop a series of substantive hypotheses about the relationship between class structure and income determination.

3

Theoretical Perspectives on Income Inequality

This then is the wit and wisdom of human capital theory—to reduce all economic relations between individuals to the relation of simple commodity exchange, all income categories to the single category interest.

—MICHAEL CARTER, 1977

Theory, Albert Einstein once said, determines what we can observe. Louis Althusser, a contemporary French Marxist philosopher, slightly transformed this proposition by saying that theory also determines what we cannot observe (Althusser, 1970a, p. 25). Theoretical questions are always embedded in conceptual structures, and if those structures lack certain pivotal elements (concepts), certain questions cannot or will not be asked. In the analysis of alternative theories, then, it is as important to establish and explain their "silences" as it is to elaborate and compare their positive claims.

This chapter will systematically compare the logical structure of a reconstructed Marxist theory of income determination with two dominant theoretical traditions in the social sciences—human capital theory within neoclassical economics and status attainment theory within sociology. Throughout the discussion particular emphasis will be placed on the structure of the concepts used in each perspective and the relationship between those concepts and the character of the questions addressed in the theory. My intention is not to offer a comprehensive summary of the details of each theory or a general assessment of their research findings. Rather, I shall focus on the essential underlying structure of the argument.

In the first section of this chapter, I shall outline the basic contours of the Marxist account of income determination. This discussion will be organized around three basic elements of the conceptual structure of Marxist theory: the *units of analysis* within the theory, the *social relations* in terms of which those units of analysis are studied, and the *logic of causation* which is used to construct theories of those units of analysis and social relations. The second section of the paper will present a parallel discussion of human capital theory and status attainment theory. There is no pretense to completeness in these summaries. They are merely designed to situate the theoretical comparisons which follow. Finally, in the third section of the chapter, I shall systematically compare the basic elements in Marxist theory with those of human capital and status attainment theories in order to show how the underlying structure of both human capital and status attainment theory excludes the possibility of asking certain critical questions which are central to Marxist theory. The actual elaboration of a series of substantive propositions about income inequality based on these questions will be postponed until chapter 4.

THE UNDERLYING LOGIC OF A MARXIST THEORY OF INCOME DETERMINATION

In a sense income inequality has been at the very heart of Marxist theory, in the form of the theory of exploitation, but there has been very little sustained theoretical work on income determination by Marxists. Marx himself mainly concentrated on the mechanisms by which capitalist income (profits or surplus value) is extracted from workers, i.e., on the income determination process *between* classes. He only casually discussed the process by which the incomes of workers themselves were determined, i.e., the income determination process *within* classes. The essential core of his analysis of workers' incomes is that:

1. Workers' income comes from the sale of a particular commodity, labor power. Its value, like that of all commodities, is defined by the socially necessary labor time that goes into its production. In the case of labor power, this is defined by the bundle of goods which are necessary to reproduce labor power, both on a day-to-day basis and intergenerationally.

2. The price of that bundle of goods—the wage—is itself determined by the level of productivity in the wage goods sector of the economy. The more productive the wage goods sector, the lower will be the value (socially necessary labor time required for production) of the wage bundle, and thus the lower will be the wage (all things being equal).

3. Variability in the magnitude of the wage goods bundle in real terms is itself determined by two basic factors: (a) variability in the costs of producing and reproducing skills within the working class—skilled labor power is generally more expensive to produce and maintain than unskilled labor power (i.e., requires a larger bundle of wage goods) and thus requires a higher wage; (b) "historical and moral" factors, in particular the capacity of the working class to struggle collectively for higher wages. In *Capital,* Marx commented,

> the fixation of the value of labor power . . . is only settled by the continuous struggle between capital and labor, the capitalist constantly trying to reduce wages to their physical minimum and to extend the working day to its physical maximum, while the working man constantly presses in the opposite direction. The matter resolves itself into a question of the relative powers of the combattants. [Marx, 1906 ed., p. 443]

These comments are very suggestive, but they provide merely the starting point for a complete theory of income determination. Later Marxists have provided only modest theoretical elaborations on these original formulations (see Baudelot et al., 1974, esp. pp. 159–236; Carter, 1977; Edwards et al., 1975).

The account of a Marxist theory of income determination which follows is not, therefore, simply a description of Marx's own theory or a distillation of various contemporary Marxist accounts of income inequality. Rather, it is an attempt to reconstruct a Marxist theory of income determination on the basis of the underlying logic of Marxist methodology. In this section the emphasis will be on the formal struc-

ture of such a theory; in the next chapter we will use that formal structure to generate a series of propositions about income determination in
contemporary American capitalism.

Units of Analysis

The choice of a unit of analysis within a scientific theory should
be a theoretical choice, not simply a pragmatic one. Implicitly or
explicitly, the choice of a given unit of analysis implies that real causal
processes are centered on that unit, that the unit of analysis in question
has real determinations and real effects.[1] In effect, the choice of a unit
of analysis is itself a theoretical proposition about the location of salient causal processes.

Marxist theory involves three basic, dialectically related units of
analysis: *social structures, classes,* and *individuals.* To say that each of
these constitutes a unit of analysis implies that they have real consequences which cannot be reduced to some other unit of analysis. This is
intuitively obvious in the case of individuals: few social scientists
argue that individual-level processes can be effectively reduced to
either biological or social-cultural phenomena. Individuals are real and
they have real, irreducible consequences in the world.

The claim that social structures and classes are as real as individuals, and thus warrant the designation "unit of analysis," is less obvious.
It has often been argued by social scientists (e.g., George Homans) that
social structures are simply aggregations of individual behaviors and
have no ontological status in their own right. Other social scientists
acknowledge the reality of social structures, but investigate them only
in terms of their effects on individuals, and thus never study structures
as proper units of analysis (see the discussion on human capital theory
below). Marxist theory, while not denying the place of the individual
within the social structure, insists that both social structures and
classes are real, that they have real determinants and real consequences

---

[1]Not all philosophers of science would accept this dictum. Some philosophers, particularly those in the positivist tradition, have argued that concepts should be seen
strictly as conventions, convenient analytical tools for describing the social world. As
analytical constructs they do not necessarily have any reality outside the head of the
theorist. Marxist social science, on the other hand, is steadfastly realist in its claims about
concepts and theories. It is always possible, of course, that a concept fails to designate
anything "real" about the world (this is indeed the fate of what can be termed "ideological concepts"), but in principle scientific concepts are not arbitrary conventions; rather,
they are tools which effectively map real relations in the social world. For an excellent
discussion of realism in science, see Bhaskar (1975). For a discussion specifically addressed to social sciences, see Keat and Urry (1976), especially chs. 1–3.

that cannot be reduced to the subjectivity of individuals, and that the logic and dynamics of these units of analysis must be investigated both theoretically and empirically.

The argument that social structures, classes, and individuals all constitute legitimate units of analysis does not imply that they are totally independent of each other. Indeed, the very heart of Marxist theory is the investigation of the complex relations of determination among these different units of analysis. The critical point is that each of these units is seen as having a genuine relative autonomy. Thus it is essential to study specific theoretical problems such as income determination in terms of dynamics located within each of the three basic units of analysis, as well as in terms of the dynamics which link the different units of analysis.

The starting point of such an investigation is the level of social structure. The fundamental premise of a Marxist theory is that the essential process by which income is determined varies from social structure to social structure. Specifically, it varies across modes of production. The decisive difference between modes of production centers on the mechanism by which dominant classes appropriate surplus labor from direct producers: in classical feudalism, for instance, surplus labor is directly appropriated in the form of labor dues to feudal lords; in capitalism it takes the form of the appropriation of surplus value (i.e., the difference between the value of labor power—the wage—and the total value produced by workers within production).

The income determination process will also vary across different stages or phases of capitalist development (competitive vs. monopoly capitalism); it will vary depending upon the location of a particular capitalist country within the world capitalist system (imperialist centers vs. periphery); and it will vary depending upon the role of the state in the accumulation process. Any fully developed theory of income determination must involve at least an implicit account of the specificities of the social structure within which that income is determined.[2]

[2]In effect, most theories of income determination, whether Marxist or non-Marxist, do involve an implicit account of social structure. The simplifying assumption within human capital theory of a perfectly competitive market, for example, is a claim about social structure that derives, basically, from the income determination process for capitalist societies in the last quarter or so of the nineteenth century. It could be argued that there are still some sectors of the U.S. economy for which these assumptions may be appropriate. But unless one is willing to claim that the essence of things in general is still represented by perfectly competitive markets, this is an inappropriate simplification for an account of income determination in advanced capitalist economies as a whole.

Within such an account of the social structural basis of the income determination process, the specific analysis of income determination at the level of classes can take place. This will be the heart of the empirical investigation later in this book. The investigation of income determination at the level of classes has two basic thrusts: first, the analysis of the income determination processes *within* classes; and second, the analysis of the ways in which the entire income determination process is shaped by class struggle.

Not only does the income determination process differ from one social structure to another, but within a given society it differs from one class location to another. Income is determined in fundamentally different ways within different classes: the process of acquisition of capitalist income (exploitation) is fundamentally different from the process of acquisition of petty bourgeois income (self-earned income, i.e., income from the sale of commodities produced by one's own labor); and both of these are different from the process of acquisition of income within the working class (sale of the commodity labor power). Furthermore, as we shall see in the following chapter, the process by which income is determined within the working class (the tendential equalization of wages to the value of labor power) is different from the process by which it is determined for contradictory locations between the working class and other classes (wages are permanently kept above the value of labor power by a mechanism of social control). The income determination process does not operate homogeneously across individuals, even across all wage laborers, but is itself determined by class relations.

Classes are not just locations within a social structure. They are also organized social forces which engage in conflict and which transform social structures. Class struggles intervene in the income determination process in two basic ways: first, through union struggles over wages, contracts, and unemployment insurance, and social struggles for welfare provisions and the like; secondly, by transforming the social structures within which income is determined. This is most dramatically the case where class struggles involve the transition from one mode of production to another, but it is also true for transformations within modes of production. A good example is the considerable growth of the state in advanced capitalism. The expansion of the state's role in the economy not only directly changes the income determination process through transfer payments, but indirectly affects that process by changing the structural constraints on the market, the competition among workers for jobs, the impact of unemployment on wage rates, the capacity of given employers to discriminate in various ways, etc.

The analysis of income determination at the level of individuals presupposes the analysis at the level of social structures and classes, for individuals as such acquire income only through their location within a class in a given social structure. Within this framework, the analysis of individual-level income determination processes involves two basic aspects: first, the ways in which individual choices and actions can transform the individual's location within class relations (i.e., the problem of social mobility, both inter- and intragenerational);[3] and second, the various processes which affect those specific individual choices and actions that influence the individual's income within a given class location. Both of these processes revolve around the social determinants of individual subjectivity or, as it is generally called by Marxists, individual consciousness.

A fully elaborated Marxist theory of income determination would attempt to link all three of these units of analysis, both theoretically and empirically. The present study, however, will focus almost entirely on classes. I shall, in effect, "hold constant" the social structural level by examining the class processes of income determination within American capitalism at a particular moment in history. The individual level of analysis also will not be systematically discussed, not because it is not important, but because the individual-level processes can only be tackled once the class processes are understood.

Social Relations

The concept of a "social relation" means something quite different for each of these three units of analysis. For the individual, social relations constitute the essential social environment. Individuals enter into social relations, which are, in a sense, "external" to them. Social structures, in contrast, are made up of social relations. These are the basic components of social structures, and thus they must be understood as "internal" to those structures. Classes, finally, are determined within social relations. Social relations are neither internal nor external

[3]The total amount and patterns of such movement must be considered a characteristic of the class structure itself, not simply of the individuals who move within that class structure. Precisely which people move or don't move, however, is partially determined within individual-level processes themselves. The study of socialization, personality development, and the like would play a part in this kind of analysis.

to classes, since classes are common positions within social relations (in the complex sense discussed in chapter 2).

Within Marxist theory, the global notion of social relations is broken down into several interdependent dimensions. Of particular importance are social relations of production, technical relations of production, exchange relations, political relations, and ideological relations. Although all of these are ultimately relevant to a fully developed theory of income determination, we will focus our attention on the first three.

Of these, the social relations of production play the pivotal role. When we say that the income determination process varies across classes, it is primarily because these classes are situated differently within the social relations of production. Capitalists earn their income through exploitation because they own the means of production (in the precise sense discussed in chapter 2) and employ the labor power of others; they are thus in a position to appropriate surplus labor from their employees. Petty bourgeois producers own their own means of production and are themselves the direct producers. Thus all of their income is self-earned, generated by their own labor. Workers, on the other hand, neither own their means of production nor control the labor of others; thus they depend entirely upon the sale of their labor power for their income. Because of their position within the social relations of production, therefore, their income depends upon the social conditions for the exchange of labor power (the conditions of the labor market).

Technical relations of production and exchange relations also clearly play a role in the determination of income. Income is not simply a function of location within the social relations of production. The ways in which technical and exchange relations affect income, however, are themselves determined by production relations. Social relations of production, in a sense, organize the causal consequences of other dimensions of social relations. To give some specific examples: changes in the technical division of labor may lead to a degradation of skills among workers and thus a devaluation of the value of their labor power; this in turn would generate a tendency for their wages to decline. Those identical changes in the technical division of labor could increase the profits of capitalists. Fluctuations in supply and demand conditions (exchange relations) may have serious effects on the wages of many workers, but very little effect on the wages of managers, because their incomes are fairly insulated from direct market pressures (for reasons to be discussed in chapter 4). Technical and exchange relations, therefore, are consequential for income, but the ways in which they are consequential are themselves determined by the social relations of production.

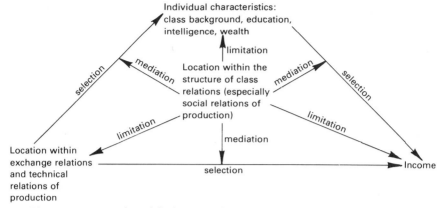

Figure 3.1. Formal model of income determination at the level of classes.

Formal Model of Income Determination at the Level of Classes

The formal model of income determination presented in Figure 3.1 will serve as the basis for the substantive hypothesis developed in chapter 4.

To know how to read this kind of model of determination, one must understand the various relations of determination indicated in the diagram: limitation, selection, and mediation.[4]

1. *Limitation* is a mode of determination in which one structure or process establishes limits of variation on another structure or process. Limits of variation imply that (a) there are certain excluded possibilities for the determined (limited) structure, and (b) within the range of included possibilities, there is a determinate distribution of probabilities for one outcome or another. In the model of determination in Figure 3.1, the location within class relations establishes limits of variation on income, on the location within exchange and technical relations, and on personal characteristics. This implies that within the working class, for example, certain incomes are totally impossible, and that among all possible incomes, certain incomes are systematically more likely than others.

[4]Three other modes of determination are not included in this particular model: transformation, reproduction/nonreproduction, and limits of functional compatibility. For an extended discussion of the logic of modes of determination and their role in Marxist theory, see Wright (1978a, ch. 1).

2. *Selection* is a mode of determination which establishes limits within limits. Selection always presupposes a broader limiting process within which it operates. In Figure 3.1, for example, individual characteristics have a selective effect on income within the limits established by the location within class relations.

3. *Mediation* defines a causal relation in which one structure or process determines the causal relationship between two other structures or processes. In Figure 3.1, the location within class relations (in particular, within the social relations of production) mediates the other causal relations in the model. The ways in which the location within exchange and technical relations, for example, influence income are themselves mediated by class location. The most important results in the empirical sections of this study all concern these relations of mediation.

In interpreting this model, it is crucial to realize that the relations of determination are not necessarily temporal. For example, to say that class location places limits on the individual characteristics of incumbents of those positions, while exchange and technical relations select characteristics from within those limits, does not imply that the limiting process comes "before" the selection process in time. If anything, concrete individuals enter into exchange relations before actually becoming incumbents of a class location (and they certainly acquire many of their individual characteristics before even entering exchange relations). The argument, therefore, is not a temporal one, but a structural one. The structural characteristics of the class locations themselves determine (i.e., limit) the basic distribution of personal characteristics recruited into those positions. Exchange relations have their effect on individual characteristics within the limits established by production relations.

This atemporal character of the relations of determination in Figure 3.1 will not cause any difficulty so long as it is remembered that this is not a model of the individual-level income determination process, but rather of the class-level process. As it stands, the model says little about how individuals as such acquire their income. Obviously, from the individual's point of view, personal characteristics are a determinant of location within class relations (and within exchange and technical relations as well). But from the point of view of the class structure as such, the individual characteristics which are selected into a given class location are themselves determined by the interplay of production relations, exchange relations, and technical relations.

If we look just at the immediate process of income determination in

Figure 3.1 (the relations of determination directly affecting income) the model should be interpreted in the following way:

1. Income is fundamentally determined by the location within the structure of class relations. This relation of determination defines the basic income differences *between* classes.

2. Individual characteristics and the location within exchange and technical relations also influence income, but only within the basic limits established by the location within class relations. No working-class position within the social relations of production can possibly receive an income as high as a large capitalist, regardless of the brilliance or education of the incumbent of that position, the tightness of the labor market, or the technical functions performed within that position. Within those limits, however, personal characteristics and exchange or technical relations can have a real impact.

3. The precise way in which exchange relations, technical relations, and individual characteristics influence income is itself determined by (mediated by) the location within class relations. For example, as we shall see in chapter 6, education (one aspect of the position within exchange relations) makes a much bigger difference for the income of managers than it does for the income of workers.

THE UNDERLYING LOGIC OF HUMAN CAPITAL
AND STATUS ATTAINMENT THEORIES OF
INCOME DETERMINATION

In this section, we will examine the basic arguments of human capital theory in economics and status attainment theory in sociology.[5] Since the main purpose is to establish the critical differences with Marxist theory, the accounts which follow will not pretend to be comprehensive.[6]

[5]The classic statement of human capital theory, which still serves as a general overview of the theory, is that of Becker (1975). For an assessment, by a human capital advocate, of recent criticisms of human capital theory, see Cain (1976). Probably the most useful critique of the tradition from within economics is that by Thurow (1975). For a very useful Marxist critique which has influenced my analysis of human capital theory, see Carter (1977). The basic argument of the status attainment approach to income determination can be found in Sewell and Hauser (1975, ch. 1).

[6]The discussion of human capital and status attainment theories which follows is not "innocent," to use a favorite expression of Louis Althusser's. The categories used to assess theories, just as the categories used to assess the world, are themselves inevitably rooted in a theoretical structure. Any comparison of theories, therefore, is

Human Capital Theory: A Brief Summary

At any given point in time, individuals make a variety of choices which shape their present consumption and future income. Particularly important among these choices are decisions about how to spend one's time and one's resources. In terms of human capital investments, the decisive choice is over allocating one's time toward obtaining income in the present, thus maximizing present consumption, or allocating one's time toward obtaining skills in the present, thus maximizing future consumption.

Why should increasing one's skills lead to increases in consumption in the future? The assumption is that skilled labor is more productive than unskilled labor, and that as a result employers are willing to pay such labor higher wages (since in neoclassical theory, wages = marginal productivity in equilibrium situations). Exactly how much higher these wages will be depends upon the technical conditions of production (which determine substitution effects) and the supply and demand conditions of the market. The actual choices by individuals, therefore, will depend upon their subjective time preferences on the one hand (utility functions), and the conditions which determine the rate of return on human capital investments (market and technical conditions) on the other.

Status Attainment Theory: A Brief Summary

Status attainment theory has a less formally developed account of the income determination process than does human capital theory. Nevertheless, the basic contours of the argument can be easily summarized. Since income varies across individuals, the causes of this outcome must be sought in variations in the characteristics of individuals. Two clusters of such variation are particularly important: first, variation in various *ascriptive* characteristics of individuals (social origins, parents' education, race, sex, intelligence, etc.) and second, variation in various *achieved* or acquired characteristics of individuals (principally education and occupational status, but also things like

---

either explicitly or implicitly a comparison from the vantage point of a particular theoretical structure, in this case, Marxist theory. I hope that the analysis of human capital theory and status attainment theory which follows will not do violence to the underlying logic of their conceptual structures, but it is important to remember that the "reading" of these theories is from a specific perspective and is intended to establish the domain of questions unaskable within these theories which can be addressed through a Marxist perspective. For an extended discussion of the problem of "reading" theory, see Louis Althusser's essay in Althusser and Balibar (1970, especially pp. 13–69).

geographical mobility, personality, motivations, etc.). The central research task within this tradition is to sort out the relative importance of
and interrelationships between achieved and ascribed factors in determining various outcomes, such as income.

In the investigation of income, occupational location (as measured
by occupational status) plays a particularly strategic role, since it is
viewed as the critical achieved characteristic. Occupations vary over
many dimensions—their "functional importance," their power, the difficulty of moving into the occupation, the mechanisms of selection into
the occupation, etc. The single metric which best captures these multiple dimensions of occupations is "occupational status" (or "occupational prestige"), which is basically a measure of the overall social
standing of the occupation in the eyes of average people.[7] In order to
understand income determination, therefore, it is necessary to understand the ascriptive and achievement processes through which people
are sorted into occupational statuses, and the extent to which their
personal characteristics (ascribed and achieved) continue to influence
their income once they have obtained an occupational status.

At first glance, the theoretical stances toward income inequality in
conventional neoclassical economics and in sociology seem poles
apart. Human capital theory in economics has developed a sophisticated, deductive mathematical analysis of income determination based
on a few simple, axiomatic assumptions. Sociological studies of income
determination have relied largely on statistical analysis of empirical
relations, generally avoiding any sustained mathematical formulations.
Human capital theory couches the analysis of income determination
in the language of utility functions, marginal productivity, supply
and demand; sociological studies use a language of social background,
occupational status, and achievement motivations.

Nevertheless, in spite of these real differences, there is a sense in
which both bodies of theory share a basic underlying structure. While
they may develop one aspect or another to differing extents, and while
they may formulate different kinds of propositions within this structure, they both adopt the individual as the central unit of analysis, and
they both analyze individuals primarily in terms of exchange relations
and technical relations of production.

---

[7]There are secondary differences between the concepts of status and prestige: *prestige* is understood as measuring the overall social rankings of occupation; *status* is often
used more narrowly to designate the economic standing of the occupation (thus, it is
often referred to as a socioeconomic status). For our present purposes this distinction is
largely irrelevant: in both cases the variable defines a one-dimensional metric of occupations which is viewed as relevant for the determination of the individual's income.

The Unit of Analysis

In both human capital and status attainment theory, outcomes which are attached to individuals are the essential objects of investigation, and the causes of those outcomes are largely seen as operating through individuals (or quasi-individuals, in the case of firms in neoclassical economics).

This individualistic premise is much more explicit within human capital theory. The ultimate regulator of the entire process of income acquisition is the subjective preferences of individuals, particularly their time preference for present over future consumption. Indeed, within human capital theory, as Mincer has argued (1970, p. 7), if individuals all had the same initial endowments and all faced the same market and technical conditions, then they would essentially choose their own incomes on the basis of their time preferences (subject to various random factors).

Status attainment theory appears somewhat less wedded to an individualistic premise. The metric for discussing occupational positions, after all, is based on social evaluations of position, and thus has a supraindividual character. The essential dynamic of the theory, however, is conceived almost entirely at the level of atomistic individuals. Social structures have their consequences because they are embodied in individuals, in the form of personal characteristics. The class structure, for example, is seen as relevant in the analysis of income determination only insofar as it constitutes one of the factors which shape the individual's own achievements and motivations. The preoccupation of the theory is with ascription vs. achievement as determinants of individual outcomes, not with the structure of the outcomes themselves.

This is not to suggest that social structure plays no role in human capital nor in status attainment theory. At least implicitly, it plays an important role in shaping the functioning of the market and individual utility functions within human capital theory, and social structure certainly operates as a systematic constraint on individual action in status attainment theory. While methodological individualism may be a strong tendency in both sociology and economics, very few serious social scientists take this individualistic thrust to the point of ignoring social structures altogether. The point is that in both status attainment and human capital theories of income determination, social structures are viewed as theoretically interesting largely as determinants or constraints on individual actions and outcomes. With few exceptions, they have little theoretical relevance in their own right.

As we have seen, within Marxist theory, both social structures and classes are considered basic units of analysis as such. While the choices and actions of individuals are legitimate objects of investigation, they are seen as theoretically intelligible only within a broader analysis of the determinations and contradictions of social structures and classes.

Social Relations

Both human capital and status attainment theories see individuals as entering into two different kinds of social relations: *exchange relations* (market relations) and *technical relations* of production.

In human capital theory, exchange relations provide the essential mechanism by which people obtain the actual income returns to their investments in human capital. To the extent that there are impediments to the free functioning of the market—including impediments to the individual's information about the market—then it would be possible for someone to invest in skills and in the end be unable to realize a full return on that investment. As in all neoclassical theory, the market constitutes the essential process for the mutual adjustments of supply and demand which make rational choice based on utility functions possible.

Technical relations of production enter into human capital theory in three ways. First, the technical relations of production of *skills* define the trade-offs in time and resources the individual has to make in order to obtain those skills (i.e., in order to increase productivity). Secondly, the technical relations of production of *commodities* determine the mix of different levels of skills which will be demanded by employers for a given level of output. Thirdly, technical relations determine the marginal productivity of those skills for a given output, and thus what the employer is willing to pay for them. Taken together, these technical and exchange relations determine what the actual income of an individual with a given level of human capital is likely to be.

Exchange relations play a more tacit role within status attainment theory. Following Weber (1922), most status attainment theorists implicitly view "market capacity" as the essential immediate determinant of the individual's "life chances." Markets are treated, in this perspective, less as an arena for the equalization of supply and demand than as a bargaining arena. Individuals with greater achieved and ascribed statuses, it is argued, have greater bargaining power within an exchange relation, and thus can negotiate better terms of exchange, i.e., higher income.

Technical relations of production might at first appear to be absent from status attainment treatments of income determination. There is certainly no formal discussion of production functions, technology, marginal productivity, and so on. However, they enter the analysis in a fundamental way through the emphasis on occupational position.

Occupations, as was argued in chapter 1, can be understood as designating positions within the technical division of labor. A given occupation is defined by a set of technical operations or functions within a given production process.[8] As such, the concept of occupation must be systematically differentiated from the concept of class, which, as we are using it, designates positions within the social rather than the technical relations of production. A carpenter, for example, is an occupational category defined by the technical operation of transforming lumber into buildings. Carpenters may be located in virtually every class location: they may be workers, semiautonomous employees, foremen (contradictory location between the working class and the bourgeoisie), self-employed artisans (petty bourgeoisie), or even small employers.

This is not, of course, to suggest that there is a random relationship between occupational positions and class positions. On the contrary, one of the basic theses of Marxism is that the social relations of production determine (limit) the technical relations of production, and thus it would be expected that given occupations would be much more concentrated in some classes than in others (see chapter 5).

Within status attainment theory, there is very little sustained discussion of what it is about the technical relations of production which enables a given occupational position to be advantaged or disadvantaged with respect to income.[9] There are periodic claims about the functional importance of occupations as determined by the technical organization of production, and some discussion about the differential power of occupations because of the command over resources that they derive from their positions in the technical division of labor.[10] But

---

[8]This is somewhat narrower than the everyday usage of the concept of *occupation*, in which it designates broadly what a person "does for a living." In much of the social science literature, the concept of occupation simply appropriates this usage without any additional theoretical specification. It is more useful, in the present context, to restrict the notion of occupation to a specific aspect of what a person "does," namely those aspects defined by the technical division of labor. For descriptive purposes, the term *job* could be used to define more inclusively all aspects of what a person does within work. In terms of our discussion of Marxist theory, a job would, therefore, consist of social relations of production (class location) and technical relations of production (occupational location).

[9]For an interesting empirical study of the characteristics which determine the average incomes of occupations, see Bielby and Kalleberg (1975).

[10]The classic statement of the functionalist view of occupational rewards is that of Davis and Moore (1945). In many ways it represents the closest thing to a marginal productivity argument in neoclassical economics, since in operational terms "marginal productivity" and "functional importance" are closely related concepts. While few em-

regardless of the specific formulation, there is in all cases the general assumption that positions within the technical relations of production—occupations—are the critical positions for understanding the income determination process. The fact that these positions tend to be scaled in terms of an ideological dimension (status or prestige) should not obscure the underlying technological determinist logic.

Thus, in both human capital theory and status attainment theory, individuals with a given set of personal characteristics (particular subjective states and objective resources) enter into exchange relations and, as a result, are sorted into positions defined by the technical relations of production. Capital and labor meet only in a pure exchange relation. Once workers enter production, they are simply a "factor of production" performing technical functions. Social relations of production, however conceived, play no explicit role in either theory.

A Formal Causal Model of Income Determination at the Level of Individuals

Figure 3.2 presents a formal causal model of income determination within status attainment theory and human capital theory. This model is obviously a considerable oversimplification. Many possible linkages or lines of causation of considerable interest to researchers are left out. Again, the point of the model is less to capture the nuances of the two theories than to reveal their common underlying logic.

The heart of this model is the individual as the nodal point for the determination of income. Various exogenous factors determine the basic characteristics of individuals. These characteristics then determine the location of individuals within exchange relations (market capacity, human capital, education, etc.). This location in turn determines the individual's attainment of a specific position within the technical relations of production (an occupation) and finally, this position determines the individual's income.

---

pirical studies of the status attainment process have attempted to elaborate the logic of functional importance or indispensability, a diffuse notion of functional importance is often implicit in much of the discussion of status attainment.

"Postindustrial" theorists such as Bell (1973) have stressed that the "real content" that gives occupations differential rewards is command over resources of one sort or another (capital, information, labor, or expertise). Such views begin to raise issues which are quite similar to those within a Marxist perspective. The distinctive feature in the present context, however, is the insistence that at root it is the *technical content* of a position which gives it its power, and thus ultimately power relations are reducible to technical relations. See, for example, Lenski (1966), Treiman (1977, pp. 5–22).

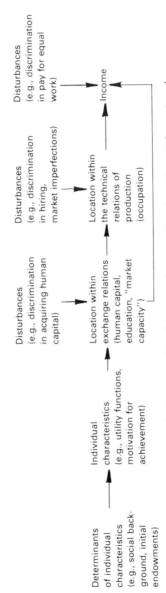

Figure 3.2. The basic model of income determination in status attainment and human capital theories. Note: For simplicity, only the central causal determinations are indicated here.

At each stage of this causal process, various kinds of disturbances may interfere with the simple translation of individual characteristics into outcomes. One of the central research tasks of both human capital and status attainment theory is to assess the magnitude of these disturbances. This is at the heart of the preoccupation of both traditions with the problem of discrimination and "equal opportunity." Discrimination is seen as an impediment to the free operation of individual choice in the determination of individual outcomes. It prevents individuals from freely acquiring all of the human capital they desire (discrimination in education); it prevents them from turning their location within exchange relations into an appropriate position within the technical division of labor (discrimination in hiring); and it may even prevent them from receiving equal pay for equal work (wage discrimination).

The logic of causation within this model is strictly temporal. Variables are ordered in terms of their biographical sequence within the life of the individual. Causes are always conceived of as prior to effects, and thus it is always possible to distinguish between "independent" and "dependent" variables. As a result, causation is always simple and homogeneous, rather than structural and heterogeneous.

QUESTIONS ASKABLE AND UNASKABLE WITHIN THEORIES OF INCOME DETERMINATION

The conceptual structures pictured in Figures 3.1 and 3.2 represent radically different approaches to the study of income determination. The differences are summarized in Table 3.1. The central thesis of this chapter is that, because of these differences in the underlying conceptual structures, human capital and status attainment theory are unable to ask certain questions which are of central importance within Marxist theory. In particular, there is no systematic way within either theory to ask questions about the determinants of the differences in income between classes or about the structural mediations within the income determination process, especially when those structural mediations are understood in terms of social relations of production.

Of course, it is always possible for status attainment or human capital theorists to include class "variables" in their equations, in spite of the fact that these variables measure concepts which have no systematic place within their theories. And it is almost always possible for human capital and status attainment theorists to provide post hoc interpretations of particular research findings generated by the questions

TABLE 3.1
Three Theories of Income Determination Compared

Elements in Conceptual Structure	Marxist Theory	Human Capital Theory	Status Attainment Theory
Basic unit of analysis	Structures, classes, and individuals	Individuals	Individuals
Critical dimensions of variability in units of analysis	Structures: mode of production and stage in the development of a mode of production; interpenetration of modes of production Classes: forms of collective organization and solidarity; level of political power; forms of class consciousness; location within production relations Individuals: location within the class structure; other characteristics elaborated in human capital and status attainment theory	Utility functions, especially time preferences. Resources: initial endowments, financial resources, already accumulated human capital, etc.	Motivations: needs for achievement, self-discipline, ability to delay gratification. Resources: IQ, social background, education, etc.
Social relations relevant to unit of analysis	Exchange relations Technical relations of production Social relations of production Political social relations Ideological social relations	Exchange relations Technical relations	Exchange relations Technical relations
Logic of causation	Structural determination	Simple temporal causation	Simple temporal causation

derived from the Marxist model. Any paradigm worth its salt can, after the fact, "explain" anything.

The point is that there would be no reason whatsoever within their theoretical frameworks for a human capital or status attainment theorist systematically to consider structural mediations in the first place. Since social relations of production play no organic role in the theory, there would be no reason to examine how the income determination process varies across production relations. Since structures are not primary units of analysis, there would be no reason to examine how different structures have different income processes. And since the theories do not countenance classes as organized social forces, there would be no reason to ask how the collective struggles of the working class and other classes transform the social structure in ways which alter the income determination process itself. These are all pivotal questions within Marxism that are excluded by the conceptual terrain of neoclassical economics and mainstream sociology.

The fact that human capital and status attainment theory are unable to ask certain important Marxist questions does not imply that the questions they do ask are irrelevant or uninteresting. Indeed, from the perspective of Marxist theory, the questions they ask are potentially relevant, if correctly situated within a social structural and class context. The basic question of status attainment theory, for example, is: What is the balance between ascribed and achieved characteristics in the determination of an individual's income? If this question is asked for people within specific class locations within specific social structures, then it becomes a meaningful question for Marxist theory: Within an advanced capitalist society, what is the balance between ascription and achievement in the determination of the income of individuals within the working class? within the capitalist class? within contradictory class locations? Asked in this way, the question directs our attention toward the process of structural mediation within the income determination process. If the class mediations are ignored, then it is assumed that the balance between ascription and achievement can be analyzed simply at the individual rather than the class-structural level.

Similarly, the basic question of human capital theory is: Why do individuals with different amounts of education (and other investments in human capital) receive different incomes? The elaborate discussions of time preferences, internal rates of return, discount rates, lifetime earnings, etc., are all designed to answer this question. If this question is posed for specific structural locations within class relations, then again it becomes a meaningful one within Marxist theory. Indeed, as we shall see in chapter 4, there are even certain circumstances when the conventional human capital answers (with some modifications) to this question become meaningful within Marxist theory, if structural mediations are taken into consideration (that is, for *pure* working-class locations under competitive market conditions).

The appropriate rejoinder to the above claims is that the Marxist questions are ill-posed. What appear to be "structural mediations," it could be argued, can ultimately be reformulated as outcomes of individual actions and choices. Thus, such "variables," if they have any relevance at all, can be incorporated into an individual-level analysis. No such reformulation has yet been produced, so any assessment of its effectiveness as a counter to the theoretical and empirical arguments of this study will have to wait.

Let us now leave this discussion of the underlying logic of a Marxist approach to income determination and develop a series of substantive propositions about the income determination process in contemporary American capitalism. The compelling quality of a Marxist approach lies not simply in its capacity to ask different questions, but in its capacity to provide a strategy for answering them as well.

4

Class and Income: Hypotheses

> It seems paradoxical that almost any scholar invited to discuss social class in historical context will refer to the works of Karl Marx, while virtually no contemporary empirical studies of social class use definitions of social class which could be called Marxian under the most liberal construction.
>
> —THOMAS E. LASSWELL, 1966

A central thesis of chapter 3 was that, in Marxist theory, *class location mediates the income determination process.* In this chapter we will try to give substance to this proposition by examining the income determination process within each of the class locations discussed in chapter 2 and then developing a series of concrete, operational hypotheses about these structural mediations. These hypotheses will provide the basic framework for the empirical investigation in chapters 5–10.

INCOME DETERMINATION IN THE WORKING CLASS

The working class, as defined in chapter 2, consists of those positions within the social relations of production which are excluded from control over money capital, physical capital, and labor. They neither own nor possess the means of production, and thus must sell their labor power to capitalists in order to work. The fundamental determinants of income within the working class, therefore, center on the determinants of the exchange value of this commodity, labor power.[1]

As I argued in chapter 3, Marxists have generally seen three factors as the primary determinants of the value of labor power: (a) the productivity of the wage goods sector; (b) the specific costs of producing and reproducing different types of labor power, i.e., of producing skills within the working class; and (c) the "historical and moral" standard of living of the working class (in real terms), won through class struggles.[2]

The last of these is the most poorly defined. The "historical and moral" factor in the value of labor power can be given two quite different interpretations. One interpretation is that all enduring wage differentials within the working class (other than those directly attributa-

---

[1]It is important to be absolutely clear on the theoretical content of this concept, "the *value* of labor power." There is certainly a relationship between the Marxist concept of the value of labor power and the neoclassical concept of the marginal productivity of labor, but the two concepts do not designate the same reality. The value of labor power simply refers to the socially determined costs of producing and reproducing the commodity, labor power. Marginal productivity refers to the price of the product produced by the last worker added to a production process (that is, added at the margin). Throughout this section we are discussing the determinants of the value of labor power and the conditions under which the actual wage of workers might deviate from that value. We are not discussing the productivity of workers as such.

[2]Marx introduces this notion of the "historical and moral element" in the value of labor power in a well-known passage in *Capital* (1867): "the number and extent of his so-called necessary wants, as also the modes of satisfying them, are themselves the product of historical development, and depend therefore to a great extent on the degree of civilization of a country, more particularly on the conditions under which, and consequentially on the habits and degree of comforts in which, the class of free laborers has been formed. In contradistinction therefore to the case of other commodities, there enters into the determination of the value of labor power a historical and moral element [1967 ed., p. 171]." It would probably be somewhat more appropriate to refer to this as an historical and cultural element, but since the earlier expression has been used traditionally in Marxist writing, I shall adopt it here.

ble to skill differences) should be considered the result of "historical and moral" factors. Thus, for example, the lower wages of black workers relative to white workers with the same levels of skills would be considered a result of historical processes—racism—which have depressed the socially defined standard of living of blacks. Black labor power, in effect, would be seen as having a lower value than white labor power. (Note that this is not equivalent to saying that black labor power is less *productive* in any sense, but simply that it takes a smaller bundle of goods to reproduce because of historical and cultural factors.) In such an interpretation, it is impossible by definition, except in a very transient way, for wages (the price of labor power) to ever be above or below the value of labor power.

Another way of understanding historical and moral factors, however, in the value of labor power is to see them as defining the wage bundle of socially average labor power, labor power of average skills and education. The actual wage of any given category of workers could then be broken down into three components: (a) a component representing the social standard for average labor; (b) a component representing the increased costs of (re)production of labor power due to greater skills (or other factors which raise the reproductive costs); and (c) a component representing that part of the wage which is above or below the value of labor power. This third component would constitute a wage-privilege or wage-discrimination element.

The investigation of the income determination process within the working class thus involves assessing the specific determinants of each of these components. The first two involve an examination of the determinants of the value of labor power; the third, of the discrepancy between the actual wage and this value.

In many ways, the most complex of these three components to investigate is the first. The average wage of workers of average skill is determined by a wide range of intersecting structural and historical factors: the position of the national economy in the world capitalist system; the historical trajectory of class struggles between the working class and capital; the ways in which these struggles have been crystalized in state institutions and interventions. The problem becomes especially complex since it is not sufficient to look at the determinants of average income per capita; the issue is the average wage of *workers* of average skill, and this, depending upon the class structure of a society, may be considerably below (or possibly above) the average income in that society. Furthermore, the content of "average skills" itself is difficult to operationalize and it changes over time, so that there is a considerable problem in even defining the appropriate category of worker by which to measure the "historical and moral" standard. In any event, since an empirical investigation of this question necessarily involves long-term longitudinal and cross-national data, neither of which are available for the present research, I shall focus most of my attention on the determinants of the second and third components of the wage of workers.

The second component—the part of the wage necessary to produce and reproduce the skills of the worker—is the aspect most familiar to economists. Marxists do not call this component "human capital" but in practical terms it is a closely related notion.[3] Skills cost something to produce and maintain and unless the wage of skilled workers more or less covers those costs, the skills will cease to be produced. Marxist theorists generally do not consider the foregone interest on savings spent in training or the interest on foregone earnings as an additional cost of training, since it is assumed that workers have negligible savings anyway, and that the increased security of skilled employment more than compensates for foregone earnings. They do, however, share with human capital theorists the basic assumption that the wages of skilled workers will, in an equilibrium situation, be high enough both to cover the costs of the training and to reproduce the skills over time. Under conditions when the third component of income is close to zero, and the historical and moral standard of average labor is taken as a given, the human capital theory's account of income determination is a reasonably correct description within the working class.[4]

In many ways, the third component of the wage—the privilege/ discrimination component—is the most critical for a developed theory of class mediations in the income determination process. As we shall see, the decisive impact of contradictory locations within class rela-

[3]Marxists object to the expression "human capital," since the skills embodied in a worker are not "capital" in the same sense that physical machinery and financial resources of the capitalist are "capital." Skills cannot be alienated; they cannot be sold; they cannot be used as collateral, etc. Above all, skills play a *qualitatively* different role in class relations from capital in the conventional sense. Whereas the accumulation of capital is based on the exploitation of labor, the accumulation of human capital (skills) is not. (For a very useful Marxist critique of human capital theory in these terms, see Carter, 1977.) In spite of this criticism, there is an essential similarity in Marxist and human capital theory, since both see the costs of production of skills as the basic determinant of the income return to skills.

[4]In these terms, the essential limitation of human capital theory is not that it is wrong, but that it is incapable of adequately defining the structural conditions of its own theoretical adequacy. Most human capital theory recognizes that market conditions (monopoly and monopsony conditions within exchange relations) affect the operation of the human capital model; but there is no recognition that the theory is adequate only under certain conditions of class relations as well.

tions on income determination is to generate large positive values for this component. Within the working class itself, it would be expected that this component is generally fairly close to zero or negative; rarely is it substantially positive.

The privilege/discrimination component of the wage is generally large and negative for women and racial minorities. As I shall demonstrate in subsequent chapters, even when we compare people whose labor power has the same value, women workers receive substantially less income than men workers, and black workers less than white. These categories of workers, therefore, are forced to sell their labor power at a price kept permanently below its social value because of racial and sexual discrimination. Except in situations where such discrimination results in shortages of certain types of skilled labor great enough to force the price of such labor above its value, discrimination against blacks and women raises the overall rate of exploitation.

Under certain circumstances, the privilege/discrimination component of the wage can be positive, even within the working class proper. Several possibilities are especially important:

1. Situations in which there is a temporary shortage of a specific category of labor power because of market fluctuations which temporarily push the price of labor power above its value.

2. Situations in which there is a permanent shortage of a specific category of skilled labor power because of institutionalized restrictions on the entry of people into the market such as credentialing, entrance requirements into training programs, and control over training programs by unions or other associations. This is a situation that has been extensively studied by neoclassical economists, since it potentially produces what they term a "monopoly rent" component in the wage. From our point of view, such situations constitute one example among several of mechanisms which push the wage of skilled labor power above its value (again, the value of skilled labor power = the value of socially average labor power + the costs of producing and reproducing the skills of skilled labor power).

3. Situations in which workers are paid a wage above the value of their labor power as part of a strategy of social control on the part of employers. This third possibility is the most important for our general analysis of class mediations in the income determination process, and needs to be discussed in some detail.

Social control is a central problem in all capitalist production processes. Capitalists purchase labor *power* on the labor market; that is, they purchase the capacity of workers to work. They do not purchase a certain quantity of *labor* as such; they only purchase the right to use that labor power for a certain period of time. Capitalist profits, however, depend upon the actual performance of labor within production, and thus the extent to which the actual labor performed will exceed the costs of the labor power purchased on the market is always problematic. Of course, capitalists face a parallel problem when they purchase raw materials and machines on the market. If a machine breaks down prematurely, the capitalist may not receive the full expected value from it (in technical terms, the machine may be destroyed before all of the value embodied in it is transferred to products). But waste of machines is largely an engineering problem of proper maintenance; "waste" of labor is a social problem. The relationship between capitalists and machinery is not a contradictory one; the relationship between capital and labor is. Labor power cannot simply be considered a "factor of production," because it exists within real people, real workers, and workers resist their own exploitation; machines do not.

Because of the antagonistic character of class relations, capitalists are forced to devise strategies for ensuring the adequate transformation of labor power into labor, or as Burawoy has put it, for securing the surplus.[5] These strategies of social control can be seen as specific combinations of repressive sanctions for misbehavior (principally the threat of being fired) and inducements for good behavior or good performance (principally income and promotions).[6] The balance between these two modes of social control varies, both historically and structurally. In certain periods of capitalist development, repressive controls were both much more severe and much more heavily relied upon. In contemporary capitalism, inducements play an important part in the dynamics of social control.

Inducements are much more important for certain locations within the social relations of production than others. As I shall argue in the following two sections, they play a decisive role among semiautono-

[5]Burawoy (1978, 1979) sees the central problem of all dominant classes as the *obscuring* and *securing* of surplus appropriation. Modes of production, he argues, differ both in the mechanisms by which the surplus is obscured and the mechanisms by which it is secured. The wage relation itself obscures the surplus in capitalism (i.e., obscures the fact of exploitation); the mechanisms of social control help to secure that surplus within production.

[6]Ideological commitment to the "goals" of the enterprise could be considered a third mode of control—one which is especially important for the managerial hierarchy (see Edwards, 1979). Except in very special circumstances, however, a specific commitment to the goals of the employer's business is unlikely to be as important a mode of control as coercion or inducements within the working class. This is not to say that ideology in general is not important. Individualism, competitiveness, or racism all contribute in various ways to the reproduction of social relations of production, and thus to the ideological control of labor within production.

mous employees and managers. But even among workers, especially highly skilled ones in the monopoly or core industries of the economy, positive inducements can be significant. As Stone (1974) has argued in an analysis of the steel industry, many job ladders and pay differentials were consciously introduced precisely as mechanisms of social control. Such structures both divide the workers within a given labor process into competing groups and provide incentives to individual workers to behave themselves on the job.

To the extent that such inducements are generalized throughout the economy and eventually raise the average income of workers of average skill, they cease to function as inducements and become part of the "historical and moral" component of the value of labor power. To function as inducements, such increments to income must represent pay differentials and must to some extent be contingent upon good behavior on the job (or at least, on the absence of significant bad behavior).

Two factors are particularly important in determining the extent to which such wage inducements—and thus income privileges—are significant forms of social control of workers. The first is simply the capacity of capital to use such inducements. A complex inducement structure of control presupposes that the capitalist has a large and fairly stable market. While inducement structures may help to guarantee a certain level of productivity on the part of workers, they also raise the built-in overhead costs of production. Workers develop rights to positions, rights to promotions, rights to pay raises, etc. Unless the capitalist is in a relatively strong position in the market—i.e., located in what Marxists call the monopoly sector—it may simply not be feasible for the capitalist to use such mechanisms of control in a serious way.

Secondly, the balance between inducements and repression adopted by capital will depend in part upon how costly it is to a capitalist to use repression as a control device. When, for example, a capitalist invests a fair amount of resources in on-the-job training, firing employees may simply not be a cost-effective device for control since it would involve a potential waste of training resources. In such a situation, wage inducements may simply end up being less costly.[7]

[7]The sunk costs of capitalists derived from on-the-job training have been emphasized by human capital theorists as well as their critics (see, e.g., Thurow, 1975). Indeed, the logic of on-the-job training is used by Becker (1975) as the paradigmatic problem for human capital theory. It is the very first example he discusses in his basic text on the theory (pp. 16 ff.). The point made here is somewhat different from the one made by Becker or Thurow. I argue that the capitalist's choice of modes of social control will depend in part upon what it costs him to fire workers for misbehavior. Both Becker and Thurow are more concerned with keeping workers from quitting, and with the related problem of laying workers off in market downturns.

Taking these two factors together, it would be expected that, within the working class, the wages of workers will tend to be somewhat above the value of their labor power in situations where: (a) they are employed in the monopoly sector of the economy, and (b) they have considerable on-the-job training which was paid for by the employer.[8] Even in these cases, however, the income privilege should be relatively small. The working class, it must be recalled, is defined by positions which lack any real control over the immediate labor process; this implies that it is fairly easy for capital to monitor the performance of labor on the job. Direct supervision of behavior can generally function as fairly effective means of control, and except under unusual circumstances it would not be expected that systematic inducements beyond the value of labor power would form a large proportion of the wage of fully proletarianized workers.

Briefly, then, to recapitulate the arguments: working-class income is determined by:

1. The historical and moral standard of average workers of average skills, which itself is determined by the historical trajectory of class struggles, technological developments, the position of the national economy in the world capitalist system, and other factors.

2. The specific costs necessary to produce and reproduce skills above the socially average skill level.

3. Special market conditions that may push the wage of workers either temporarily or permanently above the value of labor power.

4. Forms of discrimination and oppression that may push the wage of certain categories of workers below the value of labor power.

5. Imperatives of social control within production, which may add an increment of inducement-income to the wage of workers, particularly those in positions involving much on-the-job training within the monopoly sector of the economy.

INCOME DETERMINATION IN THE CONTRADICTORY CLASS LOCATION BETWEEN THE WORKING CLASS AND THE PETTY BOURGEOISIE (SEMIAUTONOMOUS EMPLOYEES)

Unlike workers, semiautonomous employees have genuine control over their immediate labor process, especially over aspects of what they produce, and this places them in a particularly advantageous position

[8]For a very interesting empirical investigation of the relationship of industrial sectors (monopoly vs. competitive vs. state) to wages, see Hodson (1978).

to control their own productivity. Not only can they influence that productivity by controlling the pace of their work—many workers can do that as well, at least in limited ways—but because of their partial control over design and planning aspects of production, it becomes more difficult for capital to monitor effectively the performance of their jobs in ways which would allow for discipline; except in extreme cases. The critical aspects of productivity for semiautonomous employees are qualitative rather than quantitative, since such positions involve to a greater or lesser extent the relatively "creative" aspects of the production process—planning, designing, researching, etc. For such employees it is not enough that they mechanically obey the rules and follow orders to the letter. It is also important that they feel some real commitment to their jobs and act creatively and responsibly within them. Repressive control may be fairly effective in preventing misbehavior and active disobedience, but it is hardly an effective tool for stimulating innovation and creativity.

Capital responds to this situation in two basic ways. Perhaps most important historically is the continual attempt by capital to transform the labor process in ways which undermine the autonomy of semiautonomous employees, which destroy their capacity to control systematically their own productivity. In advanced capitalism, the increasing use of computers in design and planning functions may begin to erode the autonomy of highly skilled technicians, planners, and designers as well. Such positions have not yet become fully proletarianized, although many technical positions are becoming increasingly routine, a fact that in principle will make social control much easier.

Proletarianization, however, is not sufficient strategy to deal with the problem of autonomy within the labor process. In the first place, some positions have proven very difficult to proletarianize effectively, for either technical or social reasons. But perhaps more importantly, the very process of proletarianization tends to create new positions (although perhaps fewer in number) with high levels of autonomy and control over their immediate labor processes. For instance, computers may help to routinize many planning and designing functions, but their introduction also creates new, high-level, programmer positions. As a result, capital relies heavily on a second strategy for coping with the problems of autonomy within the labor process: the creation of fairly elaborate systems of inducements for creative and responsible behavior.

It would thus be expected that, compared to workers, semiautonomous employees would have a considerably greater income privilege component of the wage generated by imperatives of social control. That is, in general, the actual wages of semiautonomous employees would deviate from the average value of their labor power to a much greater extent than would be the case for workers.

Actually, we can make an even more precise prediction. Not all semiautonomous employees pose an equal problem of social control for their employers. The extent to which a given semiautonomous position poses this kind of problem depends upon two factors: (a) the centrality and scope of the planning and design activities within that position; (b) the extent to which the position also involves substantial levels of control over how that planning and design activity takes place. Taken together, these two aspects define how close to the petty bourgeoisie the contradictory class location is situated. In general, it would be expected that the income privilege component of the wage of semiautonomous employees will tend to increase as the petty bourgeois character of that position increases. Furthermore, since it is likely that formal education will itself vary positively with the degree of semiautonomy, it would be expected that the income privilege component of the wage— that part of the wage above the value of labor power—will itself increase with education. To state this proposition in slightly different terms: among semiautonomous employees, the income privilege component above the value of labor power will increase with the value of labor power itself. In formal statistical terms this would imply that the income return to education for semiautonomous employees should be greater than for workers.

INCOME DETERMINATION IN THE CONTRADICTORY CLASS LOCATION BETWEEN THE WORKING CLASS AND THE BOURGEOISIE (MANAGERS/SUPERVISORS)

The income determination process in this class location is even more complex than among semiautonomous employees. Not only do managers/supervisors have relatively high degrees of control over their own labor process, they also have control over the labor of others. And they often have control over the physical means of production as well. Top managers even have some degree of control over investments and accumulation. The actions of managers, therefore, not only influence their own immediate productivity, but potentially the productivity of substantial sections of the enterprise as a whole. The problem of the social control of managers, in other words, is basically: How to control the controllers?

Managers, like semiautonomous employees, must provide responsible and creative behavior, not simple conformity. Repressive control mechanisms are thus likely to be counterproductive, and so the social control of managers is likely to rely heavily on a structure of inducements: regular pay increases, career ladders, increasing fringe benefits over time, and so on.

The story for the managerial class location, however, has another critical aspect, which poses an entirely different problem from that of semiautonomous employees. The managerial structure poses a double problem of social control for capital: it is important to create conditions under which not only do managers give the right orders, but those orders are also seen as authoritative, and are thus willingly followed by other managers at lower levels of the hierarchy. Individual managers need to be simultaneously creative and responsible in their own decisions and activities and obedient and effective in carrying out orders from above.

Controlling the controllers thus ultimately poses the question of mechanisms which establish the legitimacy of the entire structure of control and authority, rather than simply of mechanisms which control each individual location within that structure. In Weberian terms, mechanisms are necessary to ensure that the managerial structure functions as a hierarchy of authority and not simply a hierarchy of power.

This imperative need for legitimation has several immediate consequences for income determination.

1. Hierarchical levels within the managerial structure need to be differentiated by fairly substantial differences in income. Since income in a capitalist society is the central criterion for status and success, large income differentials between hierarchical levels are essential for underwriting the legitimacy of authority. (For the same reasons, managerial structures are typically characterized by systematic gradations in the size and elegance of offices based on hierarchical location.) Individual managers will thus be able to increase their pay over time through two primary mechanisms: first, they will receive automatic increases in pay simply by dutifully and responsibly doing their jobs (pay as an inducement within a given position); and secondly, they will receive substantial promotional pay increases by moving up the managerial hierarchy (pay differentials as a structure of status and legitimation).

2. The larger and more complex the authority structure, the steeper the pay differential between positions would be expected to be.

Not only would the range of incomes be greater, simply because there are more levels within the hierarchy, but the increments for each step in the hierarchy should be larger. If it is correct that the pay gradient within a managerial hierarchy reflects in part a logic of legitimation of authority, then it would be expected that the problem of legitimation would increase with increasing complexity and differentiation in the hierarchy itself. Large-scale, monopoly corporations, therefore, would be expected to have steeper income gradients within their managerial structures than would smaller, competitive enterprises.

3. Hierarchy is not legitimated only by income differentials. The pivotal ideological justification for hierarchy, especially in the modern corporation of advanced capitalism, is merit: people at the top are supposed to be there because they are brighter or more capable. The most accessible criterion of merit is the individual's formal educational credentials. Within managerial hierarchies, therefore, it is expected that individuals will tend not to be promoted above others with higher credentials. It would therefore be expected that the educational gradient associated with managerial hierarchies would be steeper than would be predicted simply on the basis of the technical requirements of different positions.

This conception of the function of education within hierarchies is based on a general theory of education in capitalist society developed by such theorists as Bowles and Gintis (1976), Edwards (1979), and Bourdieu (1977). At its core is an analysis of three critical functions of education in reproducing capitalist relations of production. First, and most obviously, education creates various kinds of competence and thus produces skilled labor power (i.e., it reproduces the technical relations of production). This particular function of education has preoccupied human capital theorists and status attainment theorists alike. Secondly, education socializes, by reproducing the work habits, attitudes, and values necessary for different positions within the class structure. Especially for middle and upper managerial positions, where individual initiative and responsibility are desired, this function is important. Finally and most centrally for our present purposes, education legitimates, by providing the institutional basis for the ideological justifications of inequalities in terms of meritocratic myths of equal opportunities, success through achievement, etc.[9] The net result of all

[9]Of course, education has many other functions. It provides a convenient certification process which makes it easier for employers to filter prospective employees. Education provides a means of social control by keeping large numbers of youths off the streets, and by absorbing potential labor during periods of unemployment. The three functions that have been singled out here are the ones which bear most directly on the question of income differences between workers and managers.

of these processes is that managerial hierarchies will be characterized by rather steep education gradients.

4. Since among managers income should rise steeply with position within the hierarchy, and education should also be closely associated with position, income, therefore, should rise steeply with education. Among managers, then, there should be an especially large, positive, income privilege component of the wage, and this component should rise rapidly with education itself.

There is one final complication in the determination of incomes for positions within the managerial class location. As one moves closer to the bourgeoisie within the contradictory class location between the working class and the bourgeoisie, the positions begin to have an actual capacity to partially determine their own incomes. Top executives participate in policy decisions concerning stock options, fringe benefits, expense accounts, and the like, as well as formal salary schedules. In effect, they determine what proportion of the surplus value appropriated from workers will be redistributed to managers in the form of direct and indirect wages. The managerial hierarchy, therefore, is not just a hierarchy of authority posing problems of social control; it is also a hierarchy of appropriation in which top positions shape their own incomes, within limits.

INCOME DETERMINATION IN THE CAPITALIST CLASS

Capitalist income is derived from the appropriation of surplus labor from workers in the form of surplus value. Capitalists hire the labor power of workers for a certain number of hours, during which the worker produces new commodities for the capitalist. The basis of capitalist income is that during this production process workers produce more than the value of their own labor power (i.e., the costs to the capitalist of hiring the worker). Ultimately, regardless of the specific form of capitalist income (profits, interest, rent, etc.), the source of that income is this surplus value appropriated from workers.

The magnitude of capitalist income is determined by several interconnected processes:

1. The amount of surplus value appropriated directly from the capitalist's own workers within production. This, in turn, is a function of the number of workers employed and the rate of exploitation of those workers. This particular determinant of the income of capitalists forms

the heart of Marx's analysis in *Capital*, volume I, and has certainly been given the most attention by Marxists since Marx. At least two other mechanisms of income determination, however, can play an important role in determining the income of specific capitalists.

2. The amount of surplus value appropriated from workers *through market relations*. Value itself, of course, is not created in the market, but the division between surplus value and variable capital (the total costs of employing workers) can be influenced through market relations. This will undoubtedly seem obvious to most neoclassical economists, but many Marxists have insisted that surplus value itself is only appropriated directly within production relations.

Sweezy (1974) has been particularly insistent that surplus value can be appropriated within exchange relations:

> Monopoly does not change the total *amount* of value produced—except indirectly to the extent that it affects the total volume of employment—but it does bring about a *redistribution* of value. Marx indicates that this can take two forms: first a transfer of surplus value from competitive to monopolistic capitals; and second, a transfer of value from wages to surplus value. [p. 41]

The passage in *Capital* to which Sweezy refers is especially instructive on this point:

> If a commodity with a monopoly price should enter into the consumption of the laborer, it would increase the wages and thereby reduce the surplus value if the laborer would receive the value of his labor power the same as before. But such a commodity might also depress wages below the value of labor power, of course only to the extent that wages would be higher than the physical minimum of subsistence. In this case the monopoly price would be paid by a deduction from real wages (that is, from the quantity of use values received by the laborer for the same quantity of labor) and from the profit of other capitalists. [quoted in Sweezy, 1974, p. 41]

This means that in the era of monopoly capitalism, surplus value is appropriated from workers through at least two mechanisms, not one: it is extracted in the labor process itself, and it is appropriated in the sphere of circulation through the manipulation of monopoly prices.[10]

3. Finally, capitalists also derive part of their incomes from the redistribution of already existing surplus value among capitalists themselves. First, monopoly corporations are able to appropriate

---

[10]There are other mechanisms of exploitation in capitalist society besides these two—in particular, taxation. Tax exploitation did not die with the feudal mode of production simply because wage exploitation has become the dominant mechanism of appropriating the surplus product in capitalist society. For a fuller discussion of these issues, see Wright (1978a, pp. 154–56).

surplus value from competitive firms by charging those firms prices above the value of the commodities they sell. Secondly, capitalists who introduce advanced technologies into their production processes and are thus able to produce commodities in less than the socially average labor time (the time necessary to produce those commodities using average technology) are able to realize extra profits in the market, since they have reduced the value of the commodities and are still able to sell them at the prevailing price. Such transition profits, as they are often called, can considerably augment the income of individual capitalists. Thirdly, in periods of economic crisis, when many capitalists go bankrupt, the surviving capitalists are able to purchase capital at prices well below value (this is called the "devaluation of capital"). This, again, allows them to make additional profits, and thus potentially augment their incomes.

Taken together, these various mechanisms suggest that, on the average, the incomes of individual capitalists will be largely determined by the absolute and relative magnitudes of their capital and by the existing balance of class forces, which determines the degree of exploitation of the working class. Education and other human capital factors should have no systematic bearing on income determination within the capitalist class.

INCOME DETERMINATION IN THE CONTRADICTORY LOCATION BETWEEN THE CAPITALIST CLASS AND THE PETTY BOURGEOISIE (SMALL EMPLOYERS)

Small employers differ from proper capitalists in two crucial respects: first, quantitatively, the magnitude of their capital is much, much smaller. Among small employers it is generally very difficult to actually accumulate a substantial portion of profits from the business. A large part of those profits is consumed in the form of a higher standard of living than the working class, and much of the rest is needed as reserve to guard against economic fluctuations. Except in unusual circumstances, small employers are unable to save sufficient quantities of their income to be able to engage in a systematic and sustained expansion of production (i.e., accumulation of *capital* as opposed to accumulation of savings in the bank).

The second essential difference is qualitative, in that small employers occupy an objectively different location within class relations from capitalists, even from small capitalists. Small employers are directly engaged in the process of production. The farm owner who hires workers is also a farmer, directly engaged in the transformation of nature, in the production of commodities. A farmer-capitalist manages the investments and capital accumulation within agribusiness, but does not actually engage in the labor of farming. A small shopkeeper-employer is directly involved in selling commodities to customers; the merchant capitalist spends most of his/her time in organizing investments in commercial activity.

A substantial part of the income of small employers, then, comes directly from their own labor and that of their immediate families, rather than from the appropriation of surplus labor from employees. To be sure, exploitation does take place within small businesses, but such exploitation only augments the income of the small employer; it is not the exclusive basis of that income.

The size of the income of small employers is thus determined by two basic factors:

1. The exact position of the small employer in the contradictory class location between the petty bourgeoisie and the capitalist class. The closer to the petty bourgeoisie, the more the small employer's income is determined by the self-earned component of income (income directly derived from the small employer's own labor); the closer the small employer is to becoming a proper capitalist, the more income is determined by the rate of exploitation and the amount of labor power employed.

2. The degree of vulnerability of the small employer within the market. Some small employers are directly subordinated to monopoly capital within market relations (e.g., franchise operations, dependent suppliers of monopoly firms, etc.). It would be expected that many such small firms would have a substantial proportion of their profits redistributed to monopoly capital via exchange relations. Other small employers are located within very restricted and protected markets, with high barriers to entry and organized, collective systems of monopoly pricing. This is particularly the case for small employers engaged in the delivery of professional services (law offices, private medical offices, etc.). Such employers are able not only to maintain control over the surplus value appropriated from their own employees, but to obtain additional income from their control of prices within the market itself. In investigating the income of small employers, therefore, it is especially important to study the effects of exchange relations on their income determination process.

INCOME DETERMINATION FOR THE
PETTY BOURGEOISIE

When we shift our attention to the income determination process within the petty bourgeoisie, we are in effect shifting out of the capitalist mode of production proper and into simple commodity production. To be sure, petty bourgeois producers earn their income in a capitalist society, and the conditions under which they ply their trade are heavily shaped by that fact. But the process of income determination rests in large part on a logic which is distinctively noncapitalist. Income depends neither upon the sale of the commodity labor power nor on the realization of a difference between the value of the commodity labor power and the value of the commodities produced by labor. Rather, income is determined by the actual performance of labor by the petty bourgeois producer and by the conditions for the sale of the commodities embodying that labor. In a purely competitive market, the income of the petty bourgeoisie would be entirely determined by the amount of labor performed by the petty bourgeois producer.

"Amount" of labor, of course, is a rather vague notion. Just as in the analysis of the performance of labor by workers in a capitalist labor process, it is important to include skills in the evaluation of the labor of the petty bourgeois. An hour's worth of labor performed in production, therefore, must be seen as having two quite distinct components: (a) one hour of new labor, of actual living labor performed in the labor process; (b) a certain quantity of past labor, previously performed in the production of skills, which is transferred to the products produced in the hour. In the course of the work life of the producer, the quantity of labor used in producing skills is transferred to the commodities produced with those skills. In every hour of production, therefore, a fraction of that skill-producing labor is transferred. Depending upon how much time it took to produce the skills of a given category of labor within the petty bourgeoisie, therefore, a given hour of work will produce more than an hour's worth of value. The income of the petty bourgeois producer, then, is equal to the total price of the commodities which embody those values.

Variation in income within the petty bourgeoisie is, therefore, determined by the following processes:

1. The amount of labor time embodied in the skills of the petty bourgeois producer. Under competitive conditions, petty bourgeois income should increase with skill level in a fairly systematic way.

2. The effort and talent of the petty bourgeois producer. The skill component of the income of petty bourgeois producers is based on the socially average labor time necessary to produce those skills. Individual petty bourgeois producers, however, differ in the amount of time it takes them to acquire those skills. An especially talented petty bourgeois producer would have an income above the labor time embodied in that individual's labor. Similarly, if the individual were to apply his/her skills with particular effort and dedication, above and beyond the socially average application of skills, the income of the individual could exceed the actual labor times embodied in the commodities produced. It would thus be expected that the dispersion of incomes within the petty bourgeoisie would in significant ways be shaped by the choices and predispositions of the individuals within that class, even though the average income within the class is a function of the socially necessary labor times embodied in the production of the commodities produced by the class.

3. Market conditions can decisively affect the income of the petty bourgeoisie just as they affect the income of small employers and small capitalists. To the extent that the petty bourgeoisie is exposed to market exploitation by monopoly capital, its income will be depressed. Throughout the history of capitalism, the dependence of the petty bourgeoisie on merchant capital has had precisely this effect, especially for the agrarian petty bourgeoisie. Market pressures operate to prevent the income of the petty bourgeoisie from rising very much above the socially necessary costs of the reproduction of their labor power. Although they are not exploited within production itself, they are exploited through the market, and this prevents them from retaining the full value of the commodities which they produce.

Overall, these various factors would suggest that the incomes of petty bourgeois producers should generally not be very much higher than the incomes of workers. If petty bourgeois producers were not exploited through market relations, then their incomes would be rather higher than workers' incomes, since they would be able to realize the added value of their own surplus labor. Market exploitation, however, will tend to reduce their incomes to levels at most slightly above those of workers, and in some cases even below. In fact, petty bourgeois producers are often willing to work for an income below what they could earn as workers precisely because they value the social relations of production embodied in simple commodity production. The desire to be one's own boss, to work for oneself rather than directly for the enrichment of capital, may keep many petty bourgeois producers from seeking employment as workers.

FORMAL HYPOTHESES

We are now in a position to formulate a series of testable propositions about the relationship between class and income. These hypotheses can be broken down into three categories: (a) comparisons between class and occupational status; (b) the structural mediations of class in the income determination process; (c) the relationship between class mediations and the effects of race and sex on income determination. These are genuine hypotheses based on the analysis of class relations, not simply post hoc interpretations of the actual findings. As we shall see, most of the hypotheses are strongly supported by the data, but there are a number of unexpected results and some unresolved anomalies.

Because of limitations in the available data, not all of these hypotheses will actually be tested in this study. In particular, it was impossible to test any of the hypotheses concerning semiautonomous employees, since there were no measures of control over the labor process in the data used in the research. Similarly, there were so few capitalists, properly speaking, in the data set that none of the hypotheses about capitalists could be tested, although it was possible to test the propositions about small employers and the petty bourgeoisie. The list of hypotheses which follows, therefore, should be seen as a research agenda rather than simply as an introduction to the empirical part of the present research. Those hypotheses which I shall not formally examine will be preceded by an asterisk.

Class and Status

The hypotheses under this rubric are not, strictly speaking, grounded in the logic of class mediation which we have been stressing throughout this chapter. Instead, class will be treated simply as an individual-level "variable" and compared in various ways to occupational status. This exercise clearly violates the basic logic of a Marxist analysis of income determination, but it serves a useful polemical purpose in demonstrating the explanatory power of class in the kinds of income determination equations most familiar to sociologists.

The basic model which underlies these hypotheses about class and status at the individual level of analysis is presented in Figure 4.1. The causal ordering of the variables in the model is based strictly on their biographical ordering within the life cycle. Since an individual's class location and occupational status are determined simultaneously in time, there is no causal ordering between them in the model.

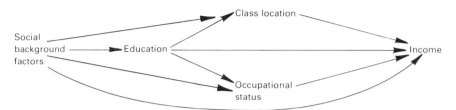

Figure 4.1. An individual-level model of income determination for comparing class and status.

The hypotheses in this section are argued in a somewhat looser fashion than are the hypotheses in the following sections. They should be understood as statements of minimal expectations rather than as the basis for a rigorous analysis of class and status at the individual level.

Hypothesis 1.1. *The individual's position within class relations will have a significant impact on income, independent of occupational status.*

Virtually all of the recent sociological work on income inequality has used occupational status or some closely related metric of occupations as the key intervening variable between the individual's social background and education and his or her income. The concept of class, defined in terms of capitalist social relations of production, is an alternative paradigm for understanding social inequality. If class relations are in fact the basic social relations which structure the income distribution process, then it would be expected that at the individual level, class position would have a significant impact on income even when occupational status is controlled for.

This hardly means that occupational position is irrelevant for income. Most people, in fact, gain most of their income through earnings; and earnings are at least in part attached to occupational positions, not simply class positions. It would, therefore, be expected that any plausible metric of occupations would have some relationship to income.

Hypothesis 1.2. *When education is controlled for, class position will have a greater impact on individual income than will occupational status.*

The simplest model of income determination in the status attainment literature views education as a cause of both income and occupational status, and occupational status as a direct cause of income. Consequently, when education is held constant within a regression equation, the effect of occupational status on income should be reduced. This is, in fact, generally observed.

This same prediction can be made within a class analysis. Education can be viewed as one of the basic causes of variation in the value of labor power, and that, in turn, is a cause of income variation among wage laborers. Since, in general, the value of labor power employed in positions of high occupational status will be greater than the value of labor power in positions of lower occupational status, status can be interpreted as a rough indicator of the value of labor power. Again, this implies that if education is held constant (and thus the value of labor power is held approximately constant), then the effect of occupational status on income would be reduced.

It would be expected that there would be a much weaker association between class position and the value of labor power than between occupational position and the value of labor power. Most of the variation in the value of labor power should occur within classes rather than between them. This suggests that the correlation between class and education should be considerably less than the correlation between occupational status and education. This, in turn, implies that controlling for education would have a smaller effect on the relationship of class to income than on the relationship of status to income. As a result, net of education, class should have a larger effect on income than will occupational status.

Class Mediations and Income Determination

The hypotheses in this section constitute the heart of the theoretical and empirical investigation of this study. They are all directly based on the arguments made earlier concerning the specific processes of income determination within each class location. It is very important to remember that each of these hypotheses is formulated at the level of classes, not individuals, as units of analysis. They are hypotheses about the ways in which class relations mediate the income determination process. The basic model on which these hypotheses are based is presented in Figure 4.2, which represents a simplified version of the more complete model of determination presented in Figure 3.1. In Figure 4.2

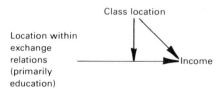

Figure 4.2. Basic model for investigating class mediations of the income determination process.

only those relationships which will be systematically investigated in this study are indicated.

Hypothesis 2. *Managers/supervisors will have higher incomes than workers, even after controlling for education, age, seniority, family background, and occupational status.*

We argued above that the use of income as a mechanism of social control was especially important for the contradictory class position between the proletariat and the bourgeoisie. If that analysis is correct, then it would be expected that managers and workers whose labor power has approximately the same value will still differ substantially in their incomes.

The value of labor power, it will be recalled, is defined by two components: first, the socially necessary costs of producing and reproducing labor power of average skills, and second, the costs of producing and reproducing the skill level of labor power beyond the social average. It is extremely difficult to actually measure the value of labor power defined in this way. As an alternative, I shall use education, one of the important determinants of the value of labor power, as an indirect way of controlling for the value of labor power itself. I shall assume that for two individuals with the same levels of education the costs of production/reproduction of skills are approximately the same.[11]

An obvious objection to this comparison of workers and managers is that whatever differences are observed might be due to various personal characteristics other than education. A sociologist, for example, might argue that instead of viewing these income differences as reflecting class position per se, we might see them as artifacts of the distribution of occupational status, IQ, family background, age, motivations, etc., among workers and managers. It is always possible, of course, to make the claim that some unmeasured variable will account for ob-

---

[11]To my knowledge, the only empirical investigation which has attempted to measure such income privilege by actually calculating the absolute value of labor power is that of Baudelot et al. (1974). The authors estimated the value of labor power of various categories of wage earners through a complicated procedure which imputed various costs to training, reproduction of skills, reproduction of the skills of the next generation, and other factors which could conceivably be considered part of the value of labor power. They even included estimates of the necessary recreation costs to enable "mental laborers" to revitalize their mental energy. In effect, all of their estimates were designed to minimize the extent of income privileges by maximizing the value of labor power within any given wage. After adding up all of these costs, they found that 55% of the salary of top managers, 43% of the salary of middle managers, 27% of the salary of technicians, 24% of the salary of lycée professors and 7% of the salary of school teachers was in excess of the value of their labor power (pp. 210–35).

served differences between groups. The burden of proof in such cases rests with the critic. Nevertheless, since family background, occupational status, and age are generally included in sociological analyses of income inequality, we will include these as additional controls, not so much because of their intrinsic interest, but to demonstrate that the differences between classes should be viewed as characteristics of the empty places within class relations, rather than as consequences of the characteristics of the incumbents of the empty places.

Hypothesis 3. *Within the managerial category, incomes will increase sharply as one moves up the authority hierarchy, even after controlling for education, age, and seniority.*

This follows directly from the analysis of inducements as a mechanism of social control. The essential way that income operates as an inducement is by being pegged to stages in a career ladder. For managers, this means tying income gradients to positions within the managerial hierarchy. Furthermore, at the very top levels of the managerial hierarchy, managers directly participate in the various ownership functions of capital, including the setting of pay scales. In a sense, therefore, top managers partially choose their own pay, and this would tend to increase the income gradient within the managerial hierarchy.

As in hypothesis 2, one might argue that the steep income gradient associated with managerial hierarchies simply reflects the different levels of human capital investments of managers at different levels of the hierarchy. The income gradient would thus be seen as a consequence of the characteristics of the incumbents of different levels of the hierarchy rather than of the hierarchy itself. We will, therefore, control for certain ingredients of "human capital" in order to see if it is reasonable to regard the income gradient associated with the managerial hierarchy as a characteristic of the structure itself.

Hypothesis 4.1. *The income returns to education will be much greater within the managerial category than within the working class, even after controlling for age, seniority, background, etc.*

This proposition is based on the conception of the relationship between hierarchy and education discussed in the general section on managerial income. There will be a fairly steep gradient for the *educational credentials* associated with the managerial hierarchy. If hypothesis 3 is also correct—that there is a steep *income* gradient associated with the managerial hierarchy—then we would expect relatively high income returns to education within the managerial category as a whole.

It is still expected that workers will have some returns to education. Education is, after all, one of the basic determinants of the value of labor power within the working class, and thus it should be reflected in higher wages. The hypothesis is not that workers receive no income returns to education, but that these returns will be substantially less than for managers/supervisors.

Hypothesis 4.2. *The difference between the managerial category and the working class in income returns to education should be greatest for college and postcollege levels of schooling.*

If the argument in hypothesis 4.1 is correct, then the returns to education among managers/supervisors and among workers should differ most for those educational credentials which are most important for legitimating the managerial structure and socializing people for positions of authority. In advanced capitalist societies, this would correspond to a college degree and postcollege training.

Hypothesis 4.3. *The income returns to education among managers/supervisors will be much closer to the returns among workers when position within the managerial hierarchy is held constant.*

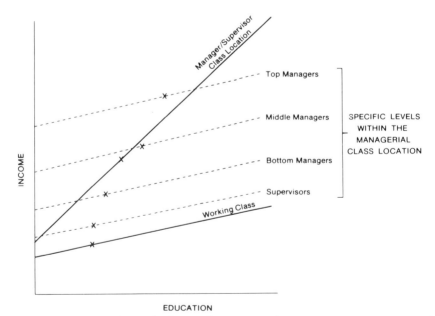

Figure 4.3. Hypothesized relation of income to education. x = Mean income and education for each category. Figure courtesy of the UW Cartographic Laboratory.

The logic for claiming that the managerial category as a whole will have greater returns to education than the working class as a whole is based on the link between education and position in the hierarchy on the one hand, and between position in the hierarchy and income on the other. If this reasoning is correct, then controlling for position within the hierarchy should considerably reduce the returns to education among managers/supervisors. This hypothesis can be tested both as an additive model (i.e., position in the hierarchy is held constant by entering a hierarchy scale into the regression equation), and as an interactive model (i.e., the returns to education are calculated separately for each level of the hierarchy). The interactive form of the hypothesis is illustrated graphically, in a somewhat exaggerated form, in Figure 4.3.

*Hypothesis 5.1. *The incomes of semiautonomous employees will be greater than for workers and less than for managers/supervisors, controlling for education, seniority, etc.*

This hypothesis follows essentially the same logic as hypothesis 2. The use of income as a mechanism of social control should be more important among semiautonomous employees (the contradictory location between the working class and the petty bourgeoisie) than among workers, but less important than among managers. We would, therefore, expect that, controlling for the value of labor power, their incomes should fall between those of managers/supervisors and workers.

*Hypothesis 5.2. *The income returns to education within the semiautonomous employee class location should be greater than within the working class but less than within the manager/supervisor class location.*

As has already been argued, the problem of social control of semiautonomous employees depends upon the degree of control over the labor process and the centrality of design and planning functions within the position; thus the income privilege component of the wage should vary with these two aspects of autonomy. Both of these aspects of autonomy should also vary with education. As a result, the income returns to education should be greater among semiautonomous employees than among workers, but since these employees are not part of the authority hierarchy, their income returns to education should be less than among managers.

Hypothesis 6. *Within the pure petty bourgeoisie, the average level of income should only be slightly greater than within the working class (controlling for education, age, background, etc.), and the returns to education should be very close to that of the working class.*

Petty bourgeois income is self-earned income. If the market were perfectly competitive and petty bourgeois producers not dominated by the capitalist class within exchange relations, they would receive the entire value of the commodities they sold on the market as income, and their income would thus be significantly larger than that of workers. The petty bourgeoisie, however, has always been subordinated to merchant and banking capital through various exchange relations. Furthermore, although there is undoubtedly a great deal of competition among petty bourgeois producers, they operate in factor markets which are typically dominated by monopoly capital. The result is that at least part of the value of the commodities they produce is appropriated by capitalists through exchange relations, and this will tend to push the average income within the petty bourgeoisie toward that of the working class.

The value of the commodities produced by the petty bourgeoisie includes a portion that represents the costs of the training and education that produced those commodities. Under competitive conditions, it would be expected that the price of the commodities sold by the petty bourgeoisie, and thus their associated income, would in effect reimburse the producer for the costs of that education. This is essentially similar to the logic of returns to education for workers, where the value of labor power includes a component which covers the costs of producing and reproducing skills. The circumstance that the factor markets for the petty bourgeoisie are not competitive does not necessarily affect the competitive adjustments in the product markets; and thus the petty bourgeoisie still should get a return to education comparable to that within the working class.

Hypothesis 7.1. *The expected incomes of small employers should be higher than those of either workers or managers, even when controlling for education, age, experience, etc.*

Small employers occupy the contradictory class position between the petty bourgeoisie and the capitalist class. At least part of their income, therefore, represents self-earned income and part of it represents surplus value appropriated from workers. In general, therefore, the income of small employers should be well above that of workers.

It is somewhat less obvious that, on the average, small employers should have higher incomes than managers. It would certainly not be anticipated that the average small employer would have a higher income than top managers in large corporations. Such top managers also receive a substantial part of their incomes from surplus value, and because of the size of the capital for which they work, their incomes are apt to be much greater than those of an employer of ten workers.

The average manager, however, is nearer the bottom than the top of managerial hierarchies, and a large number of managers work in relatively small and medium-sized capitalist firms. While such managers are still likely to have income privileges, it is unlikely that a very large part of their income represents surplus value. Compared to the average manager, then, small employers would be expected to have relatively high incomes.

Hypothesis 7.2. *Small employers will have especially high income returns to education.*

As was argued in the general discussion of small employers, their incomes should be especially sensitive to market forces of various sorts. Two such market relations are especially important: (a) the degree of competitiveness of the markets in which the small employers operate; and (b) the vulnerability of the small employer to monopoly capital. The first of these determines whether or not the small employer is able to appropriate surplus value in the market as well as in production; the second determines the extent to which surplus value will tend to be transferred from the small employer to monopoly capital. Highly educated small employers are more likely to operate in relatively uncompetitive markets (i.e., markets with high barriers to entry), especially markets for professional services, which are partially sheltered from monopoly capital; uneducated small employers are likely to operate in very competitive markets (farming, retail stores, etc.), which are often quite dependent upon monopoly capital. Because of this relationship of education to the market conditions of small employers, we would expect them to have high returns to education.

If this interpretation of small employers' income is correct, then we would also expect two subsidiary hypotheses to hold:

Hypothesis 7.3. *If the industrial sector and occupational status of small employers are held constant, the returns to education will be considerably reduced.*

Industrial sector and occupational status can be considered rough proxies for the market conditions within which small employers operate. To the extent that the market mediates the relationship of education to income for small employers, as discussed in hypothesis 7.2, the returns to education should be considerably reduced when market situation is controlled for.

Hypothesis 7.4. *The returns to education for small employers with less than a college degree should be relatively small, while the returns for getting a college or graduate degree should be very large.*

Academic credentials define legal access to many of the privileged markets referred to in hypothesis 7.2. If a small employer does not have a college degree or more, then education is not particularly important in influencing the markets within which he or she operates. Thus we would expect the income-education function for small employers to be a kind of step-function: it should be relatively flat below the college level, with a substantial jump at the college degree.

*Hypothesis 8. *Among proper capitalists, there should be relatively little relationship between income and education; income will be much higher than for any other class position, even controlling for education, age, etc.*

This proposition emphasizes the qualitative difference between the incomes of the capitalist and noncapitalist classes. Capitalist income reflects relations of exploitation rather than the reproductive costs of labor power, in any meaningful sense. Capitalist income will, therefore, vary with the magnitude of the capital owned by the capitalist; neither the expected exchange value of capitalist "labor power" nor the problems of social control within the labor process have any bearing on capitalist income.

Race, Sex, and Class

If class mediates the income determination process then class relations should also mediate the specific effects of race and sex on income. That is, the social consequences of race and sex, as factors in the income determination process, should themselves be determined by location within class relations. Figure 4.4 presents the general model of such mediations.

Several comments about this model are needed before we develop a series of concrete hypotheses derived from it. First, the model does not deny the reality of either race or sex effects on income, nor does it attempt to reduce racial and sexual discrimination to class domination. The argument is simply that racial and sexual discrimination have different effects within different classes.

Secondly, the causal relationship between class and race or sex must be understood strictly as a structural relation posed at the level of classes as units of analysis. At the level of individual biography, the individual clearly acquires race and sex characteristics before entering

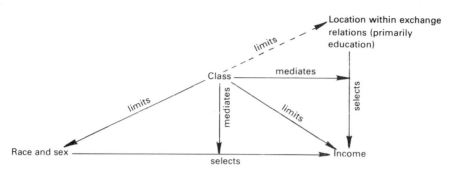

Figure 4.4.   Basic model of class mediations of race and sex effects on income.

a location within the social relations of production. But structurally, it is the class location itself that establishes limits on the distribution of race and sex characteristics within that location. Unless this kind of structural determination is accepted as legitimate, most of this discussion of class mediations will be unintelligible.

Finally, it is important to note what happens, in formal statistical terms, to this model if class is ignored, as it is in virtually all research on race and sex discrimination. Since class is viewed as mediating both the education-income relationship and the race or sex and income relation, and since class is also a determinant of race or sex, these last two would appear to mediate the education-income relationship if class is left out of the model.[12] If the argument about class mediations is cor-

[12]This argument holds even if the model is transposed to the individual level of analysis and the arrows between class and race/sex and between class and education change direction. In the equations involving race, for example, Figure 4.4 at the level of individuals as units of analysis would read:

Income $= b_1(\text{class} \times \text{race}) + b_2(\text{class} \times \text{education}) + b_3\text{class}$
Class $= b_4\text{race} + b_5\text{education}$

Substituting for class in the first equation, we would have

Income $= (b_4\text{race} + b_5\text{education}) \times (b_1\text{race} + b_2\text{education})$
  $+ b_3b_4\text{race} + b_3b_5\text{education}$

If we rewrite this equation, letting $a_1 = b_3b_4$; $a_2 = b_3b_5$; $a_3 = b_4b_1$; $a = b_5b_2$; and $a_5 = b_4b_2 + b_5b_1$, then this equation would read

Income $= a_1 \text{ race} + a_2 \text{ education} + a_3 \text{ race}^2 + a_4 \text{ education}^2 + a_5(\text{race} \times \text{education})$

In this equation race appears formally as the mediating variable (interactive term). If the claim that class structures in fact mediate the income determination process is correct, leaving class out of the analysis will tend to produce an appearance of race and sex mediations (interactions).

rect, therefore, we would expect very substantial reductions in the apparent race or sex interactions in the income determination process if class is included in the analysis as in Figure 4.4.

Hypothesis 9.1. *The returns to education of black and white males will be much closer within class positions than across all class categories.*

The analysis of differences in the status attainment process between blacks and whites has been a basic preoccupation in the stratification literature. One of the most robust findings of this body of research is that blacks in general receive less income per increment in education than do whites (Siegel, 1965; Duncan, 1969; Weiss, 1970). None of these studies, however, has controlled for class position defined in terms of social relations of production. If hypotheses 4.1 and 7.2 are correct—if managers and small employers receive much higher returns to education than workers—and if it is true that blacks are much more heavily concentrated than whites in the working class, then we would expect that much of the differential returns for blacks and whites might be due to the distribution of races across class categories. We will, therefore, compare the returns to education for blacks and whites *within* class categories in order to control for this class composition effect.

Hypothesis 9.2. *The differences between black male workers and managers/supervisors will be less marked than the differences between white male workers and managers/supervisors.*

The logic behind arguing that managers/supervisors would have higher incomes (hypothesis 2) and much greater returns to education (hypothesis 4.1) than workers was based on the analysis of social control within the labor process. To the extent that black managers are concentrated at the bottom levels of the managerial hierarchy, these dynamics of social control would be weaker. While bottom-level managers still occupy a contradictory class position between the working class and the bourgeoisie, they would be closer to the boundary of the working class and would thus tend to more closely resemble workers.

Hypothesis 10.1. *The returns to education of men and women will be much closer within class categories than across class categories.*

The argument here is essentially the same as in hypothesis 9.1: women, like blacks, will be concentrated in the working class, and thus the apparent difference in returns to education for men and women will be at least in part a consequence of the class distribution of sexes.

Hypothesis 10.2. *The differences between female workers and managers/supervisors will be less marked than the differences between male workers and managers/supervisors.*

Again, the logic is the same as in hypothesis 9.2. Even more than in the case of blacks, female managers will tend to be bottom-level supervisors and thus occupy class positions very close to the boundary of the working class.

These ten clusters of hypotheses will provide the focus for most of the empirical investigation in the rest of this study. They hardly exhaust a Marxist theory of income determination. Several critical issues have been largely ignored: the effects of internal structural divisions within classes on the income determination process; the effects of the relationship to the state on income determination; the historical transformations of the income determination process through class struggles, changes in the role of the state, changes in the location within the international capitalist system, etc. In many ways these dynamic issues are more fundamental to Marxism than the more static, structural questions addressed in the hypotheses of this study. Marxism is, after all, a theory of social change, of the role of classes and class struggle in the transformation of societies, rather than simply an analysis of structural determinations within a given system of class relations. The difficulties of embarking on a comprehensive study of the transformation of the income determination process are, however, enormous, because of limitations of data and the analytical difficulty of evaluating those data. The present study is, therefore, restricted to a narrower theoretical terrain—the analysis of class mediations in the income determination process.

II

THE EMPIRICAL INVESTIGATION OF CLASS MEDIATIONS OF THE INCOME DETERMINATION PROCESS

The next five chapters will each attempt to explore some of the hypotheses developed at the end of the previous chapter. Rather than encumber the text with lengthy descriptions and definitions of the data sets, variables, and statistical procedures employed in the analysis, I have placed these various methodological issues in three appendices at the end of the book. Although it is unnecessary to read these appendices closely in order to understand the results in the following chapters, it is probably a good idea at least to glance through the discussion of the operationalization of different variables.

5

Class and Occupation

Few issues have caused more confusion in the sociological analysis of inequality than the conflation of class and occupation. As was argued in chapter 1, most sociologists in fact view classes as no more than clusters of occupational categories arranged in some hierarchical fashion. In that chapter we discussed the distinction between class and occupation at the theoretical level; in this chapter we shall explore the empirical contours of the relationship between class and occupation.

The chapter will be divided into two main sections. The first will focus on the distribution of occupational positions within classes. The main purpose of this discussion will be to demonstrate the relative independence of the social relations of production from the technical relations of production. The second section will examine the relative explanatory power of class and occupational status (the most common

TABLE 5.1
Distribution of Occupations Within Classes

Occupation	Employers	Petty Bourgeoisie	Managers/ Supervisors	Semiautonomous Employees	Workers	All Classes	N
Upper white-collar							
Professionals	4.5%	9.8%	16.2%	4.7%	2.7%	8.1%	124
Technicians	.9	0.0	2.7	2.4	1.9	2.1	33
Managers, proprietors, and officials	70.5	30.4	16.6	3.6	.9	13.4	206
Teachers[a]	0.0	0.0	0.0	20.2	5.7	4.6	70
Subtotal	75.9	40.2	35.5	30.9	11.2	28.2	433
Lower white-collar							
Clerical	0.0	2.2	15.3	10.1	22.9	16.0	245
Sales	2.7	5.4	4.4	10.7	4.9	5.2	80
Subtotal	2.7	7.6	19.7	20.8	27.9	21.2	325
Upper blue-collar							
Craftsmen	5.4	9.8	13.4	16.7	11.3	12.1	185
Foremen	.9	0.0	7.3	0.0	0.0	2.5	39
Subtotal	6.3	9.8	20.7	16.7	11.3	14.6	224

Lower blue-collar							
Operatives	.9	8.7	13.6	18.5	28.7	19.2	294
Laborers[b]	.9	2.2	2.2	3.0	7.4	4.3	66
Subtotal	1.8	10.9	15.8	21.5	36.1	23.5	360
Services	1.8	3.3	7.8	9.6	13.5	9.6	147
Farmers[c]	11.6	28.3	.6	.6	.2	2.9	44
Total	100.0	100.0	100.0	100.0	100.0	100.0	
N	112	92	524	168	637		1,533

Source: Data from 1969 Survey of Working Conditions. Percentages do not always add to 100% because of rounding. Formal operationalizations of class are presented in Table 2.4. The estimate for each of these class locations does not take into consideration the descriptions given in the *Dictionary of Occupational Titles*. These estimates thus correspond to the high estimate for semiautonomous employers and for managers/supervisors (top and middle managers are combined with bottom managers in these tables) and the low estimate for workers. All employers in the sample are included in the small-employer category, even though 8% of these employers in fact employed more than 100 workers and should be classified, strictly, as small capitalists. No estimate of the occupational distribution for proper capitalists was attempted because the N was so small. For a more detailed discussion of this data set, see appendix A, data sources.

[a]All teachers were classified as nonsupervisors regardless of their response to the supervision question. (See appendix B, variables, operationalizations of class.)

[b]Includes farm laborers.

[c]Includes farm managers and farm owners.

TABLE 5.2
Distribution of Classes Within Occupations

Occupation	Employers	Petty Bourgeoisie	Managers/ Supervisors	Semiautonomous Employees	Workers	Total
Upper white-collar	19.7%	8.6%	43.2%	12.1%	16.5%	100.0%
Professionals	4.0	7.3	68.5	6.5	13.7	100.0
Technicians	3.0	0.0	45.4	12.2	39.3	100.0
Managers, proprietors, and officials	38.5	13.6	42.2	2.9	2.9	100.0
Teachers[a]	0.0	0.0	0.0	48.6	51.5	100.0
Lower white-collar	.9	2.2	31.7	10.7	54.5	100.0
Clerical	0.0	.8	32.7	6.9	59.5	100.0
Sales	3.8	6.3	28.8	22.5	38.8	100.0
Upper blue-collar	3.1	4.0	48.2	12.5	32.1	100.0
Craftsmen	3.2	4.9	37.8	15.1	38.9	100.0
Foremen	2.6	0.0	97.4	0.0	0.0	100.0
Lower blue-collar	.5	2.8	22.8	10.0	63.9	100.0
Operatives	.3	2.7	24.2	10.5	62.2	100.0
Laborers[b]	1.5	3.0	16.7	7.6	71.2	100.0
Services	1.4	2.0	27.9	10.9	57.8	100.0
Farmers[c]	29.5	59.1	6.8	2.3	2.3	100.0
All Occupations	7.3	6.0	34.2	11.0	41.6	100.0

Source: Data from 1969 Survey of Working Conditions. Percentages do not always add to 100% because of rounding. Formal operationalizations of class are presented in Table 2.4. The estimate for each of these class locations does not take into consideration the descriptions given in the *Dictionary of Occupational Titles*. These estimates thus correspond to the high estimate for semiautonomous employers and for managers/supervisors (top and middle managers are combined with bottom managers in these tables) and the low estimate for workers. All employers in the sample are included in the small-employer category, even though 8% of these employers in fact employed more than 100 workers and should be classified, strictly, as small capitalists. No estimate of the occupational distribution for proper capitalists was attempted because the N was so small. For a more detailed discussion of this data set, see appendix A, data sources.

[a] All teachers were classified as nonsupervisors regardless of their response to the supervision question. (See appendix B, variables, operationalizations of class.)

[b] Includes farm laborers.

[c] Includes farm managers and farm owners.

metric for occupations) in individual-level income determination equations. The purpose of this analysis, as explained in chapter 4, is less to explore the nuances of the relative contributions of social and technical relations of production in the determination of income than to demonstrate the importance of social relations of production as an independent determinant of income.

One preliminary comment on the operationalization of class that will be used in this chapter is necessary before proceeding. Except in the discussion of occupation-class distributions, I shall make no attempt to operationalize the "semiautonomous employee" class location. None of the data in this study had objective measures of control within the labor process, and it was impossible to define these class positions adequately. In the analysis of occupation-class distributions, I have used a purely subjective criterion for the semiautonomous employee category, in order to get a first-approximation impression of the contours of these distributions. In the rest of the book, however, this criterion is dropped, and the working class and the semiautonomous employee class location are merged into a single class category. For convenience, I shall refer to this combined category as the "working class" throughout the rest of this study, even though it in fact contains a certain proportion of semiautonomous employees (probably about 10% of the total in the combined category).

OCCUPATIONAL DISTRIBUTIONS WITHIN CLASSES

To argue that social relations of production (class relations) and technical relations of production (occupational relations) are theoretically independent dimensions of social relations is not to argue that they are empirically unrelated. Indeed, at the very heart of Marxist theory is the analysis of the relationship between forces and relations of production within modes of production, and this has direct implications for the relationship between occupations and classes as positions within the social structure.

Table 5.1 presents the occupational distribution within classes, and Table 5.2 the class distribution within occupations based on data from the 1969 Institute for Social Research Survey of Working Conditions (SWC). (See appendix A for details on this and other data sets.) The operationalizations of the class categories in these tables are the same as those discussed in chapter 2.

Two general observations can immediately be made on the basis of these tables. First, with very few exceptions, every occupational category is distributed across all class categories (see Table 5.2). Managers constitute at least 20% of every occupational category except farmers and unskilled laborers, and workers constitute at least a third of every occupational category except for professionals, managers, foremen, and farmers. Certain occupational categories (such as craftsmen and sales) have class distributions relatively similar to the population as a whole, and thus knowing that an individual falls into one of these occupations tells you virtually nothing about his or her likely class location. In fact, on the basis of the data from Tables 5.1 and 5.2, less than 15% of the economically active population in the United States in 1969 were in occupational categories in which more than two-thirds of the individuals fell into a single class location. Even if we drop the distinction between workers and semiautonomous employees, this would only increase to about 25%. In other words, when class is defined in terms of social relations of production, it is clearly a mistake to equate the "working class" with manual labor and the "middle class" with mental (or white-collar) labor.

The second general conclusion from these tables is that although most occupations are represented within each class location, the distribution of occupations is quite different within different classes (Table 5.1). Just under 61% of all workers occupy blue-collar occupational positions, compared to 48% of semiautonomous employees, 44% of managers, 24% of the petty bourgeoisie and 10% of employers. On the other extreme, 70% of all employers and 30% of all petty bourgeois say that their occupation is "manager, proprietor or official," compared to 17% of all managers/supervisors, 4% of all semiautonomous employees, and less than 1% of all workers.

If anything, these estimates probably understate somewhat the differences between classes in occupational composition. For one thing, since the contradictory location between the working class and the petty bourgeoisie is defined by strictly subjective criteria (see chapter 2), it is likely that this category includes many positions which, on objective criteria, should belong in the working class. Unless these incorrect classifications are evenly distributed across occupations, then an adequate objective measure of autonomy would change the occupation-class distribution. Similarly, some supervisors in the Survey of Working Conditions are undoubtedly purely nominal supervisors, lacking any real control (authority) over the labor of their "subordinates," and thus they should be classified within the working class itself.

We can get some conception of the likely error introduced by merging nominal supervisors with real managers/supervisors from a second data set, the Panel Study of Income Dynamics (PSID). Because of some limitations in the randomness of this sample, it is less useful than the Survey of Working Conditions for getting a general idea of the overall class-occupation distribution (see appendix A). It can, however, give us a rough idea of the difference in occupational distributions between nominal supervisors and proper managers, since all supervisors in the survey were also asked: "Do you have any say in the pay or promotions of your subordinates?" Table 5.3 indicates the distribution of occupation *for men only* (Tables 5.1 and 5.2 are for men and women) in three categories—the working class, mere supervisors (those who have no say in pay or promotions), and proper managers—using PSID data. There was no basis for distinguishing the working class from semiautonomous employees in the Panel Study, and thus the worker category includes both class locations. (For comparative purposes, the SWC figures for male workers combined with male semiautonomous employees are also presented in the table.) Even allowing for some error because the PSID sample was not altogether random, it is clear from Table 5.3 that a much higher proportion of male supervisors than of proper managers are in blue-collar occupations (52% compared to 25%). A much higher proportion of managers than mere supervisors, in contrast, give "manager" as their occupation (41% compared to 14%).

Another way of assessing the relationship between class and occupation is to compute the multiple correlation coefficient between a series of dummy variables (0–1 variables) for class and a metric of occupational position such as occupational status. If we use three dummy variables to represent class (one for workers, one for managers, and one for employers), the multiple correlation between class and occupational status for the PSID data is .38. The correlation of the worker dummy variable alone is −.31. These correlations indicate that class and occupational position are related, but that most of the variance in occupations (at least as measured by occupational status) occurs within class positions rather than between class positions.

These findings have two central implications for Marxist theory. First, and perhaps most important, they confirm the conceptual distinction between the technical and social relations of production. Although there is clearly an empirical relationship between the two, they cannot be collapsed into a single typology. Given technical functions within production are performed by a variety of positions within the social relations of production, and every class location contains positions involving a wide range of technical activities.

TABLE 5.3
Distribution of Occupations Among Managers and Supervisors, Males Only

| Occupation | Panel Study of Income Dynamics | | | Survey of Working Conditions |
	Managers[a]	Supervisors	Workers[b]	Workers[b] (males only)
Professional, technical, and kindred	27.0%	24.0%	15.8%	11.2%
Managers, officials, and proprietors	41.1	13.7	2.6	1.7
Clerical and sales	6.5	10.0	15.0	14.5
Craftsmen, foremen, and kindred	20.0	29.6	23.4	23.3
Operatives	3.8	13.3	29.1	31.8
Laborers, farm laborers, and services	1.1	8.6	13.9	17.4
Farmers and farm managers	.5	.5	.2	0.0
Total	100	100	100	100
N	557	528	1383	408

Note: Percentages do not always add to 100% because of rounding.
[a]Managers are defined as supervisors who report that they have some say in the pay and promotions of their subordinates.
[b]The category "worker" in this table includes people in semiautonomous employee class locations as well as the working class proper.

Second, these results suggest that occupations may constitute one critical basis for the internal divisions within classes. Occupational locations determine intraclass strata through two primary mechanisms:

1. Occupational positions reflect different market capacities and thus contribute to reproducing privileged segments of classes at the level of exchange relations (i.e., income).

2. Occupational positions are one of the central criteria for status and thus contribute to reproducing privileged segments of classes at the level of ideological relations.

To the extent that salient occupational and class divisions coincide, those classes are likely to be more united, in terms both of the life experiences of people within the class and collective action by the class. One of the striking features of Table 5.1, in these terms, is that the small-employer class location is much more homogeneous in its mix of technical activities than is any other class. Proper capitalists would, if anything, be even more homogeneous.

If this general interpretation is valid, then when sociologists study the relationship of occupational status to income, they are really studying the interconnections between two dimensions of stratification *within* classes. The limitation of such research is not so much the variables that are chosen for study, but the variables that are left out of the analysis, in particular class relations.

The rest of this chapter directly compares the explanatory power of class and occupational status within regression equations predicting income. While the results hardly prove the general interpretation of the relationship of occupational status to class discussed above, they establish the importance of studying the relationship of class to status in the analysis of income inequality.

CLASS AND OCCUPATIONAL STATUS AS PREDICTORS OF INDIVIDUAL INCOME

To compare the explanatory power of class and occupational status, data from the Panel Study of Income Dynamics will be used. This data set was chosen over the Survey of Working Conditions both because the sample size is considerably larger and because it has a much more refined measure of the managerial class location (i.e., manager = supervisor with some say in pay and promotions of subordinates). The major limitation of the Panel Study is that the questions on class location were asked only of men, and thus all analyses using these data must exclude women. Nevertheless, the greater precision in the operationalization of class is more important for the present purposes, and thus I shall rely almost exclusively on the PSID data.[1]

The basic regression equation which will be used to compare class and occupation status is:

$$\text{Income} = \beta_1 \text{ Occupational Status} + \sum_{i=2}^{4} \beta_i \text{ Class Dummies}$$
$$+ \beta_5 \text{ Number of Employees} + \beta_6 \text{ Education}$$
$$+ \beta_7 \text{ Age} + \beta_8 \text{ Seniority} + \sum_{i=9}^{11} \beta_i \text{ Background}$$

where the class dummies consist of three 0–1 variables: workers, employers, and managers (thus the category left out combines the petty bourgeoisie and mere supervisors); and the background variables consist of father's education, father's occupational status, and general parental economic condition. (All of these variables are described in appendix B.) Income will be measured by the individual's total annual taxable income from all sources before taxes, including such things as wages, interest from savings and investments, rents, etc.[2] Throughout this analysis, income will be measured in raw (unlogged) dollars, for reasons discussed in appendix B.

In this equation the effect of class on income is measured by the combined effect of the three class dummies and number of employees since, in terms of the conceptual framework developed in chapter 2, number of employees indicates how close to the petty bourgeoisie is the class position of small employers. The regressions will also be run without number of employees, in order to compare the class dummies alone to status.

---

[1] In any event, the results using SWC data are virtually identical to those reported here (see Wright and Perrone, 1977, p. 44, and Wright, 1976b, p. 349).

[2] In an earlier version of this study (Wright, 1976b), four other income variables were also used: the average income over the previous seven years (or the maximum number of years in that period in which the individual worked); a very crude measure of nonwage income; annual earnings; and imputed hourly earnings. Since the results using these variables are virtually all consistent with the results simply using annual income, I have limited the presentation to this single income variable. For a discussion of the regressions using all five measures of income, see Wright (1976b, pp. 177–79).

The strategy for comparing the predictive power of class and occupational status will be to examine how the explained variance (R^2) in this equation changes as status, class, and number of employees are included and excluded in various combinations. This is a rather crude method for comparing the explanatory power of different variables. But since the purpose of this particular exercise is to demonstrate the relevance of class to hard-nosed empiricists, it provides a useful criterion for comparing class and status.

Part A of Table 5.4 presents the results for the various regression equations predicting total annual income. Part B presents an explicit comparison of the explained variance contributed by class and status in these equations.

The full equation explains just under 35% of the variance in income. When class and number of employees are dropped from this equation, the explained variance decreases to 25% (line 3, Table 5.4); when status is dropped, on the other hand, the explained variance only decreases to 32% (line 4, Table 5.4). When status, class, and number of employees are all dropped, the explained variance declines to 20% (line 5). Thus, net of status, background, education, and the other variables, class, and number of employees explain 10% of the variance in income (line 11, Table 5.4), whereas status, net of class and the other variables, explains only 2% of the variance (line 13).

Similarly, if we examine equation (2) in Table 5.4, we see that net of education and status, class and number of employees explain 11.3% of the variance in income (line 18, Table 5.4), whereas status net of class, number of employees, and education explains only 4.3% of the variance (line 20). Furthermore, if we add variables to the equation lacking both class and status (i.e., in this case, the simple regression of income on education), we see that class and number of employees, net of education, explain 16% of the variance in income (line 22); the class dummies alone, net of education, explain 13.4% of the variance (line 23); while status, net of education, explains only 8.7% (line 24).

Finally, when we compare class and status directly, we find that each of them alone explains just about 18% of the variance in income (lines 9 and 10a, Table 5.4) while class and number of employees explain just over 20% of the variance (line 10).[3]

---

[3]If we look simply at nonwage income (asset income, interest, dividends, profits, etc.) as mentioned in note 2, the difference between the explanatory power of class and status is even more striking: the class dummies by themselves explain 23% of the variance in nonwage income, occupational status only 3%. (See Wright, 1976b, p. 178.)

TABLE 5.4
Regression Equations for Comparisons of Class and Occupational Status with Annual Taxable Income as Dependent Variable

A. Beta Coefficients for Independent Variables in Equation

	Employer Dummy	Manager Dummy	Worker Dummy	No. of Employees	Occupational Status	Education	Father's Education	Father's Occupational Status	Parents' Economic Condition	Age	Seniority	R^2
1.	.07	.12	(.01)[a]	.27	.21	.19	−.03	(.0)	.04	.15	.10	.347
1a.	.29	.12	(.01)	—[b]	.22	.19	−.04	(.0)	.04	.15	.09	.324
2.	.09	.12	(−.02)	.26	.27	.10	—	—	—	—	—	.303
2a.	.31	.12	(−.02)	—	.28	.09	—	—	—	—	—	.281
3.	—	—	—	—	.28	.20	−.04	(.01)	.05	.17	.13	.250
4.	.07	.15	(−.01)	.28	—	.31	−.03	.02	.03	.19	.10	.323
4a.	.30	.15	(−.01)	—	—	.31	−.05	.02	.04	.20	.09	.297
5.	—	—	—	—	—	.31	−.04	.04	.05	.24	.13	.204
6.	—	—	—	—	.37	.09	—	—	—	—	—	.187
7.	.11	.16	−.05	.28	—	.24	—	—	—	—	—	.260
7a.	.34	.16	−.05	—	—	.24	—	—	—	—	—	.234
8.	—	—	—	—	—	.32	—	—	—	—	—	.100
9.	—	—	—	—	.43	—	—	—	—	—	—	.181
10.	.13	.20	−.07	.28	—	—	—	—	—	—	—	.204
10a.	.36	.20	−.07	—	—	—	—	—	—	—	—	.178

B. Comparison of Explained Variance of Class and Status

	Increment in R^2
11. Class and no. employees, net of status, education, and others (1–3)[c]	.097
12. Class net of status, education, and other variables (1a–3)	.074
13. Status net of class, no. employees, education, and other variables (1–4)	.023
14. Status net of class, education, and other variables (1a–4a)	.027
15. Class and no. employees net of education and other variables (4–5)	.120
16. Class net of education and other variables (4a–5)	.093
17. Status net of education and other variables (3–5)	.046
18. Class and no. employees net of status and education (2–6)	.113
19. Class net of status and education (2a–5)	.093
20. Status net of class, no. employees, and education (2–7)	.043
21. Status net of class and education (2a–7a)	.046
22. Class and no. employees net of education (7–8)	.160
23. Class net of education (7a–8)	.134
24. Status net of education (6–8)	.087
25. Class and no. employees minus status (10–9)	.023
26. Class minus status (10a–9)	−.003

Source: Data from Panel Study of Income Dynamics.
[a]Coefficients in parentheses are less than their standard error.
[b]Dashes indicate that the variable is left out of the equation.
[c]The numbers in parentheses refer to the equations in part A of the table.

CONCLUSIONS

These results strongly confirm the first two hypotheses in chapter 4. The individual's position within class relations, measured by either the class dummies and number of employees or the dummies alone, clearly has a significant impact on income, independent of occupational status (hypothesis 1.1); and, net of education, the impact of class on income is considerably greater than the effect of status on income (hypothesis 1.2). Thus, even at the individual level of analysis, location within the social relations of production is a relatively powerful predictor of income.

There are several things which these results do *not* indicate. They do not indicate that class alone is sufficient for understanding income inequality at the individual level. Class, as we have measured it, accounts for only 20% of the variance in total annual income. While this proportion would undoubtedly be increased if we had more refined measures of class locations and contradictory locations within class relations, still it is clear from the data that a great deal of the total variation in incomes occurs within classes.

The data also do not indicate that occupational status, or other metrics of occupational position, are inconsequential for understanding income variation. Occupation, as an indicator of position both within the labor market and within ideological relations, clearly plays a role in determining individual income, as reflected in the fact that occupational position generally does account for some of the variance in income even when one controls for class and other variables at the individual level of analysis.

The individual level of analysis, however, is not the heart of a Marxist theory of income determination. Showing that class compares favorably with status as a predictor of individual income is important mainly in convincing people that class is worth studying. This chapter, I hope, has accomplished this minimal task.

We can now shift our terrain to the really interesting questions: the ways in which class structurally mediates the income determination process.

6

Class and Income

THE LOGIC OF THE ANALYSIS

In chapter 5 we analyzed the relative explanatory power of class and status within individual income determination equations. The proportions of explained variances compared were all variances in individual income. In this chapter the unit of analysis shifts from the individual as such to the class structure itself. While the data that we will explore are all tagged onto individuals, the analysis centers on structural positions, not on the individuals who fill those positions.

The logic of such an analysis might be clearer if we look at an example other than the investigation of class structure. Suppose we were interested in studying various structural characteristics of business organizations. In particular, we might be interested in the differences between large, bureaucratically organized corporations and small, less bureaucratically structured businesses. One could hypothesize that, for a variety of reasons, pay scales in the bureaucratic organization are likely to be much more closely tied to formal educational credentials than they are in the smaller, unbureaucratic organizations. Two empirical strategies could be adopted to test this hypothesis. We could look at the formal pay scales and job requirements in the business records of large and small firms and use these records to estimate the relationship between income and education in the two types of businesses. Or, if those records were unavailable, we could conduct a survey of the personnel in the two types of firms and use individual-level data to estimate the returns to educational credentials. In both cases, the resulting regression equations must be seen as tapping structural characteristics of the firms rather than the income determination process of individuals.

The fact that the data are attached to individuals does not imply that the resulting regressions are based on models of individual units of analysis. Indeed, these regression equations would be extremely misleading if they were interpreted as reflecting individual returns to education rather than as characterizing structural differences between firms. Let us suppose, in the example of the two types of firms, that educational credentials were themselves one of the important criteria determining the firm in which the individual worked. In such a situation, the estimates of returns to educational credentials *within* each firm would tell us very little about the total relationship of education to income for individuals, even though these regressions might tell us a great deal about the structural differences between firms.

To state this issue in slightly more technical terms: the correct specification of a regression equation for an analysis of the structural differences between firms might be a totally incorrect specification of the equations for an analysis of individuals. Throughout the analysis which follows, positions within class relations should be viewed as quite analogous to the firms in the above example. They constitute empty places within the class structure and the hypotheses are primarily about the structural characteristics of the empty places as such, not about the individual-level processes that occur within those class relations. Much confusion in the analysis which follows will be avoided if it is remembered that the equations are not being specified at the level of individuals as units of analysis, but at the level of classes.

SPECIFICATION OF THE EQUATIONS

The argument about the logic of a structural analysis is critical if we are to specify the equations correctly. In chapter 3 we noted that the basic directions that a number of causal processes might take in an individual-level model are reversed in a model that operates at the level of class structures. For example, in an individual-level model, social background is seen as a cause of education, and both education and background as a direct cause of income. Since education appears as an intervening variable between background and income, the equation would be misspecified if the background variables were left out. That is, potential biases in the magnitude of the education effects would be introduced by not controlling for social background since some of the apparent education effects should be properly interpreted as effects of the social background. Within a model of income determination at the level of class structure, in contrast, education acts as a *selective mechanism* on the social background characteristics of people re-cruited into class positions. (In a model at the level of social structure, causation is not understood in simple temporal terms, and the expression "intervening variable" is less appropriate, but one could regard social background as an intervening variable between education and income.) Therefore, the correct specification of the full effect of edu-cation on income *at the level of classes as units of analysis* would not include social background variables as controls. Again, unless classes are viewed as legitimate units of analysis in their own right and not simply as variables influencing individuals, then the analysis which follows will make little, if any, sense.

Most of the analysis which follows will center on three basic re-gression equations, each of which will be estimated *separately within each of the class categories* we are studying:

$$\text{Income} = a + b_1 \text{ Education} \tag{1}$$

$$\begin{aligned}
\text{Income} = a &+ b_1 \text{ Education} + b_2 \text{ Occupational Status} + b_3 \text{ Age} \\
&+ b_4 \text{ Seniority} + b_5 \text{ Father's Status} + b_6 \text{ Father's Education} \\
&+ b_7 \text{ Parental Economic Condition} \tag{2}
\end{aligned}$$

$$\text{Income} = a + \sum_{i=1}^{7} b_i X_i + b_8 \text{ Total Annual Hours Worked}, \tag{3}$$

where X_1 represents the variables in equation (2). (These variables are described in appendix B.) The education variable will be entered into these equations in two forms: first, as a single, 8-level educational credential scale, and second, as a series of dummy variables. Income, throughout this analysis, is measured by total annual income from all sources in unlogged dollars.[1] In several places we will estimate

---

[1]As in the analysis in the previous chapter, all the equations in this chapter were also run using several other measures of income: average income over the number of years

additional equations, but these three will comprise the heart of the analysis.

These equations will be used to compare class categories in two ways:

1. The coefficients of the education variable will be used as the basis for comparing the income returns to education among different classes. In the unstandardized regression equation, this coefficient indicates how many dollars of additional income an individual *within a given class location* would expect for a unit increase in education. Comparing these coefficients, therefore, enables us to test the various hypotheses concerning different returns to education within different class locations.

2. The equations will also enable us to compare the expected incomes of individuals within different class locations, controlling for various individual characteristics. I shall refer to these comparisons as analyses of the "gaps" in income between classes. Depending upon the specific analysis, two different measures of this gap will be employed. The first, to be referred to as the "average gap" in income between classes, estimates this gap at values of the control variables equal to the average of the mean values of these variables for the two classes being compared. Thus, for example, if we were calculating the average income gap between workers and managers using equation (1), this gap would be measured at a level of education, $(\bar{E}_w + \bar{E}_m)/2$, where $\bar{E}_w$ and $\bar{E}_m$ are the mean levels of education for workers and managers, respectively. The second measure of the gap, referred to as the "standardized income gap," estimates the gap at a level of control variables equal to the most privileged category in the comparison. In the above example, this would mean estimating the expected difference between workers and manager incomes at education $= \bar{E}_m$. The rationale for these different measures of the income gap between classes, and the formal statistical procedures that will be used to test the significance of such gaps, are discussed in appendix C.

Equation (1) above will be used to provide the basic estimates of the returns to education within the various class positions. This equation provides the best measure of the overall relationship between education and income within a class.

---

worked during the previous seven years, annual earnings, and imputed hourly earnings. With very marginal exceptions, all of the results which will be reported here are unaffected by the specific version of the income variable employed. The only situation in which any discrepancy of note appeared was in the analysis of hypothesis 4.1 using the imputed hourly wage variable in equation (2) (see Wright, 1976b, pp. 198–201).

Equation (2) serves two basic purposes. First, it will be used to see if the differences in returns to education between classes based on equation (1) are affected by the addition of various control variables. If in fact classes are not real structures, if they are not legitimate objects of investigation or units of analysis, but simply aggregations of the characteristics of the individuals we have classified into classes, then controlling for these various individual characteristics should substantially reduce the differential returns to education across classes. Equation (2), therefore, can be considered an indirect way of validating the underlying claim that classes are indeed real structures, irreducible to the characteristics of individuals.

Secondly, equation (2) will be used to see whether the differences in mean incomes between classes disappear as controls are added. This equation will, therefore, be the basis for analysis of income gaps between class categories. As in the analysis of returns to education, the hypotheses discussed in chapter 3 argue that the differences in incomes between classes are not a consequence of the characteristics of the individuals who occupy class positions, but rather are consequences of the structure of class relations as such. If this is true, then there should still be significant income gaps between classes in equation (2).

Finally, equation (3) is included in order to see whether or not the results from the analysis of equation (2) are simply consequences of the different number of hours worked by people in different class positions. If the income gap remains in equation (3), this gap can be interpreted as reflecting an income privilege or income discrimination component of total income (among wage earners) as discussed in chapter 4. To state the issue in more conventional Marxist terminology: in equation (3) the income gaps between managers and workers, or between races and sexes within either the managerial or working-class location, can be interpreted as reflecting differences in rates of exploitation.

OVERVIEW OF THE RESULTS

Figure 6.1 graphically presents the simple regression of annual income on education for the basic class categories in our analysis— workers, managers and supervisors, employers, and the petty bourgeoisie. Table 6.1 presents the coefficients for the regression of annual income on the variables in equation (3) for each of the class categories we shall investigate. The constant term in these equations is evaluated at the mean values of the independent variables for em-

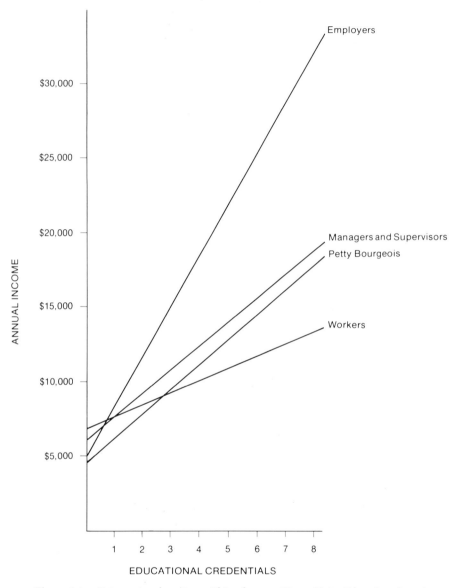

Figure 6.1. Returns to education within class positions. Note: Educational credentials are defined as follows: 0 = no education; 1 = some elementary; 2 = elementary; 3 = some high school; 4 = high school; 5 = high school + nonacademic; 6 = some college; 7 = college; 8 = graduate training. (*Source: Data from Panel Study of Income Dynamics. Figure courtesy of the UW Cartographic Laboratory.*)

TABLE 6.1

Regressions of Taxable Income on Selected Variables

Class Category	Adjusted Constant[a]	Education	Occupational Status	Age	Seniority	Annual Hours Worked	Father's Education	Father's Occupational Status	Parents' Economic Condition	R^2
Workers (N=1715)										
B	$16,069	$655	$68	$122	$124	$3.2	$249	$-30	$263	.369
(se)	(204)	(93)	(7)	(11)	(18)	(.2)	(89)	(8)	(87)	
Beta		.20	.25	.27	.16	.32	.07	-.09	.07	
All managers/supervisors (N=1014)										
B	17,583	1,169	99	140	127	2.6	-251	29	-422	.372
(se)	(255)	(153)	(11)	(21)	(29)	(.3)	(143)	(12)	(152)	
Beta		.25	.28	.21	.13	.18	-.05	.07	-.08	
Supervisors (N=535)										
B	15,451	856	55	78	176	2.7	-157	28	-513	.349
(se)	(312)	(161)	(11)	(21)	(31)	(.4)	(170)	(13)	(166)	
Beta		.26	.21	.17	.23	.25	-.04	.09	-.12	
Managers (N=479)										
B	18,640	1,403	116	184	80	1.5	-379	29	-291	.339
(se)	(392)	(20)	(37)	(48)	(.6)	(216)	(18)	(246)		
Beta	.27	.27	.24	.07	.10	-.08	.06	-.05		
Petty bourgeoisie										
B	16,307	81,375	176	-12	227	1.00	1,768	-100	-501	.317
(se)		(595)	(40)	(83)	(82)	(1.0)	(637)	(50)	w)704)	
Beta		.27	.44	-.02	.29	.09	.27	-.20	-m07	
Employers										
B	25,711	2,137	304	266	90	-.08	-1,465	-19	2,974	.256
(se)	(1,246)	(820)	(61)	(151)	(159)	(1.6)	(814)	(73)	(939)	
Beta		.18	.33	.14	.04	.00	-.12	-.02	.20	

Source: Data from Panel Study of Income Dynamics.

B = Raw coefficient

(se) = Standard error

Beta = Standardized coefficient

[a] The constant term in these equations has been adjusted to the mean values of the independent variables for employer. The difference between classes on this adjusted constant constitutes the "standardized income gap" defined in chapter 6.

ployers, and thus the difference in constants can be interpreted as the difference in expected income between classes if all classes shared the employer's means on the independent variables (i.e., standardized income gaps). These regressions constitute the heart of the results that we shall try to unravel in the rest of this chapter.

The presentation and discussion of the results will basically follow the order of the hypotheses presented at the end of chapter 4. We shall begin by comparing the working class and the contradictory location between the working class and the bourgeoisie (managers/supervisors). More refined analysis of the internal structure of the managerial category will be left for chapter 7. The comparison of workers and managers/supervisors will be followed by a brief analysis of the petty bourgeoisie, and then a more extensive discussion of the hypotheses involving small employers.

MANAGERS/SUPERVISORS AND
WORKERS COMPARED

Hypothesis 2.0.   *Managers/supervisors will have higher incomes than workers, even after controlling for education, seniority, family background, and occupational status.*

The basic strategy for testing this hypothesis will be to analyze the "average income gaps" between workers and managers/supervisors, between workers and mere supervisors and between workers and proper managers for the three regression equations discussed above. In the comparison of workers and managers/supervisors, the equations will be estimated using the six education dummy variables as well as the single education scale. The results are presented in Table 6.2.

Several generalizations can be drawn from this table:

1. There is a highly significant gap in income between workers and managers/supervisors and between workers and managers for all three regression equations. In every case these gaps are significant at the .001 level. This means that workers and managers/supervisors with equal levels of education, occupational status, age, seniority, and family background (set at the average of their respective class means on these variables) will still differ significantly in expected incomes.

2. The gap in income between workers and mere supervisors disappears completely in equations (2) and (3). This reflects the class position of mere supervisors as a marginal category located right at the boundary of the working class. As was suggested in chapter 4, many

TABLE 6.2
Analysis of Income Gaps for Comparisons of Total Annual Income of Workers with Managers and Supervisors

Class Comparisons	Mean Total Income	Expected Income, Adjusted[a] for Variables in					
		Eq 1	Eq 1[b]	Eq 2	Eq 2[b]	Eq 3	Eq 3[b]
Workers vs. Managers/Supervisors							
Managers + supervisors	$15,256	$14,571	$14,613	$13,730	$13,758	$13,444	$13,469
Workers	10,976	11,322	11,339	11,978	11,975	12,376	12,365
Income gap	4,280	3,249	3,274	1,752	1,783	1,068	1,104
% of difference in mean income eliminated by controls			24%	59%	58%	75%	74%
t-value of income gap		11.6***	11.7***	6.9***	7.0***	4.3***	4.4***
Workers vs. Managers							
Managers	$18,090	$16,903		$15,613		$15,343	
Workers	10,976	11,461		12,391		12,966	
Income gap	7,114	5,442		3,222		2,377	
% of difference in mean income eliminated by controls		24%		55%		67%	
t-value of income gap		13.1***		8.0***		5.9***	
Workers vs. Supervisors							
Supervisors	$12,266	$12,064		$11,705		$11,513	
Workers	10,976	11,177		11,557		11,782	
Income gap	1,290	853		148		−269	
% of difference in mean income eliminated by controls		34%		89%		121%	
t-value of income gap		2.9**		ns		ns	

Source: Data from Panel Study of Income Dynamics.

Independent variables: Eq 1 = education only

Eq 2 = education, seniority, age, background, and occupational status

Eq 3 = Eq 2 + annual hours worked

Significance levels on a one-tailed test:

*** .001

** .01

* .05

ns $t < 1$

[a]Incomes are adjusted to the average of the mean values of the independent variables for the groups being compared.

[b]Using education dummies.

such supervisors should probably be placed within the working class itself.

3. The use of dummy variables instead of the single education variable has essentially no effect on the income gaps between workers and managers/supervisors. In the simple regression of annual income on education, for example, the gap using the education scale is $3249, whereas using the six education dummy variables it is $3274. When the single education scale is used, the income gap tells us the expected difference in income when both classes have the same *mean* education. When education dummy variables are used, the income gap indicates the expected difference in income when both classes have the same *distribution* of individuals across education categories (although not necessarily the same income returns for each education category).[2] The results clearly indicate that it does not matter which way education is measured for the comparison of workers and managers/supervisors.

4. While the gaps in income between workers and managers remain quite significant in equations (2) and (3), the total gap (i.e., the total difference in gross mean incomes) is considerably reduced as controls are added. Overall, about 55% of the difference in mean incomes is eliminated when all of the variables in equation (2) are held constant, and 67% when the number of hours worked annually is also held constant in equation (3).[3]

This reduction in the total income gap in equations (2) and (3) suggests that at least part of the overall income differences between class positions involves, in one way or another, the characteristics of the individuals who fill those positions. Two sorts of interpretations of these results are possible. One line of reasoning would argue that this reduction in the income gap indicates that the overall difference in mean incomes between classes is in part an "artifact" of the distribution of personal characteristics within classes. These personal attributes, not the class positions in their own right, are the "real" cause of much of the observed differences between classes.

[2]In our analysis, this distribution consists of the average of the percentage of workers and of the percentage of managers who fall into a particular educational category.

[3]In interpreting these figures it must be remembered that we are evaluating the income gap at the mid-point between the mean values of the independent variables for workers and for managers. If we evaluated the gap at the managers' means, the proportion of the total difference between gross mean incomes that would be eliminated would be less than in Table 6.2. For example, the gap in income for equation (3) would only be 55% rather than 67% of the total difference in income. As explained in appendix C, the gap is being assessed at this average level of the independent variables rather than at the managers' means since we are interested in testing propositions about the structural differences between workers and managers at a typical rather than an extreme point.

An alternative view regards the distribution of the characteristics of individuals occupying class positions as itself largely a consequence of class relations. The bourgeoisie, after all, hires both workers and managers, and clearly has a stake in selecting certain characteristics for both. The result is that there will be a different mix of family backgrounds, age, occupational statuses, etc., for people who end up in managerial or working-class positions. This logic suggests that the total difference in mean incomes between classes can be broken down into two parts: one reflecting the *direct* effects of class on income, the other reflecting the *indirect* effects of class position as it operates through the characteristics of the individuals selected into the class slots. In our analysis of income gaps, the direct effect roughly corresponds to the gap in income that remains after individual characteristics are held constant, while the indirect effect corresponds to the difference between the total difference in mean incomes and this gap. In the example of total annual income, about two thirds of the total difference in income between workers and managers can be viewed as representing this indirect effect, and one third the direct effect of class.[4]

There is no way of empirically distinguishing between these two interpretations in the present data.[5] All that the data "show" in an empiricist sense is that income differences between classes are reduced by statistically controlling for individual characteristics. The results do not indicate whether such a reduction should itself be viewed as a consequence of class relations or as processes directly springing from a logic of individual action, independent of class relations.

In any event, regardless of which interpretation is chosen, all of these results strongly support hypothesis 2. Managers clearly do have

[4]In order to make this link between direct and indirect effects of class and the income gaps as we have measured them it is necessary to assume that the coefficients in the regression equations are simple characteristics of the class positions, and that they would not change if the characteristics of the individuals occupying those class positions changed. This grossly ahistorical, static assumption is really only useful for heuristic purposes, but once it is made, we can partition the total difference in incomes into a component reflecting the distribution of individual characteristics and a component directly reflecting the class positions as such.

[5]More complex ways of partitioning the total gap in income between groups, such as the method suggested by Masters (1975, pp. 104–6), in which the difference in mean incomes is divided into three parts, due respectively to differences in the means of the independent variables, in slope coefficients, and in the interaction of the two, will not help us here. The issue is not precisely how much of the total difference in income between classes involves individual characteristics, but rather how such individual characteristics should be viewed theoretically. Are they characteristics of the structure as such (through a process of structural determination as described in chapter 3) or is the structure simply a reflection of individual processes?

higher incomes than workers, and this difference remains significant even after controlling for a wide range of other variables. The income determination process within the contradictory class location between the working class and the bourgeoisie, therefore, seems to generate income privileges when compared to that within the working class. If controlling for all of the variables in equation (3) can be interpreted as holding constant the value of labor power, and if it is assumed that, on the average, labor power within the working class proper is exchanged close to its value, then these results indicate that managers receive an income which is systematically above the value of their labor power.

Hypothesis 4.1. *The income returns to education will be much greater within the managerial category than within the working class, even after controlling for age, occupational status, family background, etc.*

Table 6.3 presents, for each class category, the three basic regression equations. Figure 6.2 graphically presents the results for the simple regression of annual income on education for workers, managers, and supervisors. Table 6.4 presents the statistical tests of differences of returns to education for hypothesis 4.1.[6]

Several generalizations can be made on the basis of these results:

1. Workers, managers, and supervisors all have highly significant returns to education, regardless of which regression equation is estimated. While adding the controls in equations (2) and (3) does reduce the education coefficients somewhat, the partial education coefficients in these equations are still statistically significant.

2. Workers have significantly lower returns to education than supervisors and managers combined and than managers examined separately in the simple regression of income on education. The returns to education for workers in these equations are generally about half the returns for managers/supervisors. When the various controls in equations (2) and (3) are added, the returns to education for both workers and managers/supervisors decline, but the workers' returns remain about half the returns for managers/supervisors. These results strongly support hypothesis 4.1.

3. The various controls in equations (2) and (3) do not reduce the differences in returns to education by more than 30–40%. In terms of the preceding discussion about the income gaps between workers and

---

[6]The means and standard deviations of all the variables used in these equations and the correlation matrices used to generate the equations can be found in Wright (1976b, pp. 320–26).

TABLE 6.3
Regression Equations Within Class Categories with Annual Taxable Income as Dependent Variable

	Unadjusted Constant	Education	Occupational Status	Age	Seniority	Father's Education	Father's Occupational Status	Parents' Economic Condition	Annual Hours Worked	R^2
Workers										
Eq 1: B	$7,193	$851.4								.066
(se)		(77.3)								
Beta		.26								
Eq 2: B	214	641.2	$71.6	$118	$132	$166	$−30	$270		.267
(se)		(100)	(7.5)	(12)	(20)	(96)	(8.2)	(94)		
Beta		.19	.26	.26	.17	.05	−.09	.07		
Eq 3: B	−6,627	655.1	67.9	122	124	249	−30	263	$3.2	.369
(se)		(92.8)	(7.0)	(11)	(18)	(89)	(7.6)	(87)	(.19)	
Beta		.20	.25	.27	.16	.07	−.09	.07	.32	
Managers/supervisors										
Eq 1: B	6,382	1,689.1								.135
(se)		(133.5)								
Beta		.37								
Eq 2: B	−1,421	1,200.1	104	136	123	−302	27	−369		.340
(se)		(157.3)	(11.2)	(21)	(30)	(146)	(12)	(156)		
Beta		.26	.30	.21	.12	−.07	.07	−.07		
Eq 3: B	−7,145	1,168.7	98.6	140	127	−251	29	−422	2.6	.373
(se)		(153.4)	(11.0)	(21)	(29)	(143)	(12)	(152)	(.35)	
Beta		.25	.28	.21	.13	−.05	.07	−.08	.18	

(continued)

TABLE 6.3 (continued)

	Unadjusted Constant	Education	Occupational Status	Age	Seniority	Father's Education	Father's Occupational Status	Parents' Economic Condition	Annual Hours Worked	R^2
Supervisors										
Eq 1: B	8,065	854.6								.065
(se)		(140.4)								
Beta		.25								
Eq 2: B	2,650	816.8	59.7	78	171	−207	21	−459		.286
(se)		(168.6)	(12.0)	(22)	(33)	(178)	(14)	(173)		
Beta		.24	.23	.17	.22	−.06	.07	−.11		
Eq 3: B	−3,468	855.8	54.5	78	176	−157	28	−512	2.7	.349
(se)		(161)	(11.4)	(21)	(31)	(170)	(14)	(166)	(.37)	
Beta		.26	.21	.17	.23	−.05	.09	−.13	.25	
Managers										
Eq 1: B	6,481	2,081.6								.155
(se)		(222)								
Beta		.39								
Eq 2: B	−3,285	1,466.0	114.6	177	78	−403	29	−246		.330
(se)		(258)	(20)	(37)	(48)	(217)	(18)	(247)		
Beta		.28	.27	.23	.07	−.08	.07	−.04		
Eq 3: B	−6,903	1,402.7	115.8	184	80	−379	29	−291	1.5	.339
(se)		(258)	(20)	(37)	(48)	(216)	(18)	(246)	(.60)	
Beta		.27	.27	.24	.07	−.08	.07	−.05	.10	

Petty bourgeoisie

Eq 1: B	4,680	1,781.2								.123
(se)		(433.3)								
Beta		.35								
Eq 2: B	-3,922	1,534.3	169.5	-13	241	1,703	-110	-410		.310
(se)		(573.6)	(39.9)	(83)	(80)	(634)	(48)	(697)		
Beta		.30	.42	-.02	.31	.26	-.22	-.06		
Eq 3: B	-5,967	1,375.2	175.6	-12	227	1,769	-100	-501	1.0	.317
(se)		(594.8)	(40.4)	(83)	(82)	(637)	(50)	(703)	(.99)	
Beta		.27	.44	-.02	.29	.27	-.20	-.07	.09	

Employers

Eq 1: B	5,028	3,843.2								.107
(se)		(698.7)								
Beta		.33								
Eq 2: B	-17,711	2,135.8	303.5	266	91	-1,460	-19	2,976		.256
(se)		(817.6)	(61.0)	(151)	(157)	(805)	(73)	(935)		
Beta		.18	.33	.14	.04	-.12	-.02	.20		
Eq 3: B	-17,498	2,137.1	303.6	266	90	-1,465	-19	2,974	-.073	.256
(se)		(819.8)	(61.1)	(151)	(159)	(814)	(73)	(939)	(1.6)	
Beta		.18	.33	.14	.04	-.12	-.02	.20	.00	

Source: Data from Panel Study of Income Dynamics.

B = Raw coefficient

(se) = Standard error

Beta = Standardized coefficient

Independent variables: Eq 1 = education only
Eq 2 = education, seniority, age, background, and occupational status
Eq 3 = Eq 2 + annual hours worked

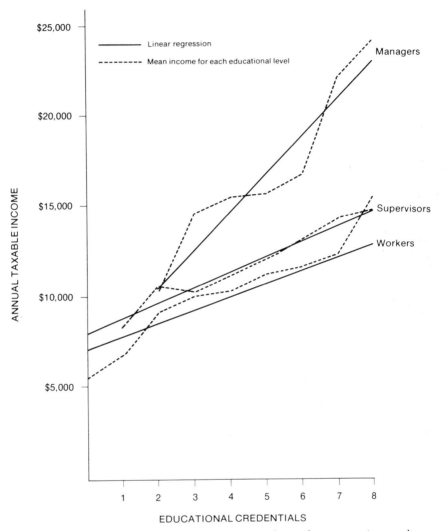

Figure 6.2. Relationship of income to education for workers, supervisors and managers. Note: Educational credentials are defined as follows: 0 = no education; 1 = some elementary; 2 = elementary; 3 = some high school; 4 = high school; 5 = high school + nonacademic; 6 = some college; 7 = college; 8 = graduate training. (*Source: Data from Panel Study of Income Dynamics. Figure courtesy of the UW Cartographic Laboratory.*)

TABLE 6.4
Returns to Education for Workers and Managers/Supervisors

Class Comparisons	Income Returns in		
	Eq 1	Eq 2	Eq 3
Workers vs. supervisors/managers			
Diff. in educ. coeffs.	$838	$559	$514
t-value of difference	5.5***	3.0**	2.9**
Worker's slope as % of mgrs/sups.	50%	53%	56%
% of slope diff. in eq 1 eliminated by controls		33%	39%
Workers vs. managers			
Diff. in educ. coeffs.	$1,231	$825	$748
t-value of difference	5.2***	3.0**	2.7**
Worker's slope as % of mgrs/sups.	41%	44%	47%
% of slope diff. in eq 1 eliminated by controls		33%	39%
Workers vs. supervisors			
Diff. in educ. coeffs.	$4	$176	$201
t-value of difference	ns	ns	1.1
Worker's slope as % of mgrs/sups.	99%	79%	77%

Source: Data from Panel Study of Income Dynamics.
Independent variables:　Eq 1 = education only
　　　　　　　　　　　　Eq 2 = education, age, seniority, background, and occupational status
　　　　　　　　　　　　Eq 3 = Eq 2 + annual hours worked
Significance levels on a one-tailed test:
*** .001
** .01
* .05
ns $t < 1$

managers/supervisors, this fact implies that most of the difference in education slopes is a direct consequence of class position per se.

4. Workers and mere supervisors differ hardly at all in any of the equations in Table 6.3. Furthermore, if we look at the coefficients of the other variables in equations (2) and (3), workers and supervisors differ significantly only on returns to age. Since both workers and supervisors have a significant income gap only in the simple regression of income on education, it seems fairly safe to conclude that many, perhaps most, supervisors probably belong in the working class. As a

result, in the rest of this chapter we will examine only proper managers in comparisons involving the contradictory class location between the working class and the bourgeoisie, rather than the combined manager/supervisor category.

One possible objection to these results is that by including age in the equations simply as an additive term, we have ruled out the possibility of more complicated cohort-effects in which the returns to education are different for different cohorts. The different returns for workers and managers could still therefore be "artifacts" of the age composition of the two classes, even though different returns are observed in equations (2) and (3).

To deal with this objection, equations (1)−(3) have been estimated separately for young, middle-aged, and older workers and managers. The results appear in Table 6.5. The simple regressions of income on education are presented graphically in Figure 6.3.

Among workers and managers over 50 and between 35 and 50, managers receive significantly higher returns to education in all three regression equations. Among workers and managers under 35, the returns differ hardly at all, although managers still receive significantly more income than workers at every level of education. These similar returns to education among younger workers and managers are entirely consistent with the general interpretation of the returns to education for workers and managers discussed in chapter 4. Among managers, it was argued, education serves as a screening device which sorts people into different levels of the hierarchy, and this is the basis for the high returns to education for managers as a whole. Among young managers at the beginning of their careers, this credential-screening process has not yet fully worked itself out. It is only after enough time has elapsed for a series of promotions to have occurred that the full effects of the relationship between education and position in the hierarchy can be felt. Thus, among younger managers it would not be expected that there would be particularly high returns to education.

A second objection to these results is that they may simply reflect a single, nonlinear relationship between income and education among all wage earners. Since workers would tend to be concentrated at the lower end of the education scale and managers at the top, the linear regression among workers would necessarily appear flatter than among managers. Two results suggest that this is not a plausible interpretation. First, in Figure 6.2 it is clear by inspection that the mean incomes for different levels of education among workers and managers are rea-

TABLE 6.5
Returns to Education for Workers and Managers, by Age

Class Comparisons	Income Returns in						Mean Education	Mean Income
	Eq 1	R^2	Eq 2	R^2	Eq 3	R^2		
35 years and under								
Workers	$683	.06	$347	.29	$460	.41	4.9 yr	$9,338
Managers	1,021	.05	389	.26	393	.27	5.7	14,460
Difference in coeff.	338		42		-67			
t-value of difference	ns		ns		ns			
36–50 years								
Workers	1,464	.18	427	.29	431	.37	4.1	13,269
Managers	2,691	.26	1,721	.34	1,388	.39	5.7	20,878
Difference in coeff.	1,227		1,294		957			
t-value of difference	3.3***		2.7**		2.0*			
51 years and over								
Workers	1,813	.22	891	.30	653	.39	3.5	12,268
Managers	2,583	.29	2,164	.36	2,168	.36	5.2	20,094
Difference in coeff.	770		1,273		1,515			
t-value of difference	1.8*		2.1*		2.6*			

Source: Data from Panel Study of Income Dynamics.
Independent variables: Eq 1 = education only
Eq 2 = education, age, seniority, background, and occupational status
Eq 3 = Eq 2 + annual hours worked

Significance levels on a one-tailed test:
*** .001
** .01
* .05
ns t < 1

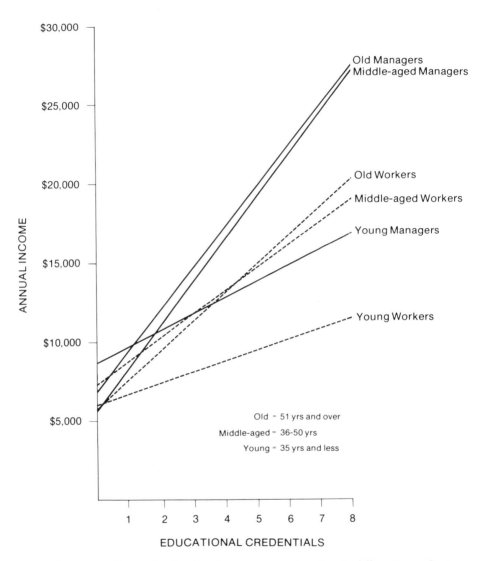

Figure 6.3. Returns to education for managers and workers in different age cohorts. Note: Educational credentials are defined as follows: 0 = no education; 1 = some elementary; 2 = elementary; 3 = some high school; 4 = high school; 5 = high school + nonacademic; 6 = some college; 7 = college; 8 = graduate training. (*Source: Data from Panel Study of Income Dynamics. Figure courtesy of the UW Cartographic Laboratory.*)

sonably linear and cannot be interpreted as points on a single curve. Secondly, as indicated in Table 6.6, the R^2 in equations using education dummy variables is virtually identical to the R^2 using the single education scale. This again indicates that the relationship between education and income is fairly linear within the managerial and working-class locations.

A final objection to these results could be that they are a consequence of problems of truncation on the dependent variable. Cain (1976, pp. 1246–47) has effectively demonstrated that the returns to education for low-income employees would generally tend to be less than for all employees simply because we have truncated the group on the dependent variable in the regression. Since workers have less income overall than managers, the comparison between the two in this study could be viewed as a comparison of a truncated category with an untruncated (or at least, less truncated) category.

There are two responses to this objection. First, while it is correct that within the working class income is truncated at the upper end of the income distribution, it is also true that the managerial category would be truncated at the bottom. This would tend to lower the slope for managers, and unless there is reason to believe that the problem of truncation is greater within one category than the other, this would not necessarily explain the differences in returns. Second, and more fundamentally, the truncation problem itself is only a problem if the regressions are interpreted as estimating income determination equations using individuals as the unit of analysis. When the equations are interpreted as measuring characteristics of class *structures*, then truncation becomes irrelevant. The fact that the income of educated workers has a constrained upper limit (i.e., is truncated) is itself a property of the working-class location within the social relations of production. Since we have not allocated individuals into the working class on the basis of their income, and our operationalization of class cannot be construed as artificially truncating the incomes of educated workers, there is no reason to see the education coefficients within the working class as artificially depressed.

All of these results, therefore, are strongly supportive of hypothesis 4.1. The relative income privilege observed among managers in hypothesis 4.0 appears to increase with education—that is, the component of income above the value of their labor power increases with the value of labor power. These results cannot be explained away by the addition of a wide variety of control variables or by arguments of age cohort effects, nonlinearity, or truncation of income.

TABLE 6.6
Returns to Specific Levels of Education for Workers and Managers

Class Comparisons	Increment in Income Expected from Attaining Education Level[a]							R^2	
	2	3	4	5	6	7	8	Using Dummy Variable[b]	Using Single Educ. Scale
Eq 1									
Workers[c]	$2,220	$431	$376	$947	$596	$1,267	$2,691	.073	.066
Managers	—	4,183	1,188	305	1,220	5,385	2,406	.180	.155
Diff. in coefficients		3,752	811	−641	624	4,118	−285		
t-value of diff.		1.6	ns	ns	ns	3.2***	ns		
Eq 3									
Workers	1,819	1,195	561	23	969	−55	864	.369	.369
Managers	—	5,181	1,351	−523	859	3,686	1,273	.354	.339
Diff. in coefficients		3,985	790	−545	−110	3,741	410		
t-value of diff.		1.9*	ns	ns	ns	3.2***	ns		

Source: Data from Panel Study of Income Dynamics.

Independent variables: Eq 1 = education only

Eq 3 = education, seniority, age, background, occupational status, and annual hours worked

[a] Education levels are: 2 elementary; 3 some high school; 4 high school; 5 high school plus nonacademic training; 6 some college; 7 college degree; 8 graduate training.

[b] This R^2 is based on the regression equation excluding the elementary school dummy variable.

[c] Entries represent the expected increase in income for obtaining a given level of education compared to the previous level of education.

Hypothesis 4.2.   *The difference between the managerial category and the working class in income returns to education should be greatest for college and postcollege levels of schooling.*

If the logic underlying hypothesis 4.1 is correct, then one would expect educational credentials to make an especially large difference in incomes between workers and managers at the college and postcollege levels. Table 6.6 indicates how much additional income an individual worker or manager would expect to get for each increment in education, using equations (1) and (3).[7] The results are not entirely as expected. Several findings are worth noting:

1. As expected, a college degree makes a much greater difference to income within the managerial class location than it does to income within the working class. Managers receive over $5000 more than workers do for a college degree in equation (1), and $3700 more in equation (3). Indeed, when all the controls in equation (3) are included, workers actually receive no returns to a college diploma whatsoever.

2. The expectation for graduate training, however, was not supported by the data. Both workers and managers received around $2500 additional income in equation (1) and within a few hundred dollars of $1000 in equation (3) for some graduate training. Two explanations of these results come to mind. First of all, it must be remembered that the working-class category in these equations contains a certain proportion of semiautonomous employees. It would be expected that there would be significantly higher income returns to higher degrees within the semiautonomous employee category than within the working class, and this may have inflated the returns to graduate training, especially since semiautonomous employees are likely to be overrepresented in this education category. Secondly, the education level is "some graduate training," not a graduate degree. The small numbers made it impossible to study separately the returns for actually receiving a credential beyond college, and this may have reduced the returns to managers (the argument was that they should receive especially high returns to credentials, not to education per se).

3. It was totally unexpected that managers should receive so much higher returns to "some high school" than workers. Indeed, while the differences are less significant statistically, the absolute magnitudes of

[7]The entries in Table 6.6 were obtained by estimating the equations several times, leaving out a different dummy variable each time. The entries under the high school variable, for example, were estimated in equations in which the "some high school" dummy was left out of the equation; the entries under "some college" were estimated leaving out "high school plus nonacademic training."

the difference in returns to some high school education for managers and workers in equations (1) and (3) are as large as they are for a college degree. I have no coherent explanation for this particular result. It is not simply an artifact of the absence of anyone with less than an elementary school education among managers. When the equations for workers were rerun leaving out both the "elementary" and "some elementary" dummies (in effect combining them into a single "less than some high school" category), the difference between managers and workers remained substantially the same. I suspect that these results reflect rather complex interactions of cohort effects with specific levels of the managerial hierarchy, but such possibilities will have to remain unexplored for the moment because of inadequate data.

Overall, these results suggest that the simple legitimating-credential interpretation of education is not sufficient to explain the differences in returns to education between the managerial class location and the working class. Such legitimation processes undoubtedly play a role, but the data do not support the claim that the managerial returns to education are consistently highest where formal academic credentials are obtained.

THE PETTY BOURGEOISIE

Hypothesis 6.0. *Within the pure petty bourgeoisie, the average level of income should only be slightly greater than within the working class (controlling for education, age, background, etc.) and the returns to education should be very close to those of the working class.*[8]

As the results in Table 6.7 indicate, the data provide at best ambiguous support for the predictions about the petty bourgeoisie. While the returns to education for the petty bourgeoisie are significantly larger than the returns for workers only in equation (1), nevertheless, in both equations (2) and (3) the absolute magnitude of the difference in slopes is relatively large. In fact, in all three regression equations the returns to education for the petty bourgeoisie were larger than for managers/supervisors combined, and nearly as large as for managers taken separately. Unless one adopts a rather naive reliance on *t*-ratios as

[8]There was one outlier in the petty bourgeois class: an individual with a high school education who earned $99,999 a year (the highest level). This is some 8 standard deviations above the mean petty bourgeois income. When this individual is included in the sample, the explained variance in equation (3) is only .11; when he is excluded, the explained variance increases to .32. Because this individual's income is so far above the mean for the petty bourgeoisie, we will exclude this case throughout the analysis.

TABLE 6.7
Income Gaps and Returns to Education for the Petty Bourgeoisie, Compared to Workers and Managers/Supervisors

Class Comparisons	Difference in Mean Incomes	Average Income Gap[a] in			Difference in Education Coefficient		
		Eq 1	Eq 2	Eq 3	Eq 1	Eq 2	Eq 3
Petty bourgeoisie vs. working class	$1,228	$1,518	−$761	−$1,358	$930	$893	$720
t-value		1.8*	ns	1.6	2.0*	1.6	1.2
Petty bourgeoisie vs. managers	−$5,886	−$3,260	−$7,261	−$7,328	−$487	$68	−$28
t-value		3.3***	6.9***	7.0***	ns	ns	ns

Source: Data from Panel Study of Income Dynamics.
Note: A negative entry means that the petty bourgeoisie has a smaller expected income or education coefficient than the class with which it is being compared.
Independent variables: Eq 1 = education only
                        Eq 2 = education, seniority, age, background, and occupational status
                        Eq 3 = Eq 2 + annual hours worked

Significance levels on a one-tailed test:
*** .001
** .01
* .05
ns $t < 1$

[a]Average income gap is assessed at the average of the means of the independent variables for the groups being compared.

the formal criterion for testing hypotheses, these results do not support the view that the petty bourgeoisie has low returns to education.

The results provide stronger support for the view that the average income of the petty bourgeoisie is close to that of the working class. While in the simple regression of income on education the expected annual income of a petty bourgeois is about $1500 greater than that of a worker (for an education level equal to the average of their respective mean educations), when various other controls are added the expected income drops below that of workers. In every equation, the expected income of a petty bourgeois is significantly below that of managers. The first half of hypothesis 6.0 is thus consistent with the data at hand.

Why should the income returns to education for the petty bourgeoisie be so high? The expectation was that since most petty bourgeois produce for competitive markets, the price of the commodities which they sold would directly reflect the value embodied in them and thus would include a component to cover the costs of producing the skills of the producer. As in the working class, therefore, the income of skilled petty bourgeois would be above that of unskilled petty bourgeois. But there was no expectation that the income of skilled petty bourgeois would rise more rapidly than the costs of reproducing their skills, and thus it was expected that the returns to skills (measured by education) should be similar to the returns within the working class. In both cases competitive pressures would keep the returns to education in line with the costs of (re)producing skilled labor power. So much for the logic of the argument.

My first thought was that perhaps the returns to education were so high for the petty bourgeoisie not because of high-income, well-educated petty bourgeois but because of low-income, poorly educated petty bourgeois. If you look at the mean incomes for each level of education (Figure 6.4), there are indeed two individuals at the bottom of the education scale with very little income. I reran the regressions omitting these cases. The returns to education were virtually the same as in the original regressions. It then occurred to me that the high returns to education might be the result of the high concentration of farmers within the petty bourgeoisie. At least part of the income of farmers takes the form of income in kind, and thus it was possible that the presence of many uneducated farmers in the regression equations could increase the slope of the education variable. So, I reestimated the equations omitting farmers. The returns to education increased rather than decreased.

Undaunted by such negative results, I looked carefully at the detailed occupational and industrial sector breakdowns for the petty

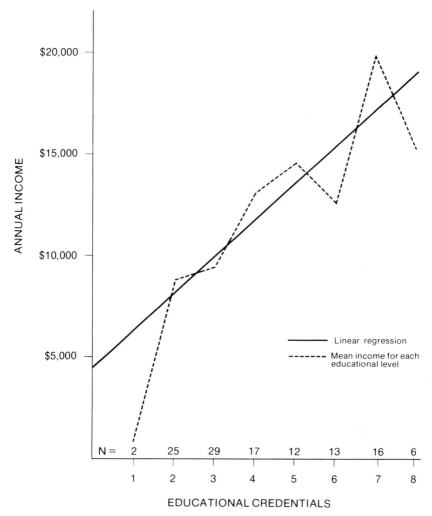

Figure 6.4. Income and education within the petty bourgeoisie. Note: Educational credentials are defined as follows: 0 = no education; 1 = some elementary; 2 = elementary; 3 = some high school; 4 = high school; 5 = high school + nonacademic; 6 = some college; 7 = college; 8 = graduate training. (*Source: Data from Panel Study of Income Dynamics. Figure courtesy of the UW Cartographic Laboratory.*)

bourgeoisie. No obvious explanations emerged. Of course, the more educated petty bourgeois tended to be in occupations characterized by higher levels of income, but as equation (2) indicates in Table 6.7, controlling for occupational status did not eliminate the relatively high returns to education within the petty bourgeoisie. Similarly, controlling for industrial sector (by entering a series of industry dummy variables into the regression) did not significantly reduce the returns to education (see Table 6.13).

The inability to "explain away" the high returns to education among the petty bourgeoisie implies that the original conceptualization is probably inadequate. Several possibilities might be worth pursuing in future research. First, there may be some problems in the responses to the question: "Do you work for yourself or for someone else?" Salesmen working on a commission may say that they work for themselves; people who do various kinds of contract work may say that they work for someone else, even though they are in fact self-employed. It is impossible to know the extent to which various kinds of semiautonomous employees (who would be expected to have high returns to education) might in fact be mixed in with the petty bourgeois category as it is currently defined. Secondly, there may be strata within the petty bourgeoisie, like within the small employer category, who work in protected markets of various sorts and thus receive a kind of monopoly rent element in their income. Finally, a much more thorough investigation of the concrete relationship between petty bourgeois producers and capital is necessary to fully understand the income determination process within this class. I have naively treated the class as involving a uniform process of self-earned income and as being uniformly subordinated to monopoly capital through exchange relations (which prevent their income from rising much above that of the working class). While these intuitions may be more or less adequate for the average petty bourgeois producer, they appear to be inadequate for more educated petty bourgeois. In any event, much more detailed study of the petty bourgeoisie is necessary before these processes can be properly sorted out and a better understanding of the relationship of income to education within this class position developed.

SMALL EMPLOYERS

Hypothesis 7.1. *The expected incomes of small employers should be higher than those of either workers or managers, even when controlling for education, etc.*

Table 6.8 presents the results for the analysis of income gaps between employers and managers and workers. These results clearly indicate that employers get considerably more income than either workers or managers, even controlling for all of the variables in equation (3). Between small employers and managers, in fact, these controls reduce

TABLE 6.8
Income Gaps and Returns to Education for Small Employers, Compared to Managers and Workers

| | Difference in Mean Incomes | Income Gaps | | | | Returns to Education | | |
| | | Average Gap[a] | | Standardized Gap[b] | | Difference in Education Coefficient | | |
Class Comparisons		Eq 1	Eq 3	Eq 1	Eq 3	Eq 1	Eq 2	Eq 3
Employers *vs.* managers	$7,621	$8,207	$7,070	$7,971	$7,071	$1,761	$670	$734
t-value		5.9***	5.3***	5.7***	5.4***	2.4**	ns	ns
Managers as % of employers	70%	69%	72%	69%	72%	54%	69%	66%
% of difference in means elim. by controls		-8%	7%	-4%	7%			
Employers *vs.* workers	$14,735	$12,530	$6,958	$13,935	$9,642	$2,992	$1,496	$1,482
t-value		9.0***	4.7***	10.3***	7.6***	4.3***	1.8*	1.8*
Workers as % of employers	43%	48%	66%	46%	62%	22%	30%	31%
% of difference in means elim. by controls		15%	53%	5%	35%	50%	50%	

Source: Data from Panel Study of Income Dynamics.
Independent variables: Eq 1 = education only
Eq 2 = education, seniority, age, background, and occupational status
Eq 3 = Eq 2 + annual hours worked

Significance levels on a one-tailed test:
*** .001
** .01
* .05
ns t < 1

[a] Average gap is assessed at the average of the means of the independent variables of the groups being compared.
[b] Standardized gap is assessed at the mean values of the independent variables for employers.

the overall gap in income by less than 10%. Virtually all of the difference in incomes between these two class positions must be considered a direct effect of the class positions per se. In the comparison between employers and workers, on the other hand, between a third and a half of the difference in income can be attributed to the characteristics of the individuals occupying those class positions.[9] When the income gap is assessed at the employers' mean values on the independent variables, the various controls in equation (3) reduce the gap between workers and employers by about 35%; when the gap is assessed at the average level of the independent variables, it is reduced by about 50% in equation (3). In either case, the direct effect of class position remains large and is highly statistically significant.

Hypothesis 7.2. *Small employers will have especially high returns to education.*

The education coefficients for employers are presented in Table 6.3. The comparisons with workers and managers appear in Table 6.8. Employers receive significantly greater returns to education than workers in each equation. The difference is especially dramatic in the simple regressions of income on education, where the returns among employers are five times greater than among workers.

The difference between small employers and managers is less marked. Employers receive significantly greater returns in the simple regressions of income on education, but not in the expanded equations. The reasons for this will be clearer when we examine hypothesis 7.3.

Hypothesis 7.3. *If the industrial sector and occupational status of small employers are held constant, the returns to education will be considerably reduced.*

In chapter 4, it was argued that education would be especially important for small employers' incomes because it created access to specialized, relatively noncompetitive markets. If this logic is correct, then we would expect the returns to education to be substantially reduced when we controlled for industrial sector and occupational status.

Two strategies can be adopted in order to control for industrial sector. First of all, a series of dummy variables for industrial sector could be entered into the regression equation. This in effect eliminates

[9]As in the earlier analysis of the income gap between managers and workers, this is not to suggest that between a third and a half of the gap can be explained by individual-level processes as such, but simply that part of the gap is determined through the characteristics of the individuals selected into class locations.

all of the variance in income that is due to the differences between industries. The slope on the education coefficient then reflects how much difference education makes for income within industrial categories. A second strategy would be to construct some sort of industry metric roughly analogous to occupational status as a metric of occupational position. The simplest such metric would be to scale industry according to the mean income of employers in that industry. In the regression equation where only industry and income appear, this is equivalent to the first procedure of using dummy variables. In regression equations where other variables besides industry appear, this industry metric has a different logic, since the internal structure of the scale cannot change as other variables are added. (In the case of the industry dummy variables, the coefficients of each dummy can change as other controls are added; in the case of a single industry scale, only the coefficient of the entire scale can change.) If we interpret this single industry scale as a very rough measure of the noncompetitiveness, arising from restricted access, of the markets in which some small em-

TABLE 6.9
Industrial Categories and Income Values Used in Industry Scale

Industry	Employers' Mean Income	N
1. Medical, health	$78,935	12
2. Education	76,000	1
3. Wholesale trade	44,116	8
4. Manufacturing, durable	32,632	13
5. Professional services	29,715	28
6. Finance, Insurance and Real Estate	29,549	12
7. Government	28,800	2
8. Mining	25,739	0[a]
9. Manufacturing, nondurables	23,255	4
10. Construction	21,913	56
11. Retail trade	21,525	43
12. Printing	19,741	3
13. Transportation	19,470	8
14. Repair services	16,874	15
15. Agriculture	16,510	34
16. Personal services, amusement	15,565	8
17. Communications	15,100	1
18. Business services	14,380	3
19. Utilities	10,766	2

Source: Data from Panel Study of Income Dynamics.
[a]Mean income for all employers assigned.

ployers operate, then the education slope in equations containing the industry scale can be interpreted as the returns to education net of the market situation of the small employer. We will control for industry using both approaches.

Industrial sector was measured using 19 industrial categories. There was at least one employer in all but one of these, and three or more in 14. So that this scale could be used for the other class categories, the mean income for all employers was assigned to the one industrial category where no employers were present in the sample (mining). The list of industrial sectors with mean employer incomes is presented in Table 6.9. There are a number of categories in this scale where the values are undoubtedly unrealistic (such as the $76,000 income for employers in the educational sector), but it is the best approximation from the present data.

TABLE 6.10
Education Coefficients Among Employers and Other Classes

Class	Education Coefficients in				
	Eq 1	Eq 4[a]	Eq 5[a]	Eq 4[b]	Eq 5[b]
All employers (N=254)	$3,843	$1,354	$847	$1,881	$1,429
(se)	(699)	(636)	(668)	(778)	(771)
R^2	.11	.38	.39	.38	.41
Very small employers					
(1–9 employees; N=190)	4,042	799	261	1,154	801
(se)	(834)	(702)	(709)	(798)	(784)
R^2	.12	.49	.50	.51	.54
Managers (N=479)	2,082	2,192	1,197	2,215	1,246
(se)	(222)	(241)	(271)	(252)	(271)
R^2	.16	.16	.24	.22	.31
Workers (N=1,715)	851	903	240	999	320
(se)	(77)	(83)	(99)	(87)	(97)
R^2	.07	.08	.15	.17	.25
Petty bourgeoisie (N=120)	1,781	1,534	1,057	1,402	1,123
(se)	(437)	(464)	(484)	(553)	(557)
R^2	.12	.14	.20	.28	.32

Source: Data from Panel Study of Income Dynamics.
(se) = Standard error
Independent variables: Eq 1 = education only
                        Eq 4 = education and industry
                        Eq 5 = education, industry, and occupational status
[a]Using industry scale.
[b]Using industry dummy variable.

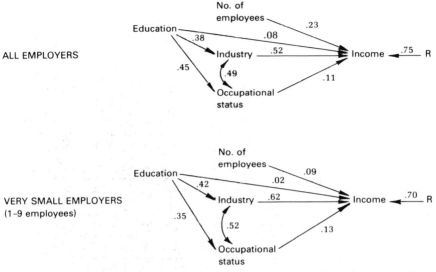

Figure 6.5. Path diagrams for relationship of education, industrial sector, and occupational status to annual income among employers. (*Source: Data from Panel Study of Income Dynamics.*)

We will use this industry scale and the industry dummy variables (construction being the left-out category) in two regression equations:

$$\text{Income} = a_1 + b_1 \text{ Education} + b_2 \text{ Industry (or } \sum_{i=3}^{20} b_i \text{ Industry}_i) \quad (4)$$

$$\text{Income} = a_1 + b_1 \text{ Education} + b_2 \text{ Industry (or } \sum_{i=3}^{20} b_i \text{ Industry}_i) \quad (5)$$
$$+ b_3 \text{ Occupational Status.}$$

The slopes on the education variable will then be compared to the coefficient in equation (1) (i.e., the simple regression of income on education) in order to assess the effects of controlling for industry and status.

These equations will be estimated separately for employers who employ fewer than ten workers as well as for all employers. Since the argument behind hypothesis 7.3 was based on an analysis of the class position of small employers, the results should be especially strong for these smallest of small employers. For comparative purposes, we will also estimate these two equations for workers, managers, and petty bourgeois. The results are presented in Table 6.10.

Whether we use the industry scale or the 18 industry dummy variables, controlling for industry in equation (4) drastically reduces the returns to education among employers. Among very small employers, the industry scale reduces the returns to education from over $4000 in the simple regression of income on education to $800 in equation (4). This is less than the returns to education for workers in this same equation. When occupational status is added to this equation, the returns to education among very small employers dwindle to only $261, compared to $240 for workers and nearly $1200 for managers. A similar pattern, although slightly less marked, occurs when the industry dummy variables are used. In both cases, controlling for industrial sector has essentially no effect on the returns to education for workers and managers, but reduces the small employers' returns to education by 50–80%.

Another way of illustrating the interrelationships between industrial sector, status, and education among small employers is through a minipath diagram. Let us assume that among employers, education is a cause of the individual employer's occupational status and industrial sector. Income in turn is caused by all three of these variables, as well as by other factors such as number of employees. Industrial sector and occupational status are correlated, but without a specific causal direction being assumed. The path diagrams for all employers and for very small employers which correspond to these assumptions are presented in Figure 6.5. This very simple model explains about half of the variance in income among both all small employers and very small employers. The direct education path in both path diagrams is quite small, while the industry path is very large.

Hypothesis 7.4. *The returns to education for small employers with less than a college degree should be relatively small, while the returns for getting college and graduate degrees should be very large.*

As in hypothesis 7.3, this hypothesis flows directly from the logic behind hypothesis 7.2. Education matters for employers not because of any incremental increase in human capital due to the content of training as such, but because credentials make it possible for employers to operate in sheltered, noncompetitive markets. This would imply that employers with less than a college degree would have very small returns to education, and Table 6.11 and Figure 6.6 indicate that this is indeed the case. Two thirds of all employers have less than a college degree. Among these employers, the returns to education are only $600; among all employers the returns are over $3800. The mean income of employers with less than a college education is just under

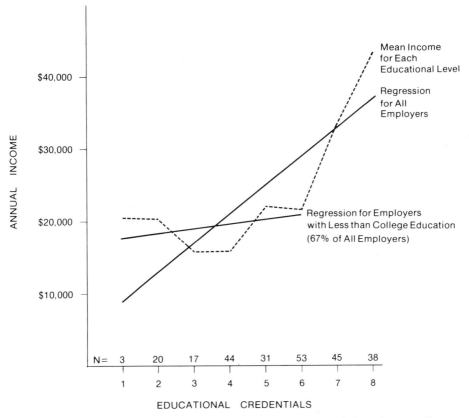

Figure 6.6. Income and education for small employers with less than a college education. Note: Educational credentials are defined as follows: 0 = no education; 1 = some elementary; 2 = elementary; 3 = some high school; 4 = high school; 5 = high school + nonacademic; 6 = some college; 7 = college; 8 = graduate training. (*Source: Data from Panel Study of Income Dynamics. Figure courtesy of the UW Cartographic Laboratory.*)

$20,000. The mean income for small employers who are college graduates is over $33,000, and for small employers with graduate training, it is $43,000. As Table 6.11 indicates, these basic results hold up even when the various controls in equations (2) and (3) are added.

CONCLUSION

The most general conclusion from the diverse results discussed in this chapter is that class consistently and significantly mediates the

TABLE 6.11
Returns to Education for Employers with Less Than College Education

Employer Category	Returns to Education in		
	Eq 1	Eq 2	Eq 3
All employers ($N=254$)	$3,843	$2,136	$2,137
(se)	(699)	(817)	(820)
R^2	.11	.26	.26
Employers with less than college education ($N=170$)	602	768	771
(se)	(743)	(870)	(875)
R^2	.004	.16	.16

Source: Data from Panel Study of Income Dynamics.
(se) = Standard error
Independent variables: Eq 1 = education only
                                    Eq 2 = education, age, seniority, background, and occupational status
                                    Eq 3 = Eq 2 + annual hours worked

income determination process. People occupying different class positions but with the same level of education and occupational status, the same age and seniority on the job, the same general social background, and working the same number of hours per year, will still differ substantially in their expected incomes. And people in different class positions can expect to receive different amounts of additional income per increment in educational credentials, even if they do not differ on a variety of other characteristics.

With the exception of the analysis of the petty bourgeoisie (hypothesis 6.0) and the prediction of high income returns to graduate training for managers, the results in this chapter generally support the specific hypotheses about class and income developed in chapter 4:

2.0 Managers ·and supervisors do have higher incomes than workers, even controlling for a range of individual characteristics.

4.1 Managers have much greater returns to education than workers.

4.2 The difference in returns to education between managers and workers is especially great for college education levels (although not for graduate training, as expected).

7.1 The incomes of small employers are higher than those of workers or managers, controlling for various factors.

7.2 Small employers have especially high returns to education.

7.3 The high returns to education among small employers are substantially reduced when industry and occupation are controlled for.

7.4 The returns to education for small employers are very small below the college level.

These various interaction patterns reflect the centrality of class relations in the structure of inequality of capitalist societies. As has been stressed throughout, this does not mean that class and class alone explains everything. But it does mean that class plays a fundamental role in mediating the income determination process. Class relations as such may not be the direct "cause" of all income inequalities, but they structure the ways in which other causes operate. The interaction patterns we have explored in this chapter can be viewed as one consequence of such structural causation.

7

The Managerial Hierarchy

One of the basic conclusions of the previous chapter was that managers receive greater income returns to education than workers. This pattern was interpreted as flowing from the imperatives of social control within the capitalist production process. More specifically, it was argued that because of the position of managers within the social relations of production, their labor would tend to be controlled more heavily through inducements than through repressive sanctions. This would tend to create a steep income gradient associated with position within the managerial hierarchy. Furthermore, for the variety of reasons spelled out in chapter 4, we would also expect to find a steep education gradient. The combination of these two gradients, it was argued, generates the steep returns to education for managers observed in chapter 6.

In this chapter, I shall attempt to support this general interpretation by looking more closely at specific layers of the managerial hierarchy. In particular, I shall show that indeed there is a steep income gradient, and that this gradient does not disappear when we control for education, age, and seniority. Once this has been established we will examine the returns to education among managers controlling for position. If the general interpretation of the high overall returns among managers is correct, then we would expect considerably lower returns when hierarchical position was held constant.

THE DATA

Very few data sets contain any information about position within authority structures, beyond the simple criterion that the individual

TABLE 7.1
Characteristics of the Sample in the Hierarchy in Organizations Study

| Plant Type | Size of Plants | | | | | |
| | Italy | | Austria | | U.S.A. | |
	Small	Large	Small	Large	Small	Large
Plastics	83	343	43	242	48	215
Foundry	62	1,081	34	1,133	80	1,354
Canning	88	650	107	405	47	499
Metal works	111	529	30	668	66	362
Furniture	76	540	41	299	58	590
Average	84	629	51	549	60	604

| Hierarchy Level | No. of Respondents at Each Hierarchy Level | | | | | | | |
| | Italy | | Austria | | U.S.A. | | Total | |
	Small Plant	Large Plant	Small Plant	Large Plant	Small Plant	Large Plant	Small Plant	Large Plant
1 (top)	5	5	5	4	5	5	15	14
2	9	8	17	21	21	33	47	62
3	52	19	44	42	32	44	128	105
4	80	44	71	37	61	44	212	125
5	22	46	5	33	54	31	81	120
6	6	31	—	9	—	13	6	53
7	—	13	—	12	—	5	—	30
Total N	174	176	142	158	173	175	489	509

Source: Tannenbaum et al., 1974.

occupies a supervisory position. One data set which does contain more complex information is the Hierarchy in Organizations study conducted by Arnold Tannenbaum and associates (see Tannenbaum et al., 1974). This study constitutes a unique source of data about managers, since it contains precise information on the number of levels in the authority structure above and below each subject in the survey.

The Hierarchy study was conducted in five countries: the United States, Italy, Austria, Yugoslavia, and Israel. For our purposes, we will confine the analysis to the three Western bourgeois democracies in the sample (Israel is not being included since only kibbutzim were studied in the survey). In each country, five large and five small plants were chosen, and within each plant individuals were sampled in such a way as to guarantee subjects at every level of the hierarchy (i.e., top levels were systematically oversampled). The number of persons employed in the various plants in the study and the number of subjects at each level of the hierarchy are given in Table 7.1. (See Tannenbaum et al., 1974, pp. 14–19, for a more detailed discussion of the sample.)

In order to keep the analysis of the managerial hierarchy as parallel as possible to the discussion in chapter 6, we will restrict the sample to males only. In any event, only about 12% of the managers in the sample were women.

DEFINING POSITIONS WITHIN THE HIERARCHY

The theoretical considerations elaborated in chapter 2 would suggest that the appropriate way to define "position" within a managerial structure is in terms of the actual kinds of decisions the position involves. The distinction between a "top" manager and a "middle" manager is fundamentally defined by kinds of participation in control over the investment and accumulation process and control over the physical means of production, not by formal position within an organizational chart. At best, positions defined by levels above and below the manager can be considered an indicator of actual managerial position. Nevertheless, since the only data available are levels above and below the individual, this will have to suffice as the basis for defining positions within the managerial hierarchy.

Even in terms of formal organizational charts, the concept of "level" is not entirely unambiguous. Different positions are located in authority chains of different lengths, and thus the number of levels above a position cannot be considered a simple complement of the number of levels below. (In the fifty plants in the Hierarchy study, the

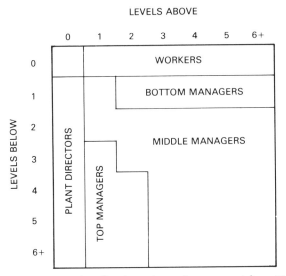

Figure 7.1. Classification schema for managerial positions.

correlation between the number of levels above and below the respondents was −.82.)

What we need is a procedure for combining levels above and levels below into a single measure of position within the authority hierarchy. Figure 7.1 indicates the criteria we will use, and Figure 7.2 shows the distribution of respondents into different layers of the managerial hierarchy. *Plant directors* constitute positions which have no levels above them, and *workers* are defined as positions with no levels below them. *Top managers* must have no more than two levels above them in the hierarchy, and must have at least two more levels below them than they have above them. *Bottom managers* are defined as positions with only one level below them, except when they also have only one level above them. Such cases constitute middle managers in very small hierarchies. All other positions in the authority structure are also defined as middle managers.[1]

Several problems with this schema deserve mentioning. To begin with, there is no information in the Hierarchy study about whether the plant is a firm in its own right, or merely a branch of a larger business. Depending upon the precise relationship between branch plants and

[1]Individuals in more than one authority chain will be placed in the longest chain. Thus, a top manager who is near the top of two chains, one with five levels below and two above, and one with two levels below and two above would be placed in the top manager category, not the middle manager category.

parent companies this could have a serious effect on the meaning of "levels" within the managerial structure.

There is also no way of distinguishing a plant director who is the actual owner of the business, and a plant director who is really just a top manager. When the plant is equivalent to a firm, the distinction is not terribly important since the plant director is, in effect, the topmost executive of the business and thus part of the bourgeoisie by the definitions in chapter 2. When the plant is a branch, however, the plant director may in fact be a mere manager, even though a very high-level manager. In any event, since in chapter 6 we adopted a fairly narrow definition of owner (i.e., self-employed employer), we will assume that plant directors are in fact part of the managerial hierarchy rather than the capitalist class proper.

Finally, it must be acknowledged that there is a certain arbitrariness in the schema presented in Figure 7.1. This is especially obvious in the distinction between middle managers and top managers. A narrower definition of middle manager could have been adopted in which anyone who had more levels below him/her than above would be classified as a top manager. Ideally, if the sample was much larger one

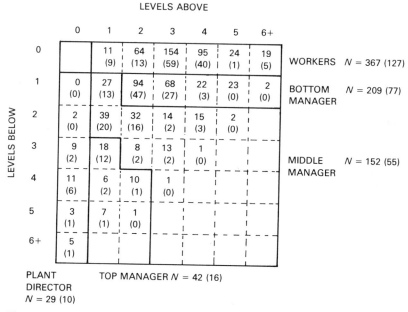

Figure 7.2. Distribution of male respondents into positions within the managerial hierarchy. Note: Figures for the United States alone are in parentheses. (*Source: Tannenbaum et al., 1974.*)

would indeed want to make finer distinctions. But given the present data, it seemed more reasonable to restrict the top manager category to positions which were fairly clearly at the top, rather than extend it downward to the upper reaches of middle management.[2]

The schema in Figure 7.1 will be used in two ways. First, we will construct a hierarchy scale in which 0 = bottom manager, 1 = middle manager, 2 = top manager, and 3 = plant director. Second, we will use the schema to break the entire sample of managers into several level-specific subsamples. Because of the small number of plant directors and top managers, especially in the American sample taken separately, we will merge these two levels into a single "upper manager" category.

OTHER VARIABLES

Education

Education was rather poorly measured in the Hierarchy study. Probably because of the small number of college-trained managers in countries other than the United States, the education variable was truncated at the post-high school level in the following manner:

1 = less than 4 years of schooling
2 = 4–6 years
3 = 6–8 years
4 = 8–10 years
5 = 10–12 years
6 = more than 12 years

The result is that for the American sample, at the top two levels of the managerial hierarchy (top managers and plant directors), all of the respondents fall into the top two categories, and over three quarters in category 6 alone.

It was because of this lack of variance within the American sample that the decision was made to pool the American respondents with the two Western European samples. Since none of the hypotheses in chapter 4 was formulated specifically in terms of U.S. capitalism, there was

[2]A manager with one level above and two levels below is especially ambiguous in this regard. Such a position is, after all, simultaneously near the middle and the top of the hierarchy. I adopted a purely empiricist strategy for deciding where to place such positions. I ran all of the regressions separately for pure top managers, for pure middle managers, and for this ambiguous category of upper-middle manager. Overall, the regression equations for this ambiguous position looked more like simple middle managers than top managers.

no reason to restrict the analysis to an American sample. Indeed, the interpretation of the high returns to education among managers was grounded in an analysis of the logic of capitalist relations of production in advanced capitalist societies, and although undoubtedly there will be important variations across countries, the basic patterns should hold in Austria and Italy as well as the United States. Thus, if the predictions are supported in the sample which includes managers in Italian and Austrian factories as well as American, this will lend added weight to the interpretations elaborated in earlier chapters. All of the results in this chapter will therefore be analyzed both for the American data taken separately and for the pooled sample of the United States, Italy, and Austria. Because of the obvious problems involved in merging data from several countries, we will rely mainly on the American sample.

Income (Earnings)

Pooling the samples in order to deal with the problem with the education variable immediately created new problems for the income variable. The subjects in each country had their income reported as monthly earnings in their own national currencies. Obviously, it would be nonsensical simply to merge dollars, liras, and schillings into a single income variable. So the question becomes, what conversion rate is most appropriate? The most natural conversion procedure would be simply to use the official exchange rates between currencies at the time of the study. This procedure has one major disadvantage. Since at every level of the managerial hierarchy the earnings in Italy and Austria are so much less than in the United States, a simple conversion to dollars would mean that most of the variance in income in the pooled sample would be due to between-country variance rather than hierarchical-level variance. In effect, we would be maximizing the variance within given hierarchical levels.

An alternative strategy is to adjust the incomes across countries by setting their means equal to some common figure. This will not, of course, affect the statistical significance of slopes within each country, but it will tend to make the separate regression equations in different countries overlap to a greater extent. This should improve the reliability of estimating the slopes for the pooled sample. In effect, we are adopting a currency conversion based on the fiction that the three samples of managers really exist within the same economy and thus have the same average incomes.

We will make this conversion by setting the Italian and Austrian incomes equal to the American mean. This adjustment is accomplished by multiplying all Italian incomes by 0.51 and all Austrian incomes by 1.56. The result is that all three countries end up with mean incomes equal to about $845 per month.

There is one final problem with the income variable. The variable on the computer tape was truncated at 997 units of income per month. For the United States, this represents $9970 per month, or over $100,000 a year, which is a reasonably high level at which to truncate an income variable. In the Italian case, however, this represents 997,000 liras a month, which comes to an annual income of just under $20,000 (using the exchange rate in the late 1960s). This is clearly a fairly low level at which to truncate income. The result is that nine of the plant directors in the Italian sample have the truncated level of income, whereas none in the American or Austrian samples is at this level. This will, needless to say, somewhat reduce our confidence in the results for upper managers in the pooled sample.

Plant Seniority and Age

Plant seniority was measured by an eight-point scale from less than six months to over 20 years:

1 = less than 6 months
2 = 6 months to 1 year
3 = 1 year to 2 years
4 = 2–3 years
5 = 3–5 years
6 = 5–10 years
7 = 10–20 years
8 = 20 or more years

As in the analysis in chapter 6, age and seniority will be included in the regression equations, not so much because of their intrinsic interest but in order to rule out the possibility that what appears to be direct effects of position within the managerial hierarchy might in fact be consequences of the age and seniority composition of different levels of the hierarchy.

EQUATIONS

Two basic equations will be estimated in the analysis of returns to education at different levels of the hierarchy:

$$\text{Income} = a + b_1 \text{ Education} \tag{1}$$

$$\text{Income} = a + b_1\text{Education} + b_2\text{Age} + b_3\text{Seniority} \tag{6}$$

No information on family background was available in the Hierarchy study, and because of the nature of the sample, occupational status would not have been an especially meaningful control even if it was available.

In order to simplify the analysis somewhat, income gaps will not be computed at the joint means for every pair of positions in the managerial hierarchy. Instead, we will simply compute an adjusted constant term for the equations evaluated at the upper managers' means for the independent variables. The income gap in this case represents the difference in expected incomes between groups if they both had the upper managers' means on the independent variables.

The computer program used to analyze the Hierarchy data (PICKLE) does not generate standard errors for the constant terms in regression equations. We will, therefore, not perform formal statistical tests on the income gaps between different levels of the managerial hierarchy.

RESULTS

Hypothesis 3.0. *Within the managerial category, incomes will increase sharply as you move up the authority hierarchy, even after controlling for education, seniority, and age.*

Table 7.2 presents the expected incomes for each level in the managerial hierarchy adjusted for education, age, and plant seniority, for both the U.S. sample alone and the pooled U.S.A., Italy, Austria sample.

These results clearly indicate that there is a steep income gradient tied to position within the managerial hierarchy. In the American sample, the expected income of upper managers is nearly twice that of bottom managers, and one and a half times that of middle managers, even when these expected incomes are adjusted to the upper managers' levels of education, age, and job tenure. Furthermore, if we use the four-level hierarchy scale to predict income among managers (workers are excluded from the regression), we find that the expected increase in monthly income for each step in the hierarchy is $293 net of education, age, and tenure in the American sample, and $560 in the pooled sample both of these returns to hierarchical position are significant at the .001 level).

TABLE 7.2
Incomes Within the Managerial Hierarchy, Adjusted for Education, Age, and Tenure

| Hierarchy Level | U.S.A. Only | | | | U.S.A., Italy, Austria | | | |
| | Mean Monthly Income | Income Adjusted for[a] | | N | Mean Monthly Income | Income Adjusted for[a] | | N |
		Eq 1	Eq 6			Eq 1	Eq 6	
Managers								
Bottom	$865	$903	$887	82	$772	$856	$864	205
Middle	1,071	1,102	1,115	55	1,093	1,157	1,210	142
Upper	1,586	1,586	1,586	26	2,287	2,287	2,287	60
All	1,049	1,119	1,119	163	1,107	1,256	1,370	406
Workers	576	659	659	124	538	644	689	351

Source: Tannenbaum et al., 1974.
Independent variables: Eq 1 = education only
                         Eq 6 = education, age, and seniority
[a]Income figures are adjusted to the means on the independent variables for the upper-manager category in the sample:

	Education	Age	Tenure
U.S.A. only	5.77	43.65	5.92
U.S.A., Italy, Austria	5.57	46.61	6.50

There is also, as predicted, a significant education gradient associated with the managerial hierarchy. Figure 7.3 indicates that, on the average, each level of the hierarchy corresponds to a .3 unit increase in education in the American sample, and just over a .5 unit increase (about one year) in the pooled sample (again, both gradients are significant at the .001 level). It would be expected that if a better education variable were available for the American data, the gradient among American managers would be considerably greater.

Another way of looking at these two gradients is through a simple path diagram relating education and hierarchical level to income. Let us assume that among managers income is caused by education, hierarchical position, plant seniority, and age, and that position within the hierarchy is caused by education, age, and seniority. Figure 7.4 presents the path model corresponding to these assumptions for the U.S. sample, and for the pooled sample. The most striking feature of these diagrams is the large path from hierarchical position to income: .60 in the pooled sample and .43 in the U.S. sample. Although it would certainly be expected that the path from education to income would be greater if education were better measured, these results do indicate the importance of hierarchical position for the income of managers.

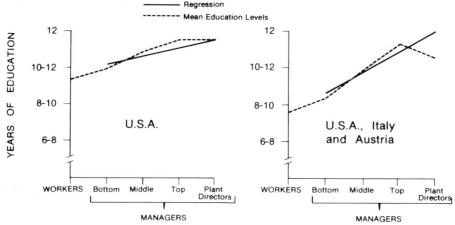

Figure 7.3. The educational gradient in the managerial hierarchy. Note: Workers are excluded from the regression equation. Thus the coefficient of the hierarchical position variable indicates the expected increase in education among managers for each step up the hierarchy. (*Source: Data from Tannenbaum et al., 1974. Figure courtesy of the UW Cartographic Laboratory.*)

It is possible that the strong path between hierarchical position and income in Figure 7.4 is the result of the inclusion of some actual capitalists in the plant director category of the hierarchy variable. When the path model is estimated excluding plant directors (Figure 7.5), the path from the hierarchical position to income does decrease to .24 for the U.S. sample and .39 for the pooled sample, but it is still larger than the path from education (.12 in the U.S. sample and .24 in the pooled sample). Since the hierarchy variable in this path diagram is only a three-point scale, and since we have clearly removed from the regressions many positions which properly belong at the top of the managerial hierarchy, these results still support the basic model.

Hypothesis 4.3. *The income returns to education among managers/supervisors will be much closer to the returns among workers when position within the managerial hierarchy is held constant.*

We have shown above that there is in fact a steep education and income gradient associated with the managerial hierarchy. If the high returns to education for managers which we observed in chapter 6 are a consequence of the link between these two gradients, then we would expect that if the level of the managerial hierarchy were controlled for, the returns to education would be much lower.

We will explore this hypothesis through two strategies. First we will simply look at the returns to education for all managers compared

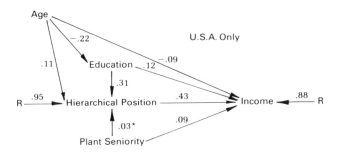

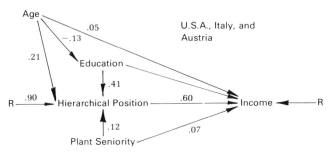

Figure 7.4. Path diagram for relationship of education and hierarchical position to income (managers only). *Coefficient less than standard error. (*Source: Data from Tannenbaum et al., 1974.*)

to workers and then see how these returns change when we control for position in the hierarchy by including the hierarchy scale in the regression. Secondly, we will estimate equation (1) and equation (6) within each broad level of the hierarchy and compare the returns to education within each level to the returns for managers as a whole.

Table 7.3 indicates the returns to education for all managers, for workers, and for managers controlling for hierarchical position. In the American sample, when position is not held constant, managers get $155 for every unit increase in education compared to $79 for workers in the simple regression of income on education, and $165 compared to $90, when age and seniority are added to the equation. Although these differences are not statistically significant using formal t-tests, the size of the difference is of the same order of magnitude as those found in chapter 6, where the returns to education for workers were about 50% of the returns for managers/supervisors, depending upon which variables other than education were in the equation. In the Hierarchy data, the returns to workers are 50% of the returns for managers in equation (1), and 55% in equation (6).

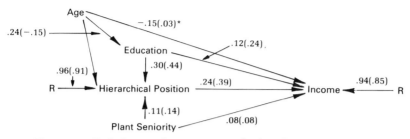

Figure 7.5 Path diagram for managers with plant directors excluded. Note: Results are for U.S.A. and (in parentheses) for U.S.A., Italy, Austria. *Coefficient less than standard error. (*Source: Data from Tannenbaum et al., 1974.*)

When we look at the pooled sample, the differences between workers and managers are considerably more significant statistically, largely because the standard errors of the coefficients are so much smaller (owing mainly to the larger sample size). The returns to education for managers are approximately three times as great as for workers in both regression equations, and the differences are significant at the .001 level.

When hierarchical position is added to these regression equations, the returns to education among managers are drastically reduced. In the American sample, the returns drop to under $80 in both regression equations, and in the pooled sample to under $70. In all of the regressions which control for hierarchical position, there is essentially no difference in returns to education among workers and managers. Hypothesis 4.3 is thus strongly supported by the additive model.

Table 7.4 and Figure 7.6 indicate what happens to the returns to education when position is controlled for in an interactive model, that is, when the regression equations are run separately within each hierarchical level. For the bottom managers and middle managers, the results are exactly as predicted in both the U.S. sample and the pooled sample. Bottom managers (like supervisors in chapter 6) have returns to education that are the same as or lower than workers'. While middle managers do have somewhat greater returns than workers, their returns to education are still less than for managers as a whole.

The results for upper managers in the American sample are not as predicted in hypothesis 4.3. Far from getting lower returns to education than managers as a whole, upper managers receive over three times the returns to education of all managers. These results, however, are quite problematic, both because of the small number of upper managers in the U.S. sample, and because of the high concentration of upper managers in the topmost education category.

TABLE 7.3
Returns to Education Among Managers and Workers, Controlling for Hierarchical Position

Independent Variables	U.S.A.			U.S.A., Italy, Austria		
	Returns to Education	Returns to Hierarchical Position	N	Returns to Education	Returns to Hierarchical Position	N
Workers						
Education only	$79		124	$63		351
(se)	(16)			(7)		
Education, tenure, age	90			68		
(se)	(17)			(7)		
Managers						
Education only	155		163	174		407
(se)	(50)			(29)		
t-value[a]	1.5			3.7***		
Education, tenure, age	165			216		
(se)	(53)			(30)		
t-value[a]	1.4			4.8***		
Education and hierarchy	77	289		40	587	
(se)	(46)	(51)		(25)	(38)	
t-value[a]	ns			ns		
Education, tenure, age, and hierarchy	78	293		64	560	
(se)	(51)	(51)		(27)	(39)	
t-value[a]	ns			ns		

Source: Data from Tannenbaum et al., 1974.
Note: The full regression equations can be found in Wright, 1976b, pp. 370–71.
(se) = Standard error
Significance levels on a one-tailed test:
*** .001
ns t < 1
[a]t-value of difference in education slopes between managers and workers.

TABLE 7.4
Returns to Education Within Specific Levels of the Managerial Hierarchy

Hierarchy Level	U.S.A. Only			U.S.A., Italy, Austria		
	Eq 1	Eq 6	N	Eq 1	Eq 6	N
Managers						
Bottom	$54	$44	82	$63	$70	205
(se)	(73)	(78)		(22)	(24)	
Middle	100	113	55	111	140	142
(se)	(43)	(46)		(26)	(27)	
Upper	543	566	26	−393[a]	−298	60
(se)	(264)	(270)		(231)	(219)	
All	155	165	163	174	216	407
(se)	(50)	(53)		(29)	(30)	
Workers	79	90	124	63	68	351
(se)	(16)	(17)		(7)	(7)	

Source: Tannenbaum et al., 1974.
(se) = Standard error
Independent variables: Eq 1 = education only
Eq 6 = education, age, and seniority
[a]The negative coefficient for upper managers in the pooled sample arises from the truncation of incomes among Italian managers.

It was hoped that the pooled sample would give us a better estimate of the returns to education among upper managers, both by increasing the dispersion of the education variable and by increasing the sample size. However, the problem of the truncation of the income variable in the case of Italian upper managers (see above) makes the results extremely questionable. The negative returns to education among upper managers in the pooled sample are entirely a consequence of a few relatively poorly educated Italian managers whose income is at the maximum level.

It is tempting to dismiss the negative results in the American sample. On the other hand, the hypothesis itself may be in need of modification. Education, after all, does not only affect the level of the managerial hierarchy a particular manager is likely to occupy; it also affects which managerial hierarchy the manager is in to begin with. It could well be, for example, that the high returns to education among upper managers in the American sample reflect the role of education in giving managers access to monopoly-sector firms or to advanced-technology firms. Our attempt at stratifying the managerial category—the contradictory class location between the bourgeoisie and the

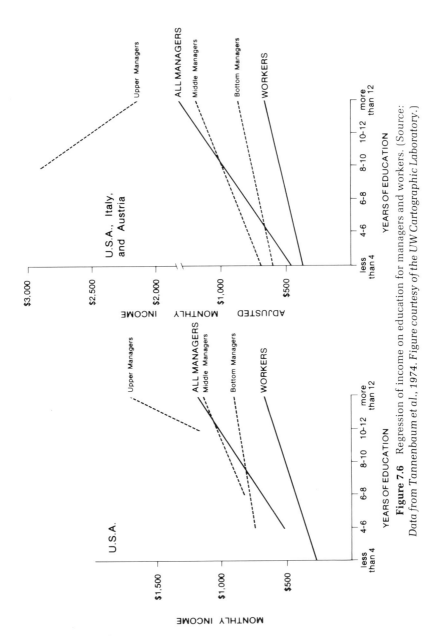

Figure 7.6 Regression of income on education for managers and workers. (*Source: Data from Tannenbaum et al., 1974. Figure courtesy of the UW Cartographic Laboratory.*)

proletariat—along a simple hierarchical continuum is obviously a considerable oversimplification, and these results may indicate the need for a more differentiated analysis. Instead of simply viewing managers in terms of the contradictory class position between the working class and the bourgeoisie, globally conceived, it might be useful to specify which segment of the bourgeoisie (for instance, monopoly capital, or competitive capital) defines the class position of a specific group of managers. Thus, in addition to defining top, middle, and bottom managers, one could define monopoly-sector and competitive-sector managers.

In spite of the limitations of the data in the Hierarchy study, the results in this chapter do lend substantial support to our general interpretation of the class situation of managers. There does appear to be both a steep education gradient and a steep income gradient tied to positions in the managerial hierarchy, and the link between these two gradients is clearly involved in the steep returns to education within the managerial category as a whole. While these results do not directly prove the argument about the relationship of income and education to the social control of managerial labor, they are consistent with the general perspective on class relations elaborated in earlier chapters.

8

Race and Class

The normative premise of most sociological research on inequality is that the ideal society is one in which all individual outcomes are simply consequences of individual choices.* Given this premise, barriers to "equal opportunity" within the existing society become the central focus of empirical investigations.

This concern with equality of opportunity has been reflected in two major lines of research: first, the enormous literature on social mobility, especially intergenerational mobility; and second, research focusing on discrimination of various sorts, especially racial and sexual discrimination. Both of these types of research attempt to sort out in one way or another how much of the variance in individual outcomes

*An earlier version of some sections of this chapter appeared in Wright (1978d).

can be accounted for by factors outside the individual's control.[1] The more sophisticated studies then attempt to discover the concrete social mechanisms through which these barriers operate: job promotion patterns within organizations (e.g., Doeringer and Piore, 1972); the functioning of labor markets (e.g., Edwards et al., 1975; Bluestone, 1974; Stolzenberg, 1975b); the occupational recruitment process (e.g., Blau and Duncan, 1967); selective processes within educational institutions (e.g., Coleman et al., 1966; Jencks et al., 1973; Bowles and Gintis, 1976); and socialization patterns within families (e.g., Sewell and Hauser, 1975; Duncan et al., 1972).[2]

None of these studies of individual mobility or discrimination has empirically examined the relationship of these diverse social processes to class, defined as positions within social relations of production, although some do interpret their findings in terms of those relations (Bowles and Gintis, 1976; Edwards et al., 1975). If our analysis in earlier chapters is correct and class does play a central mediating role in structuring income determination, then it would be expected that many of the results of these various studies would be affected if class were systematically taken into account. While the data available in the present research do not allow for an examination of the relationship of class to social mobility, we can examine the interactions between class position and some of the processes involved in racial and sexual discrimination. In this chapter we will look in some detail at the interactions between race and class, and in the next chapter, at the interactions between sex and class.

THE DISTRIBUTION OF RACE AND CLASS

Table 8.1 presents the class distribution within racial categories. Because of the problem of nonrandomness in the Michigan PSID data, this table is based on the 1969 SWC data and a similar study conducted

[1]Duncan et al. (1972) state this perspective quite explicitly: "all known complex societies are characterized by one or more forms of institutionalized social inequality. However, there are variations between societies and, presumably, within a society over time in the degree of opportunity, that is, the extent to which persons are recruited or assigned to roles bearing unequal rewards on the basis of circumstances of birth or rearing in a particular family, locality, cultural or ethnic group, or social milieu. To the extent that achievement depends upon such circumstances over which the individual has little or no control, we say that a society is stratified [p. 2]."

[2]Few studies, needless to say, actually ever measure child-rearing and other socialization processes as such. But generally speaking, variables such as parental education or status are taken as loose proxies for the "values" and "motivations" instilled in

TABLE 8.1
Distribution of Class Positions Within Racial Categories

Class Position	White Males		Black Males	
Small employers	11.5%		4.9%	
Managers and supervisors	40.2		32.5	
Managers[a]		20.9		15.3
Supervisors		19.3		17.2
Workers	43.5		61.4	
Petty bourgeoisie	4.9		1.2	
N	2,100		168	

Source: Percentages represent average of 1969 Survey of Working Conditions and 1973 Quality of Employment Survey distributions.

[a]The proportional division between managers and supervisors is estimated from the distribution in the Panel Study of Income Dynamics; the total proportion of managers and supervisors within racial categories comes from the 1969 SWC and 1973 QES data.

in 1973, the Quality of Employment Survey (QES). Since there were only about 85 black males in each of these surveys, an average of the distributions for the separate surveys was used to construct this table.[3]

These data clearly indicate that black men are considerably more concentrated within the working class than are white men: over 61% of all black men are workers, compared to only 43.5% of white men. If mere supervisors are added to this figure, then 79% of black men are workers or supervisors compared to only 63% of white men. While these data say nothing about how blacks and whites get sorted into different positions within class relations, they do show that the end result of the sorting process is a quite different class distribution within race categories.[4]

---

the individual through the family. This is especially explicit in the "Wisconsin Model" in which family background is portrayed as shaping individual aptitudes and aspirations (see Sewell and Hauser, 1975; Alexander et al., 1975).

[3]The distributions for each of these surveys taken separately can be found in Wright (1976b, pp. 353, 365).

[4]It is important to remember that only employed and self-employed participants in the labor force are included in the data used in this study. Since blacks have higher unemployment rates than whites, this clearly influences the class distribution within race categories. Since the percentages in Table 8.1 are an average of data gathered in 1969 (a year of relatively low unemployment) and 1973 (a year of higher unemployment), this understatement of the size of the working class is probably not terribly large. Nevertheless, if we assume that most unemployed people are in fact workers, then the proportion of black males who are in the working class is probably closer to 70–75% than 61%, and the proportion of white males closer to 50% than 44%.

RETURNS TO EDUCATION FOR RACES WITHIN
CLASS CATEGORIES

Hypothesis 9.1.   *The returns to education of black and white males will be much closer within class positions than across all class categories.*

Sociologists and economists have consistently found that white males get considerably higher returns to education than black males. Weiss (1970) found that within specific age groups, black males received significantly lower returns to education than white males, whether education was measured as years of schooling or achievement level. Siegel (1965) found that, net of occupation and region of the country, the difference in expected incomes of black and white males increased monotonically with education: at less than elementary education, blacks earned, in 1960, $700 less than whites; at the high school level this increased to $1400; and at the college level, to $3800. Duncan (1969) has shown that even controlling for family background, number of siblings, and occupational status, blacks still receive lower returns to education than whites.[5]

[5]The only study I know of which claims to present different findings from these results is the research of Stolzenberg (1973, 1975a). Stolzenberg (1975a) estimated a rather complicated income determination equation within 67 detailed occupational categories for both black and white males. He then compared the partial derivatives of income with respect to education for these equations and found that in nearly half of the occupational categories the partial derivative was larger for blacks than for whites. Thus, he concludes that, "Earlier findings suggesting high within-occupation racial differences in wage returns to schooling (e.g., Siegel 1965; Thurow 1967) were probably artifacts of the gross occupational classifications used. These past findings appear to have been produced by the tendency of black men to be concentrated in the lowest-paying *detailed* occupation categories within the major occupational group in which they are employed [p. 314]." The problem with this conclusion is that Stolzenberg uses a natural logarithmic transformation of income whereas Siegel uses raw dollars. This means that Stolzenberg is estimating (approximately) *rates* of returns to education rather than *absolute* returns. It may well be that the absolute returns to education within the detailed occupational categories might still not have differed significantly between blacks and whites, but Stolzenberg's results do not demonstrate this. I ran Stolzenberg's equation using the PSID data, calculated the partial derivatives for all blacks and whites and discovered that the *rates* of return for *all* blacks were significantly greater than for all whites (Stolzenberg does not report the results for all blacks and whites). Stolzenberg's results thus indicate that these higher rates of return to education for black men as a whole can also be found within about half of the detailed occupations held by black men. His results do not indicate that the absolute returns for black and white men are the same within detailed occupations.

TABLE 8.2
Regression Equations Within Race-Class Categories with Annual Taxable Income as Dependent Variable

	Unadjusted Constant	Education	Occupational Status	Age	Seniority	Father's Education	Father's Occupational Status	Parents' Economic Condition	Annual Hours Worked	R^2
Whites (N=2,145)										
Eq 1: B	$5,583	$1,818.6								.087
(se)		(127.1)								
Beta		.30								
Eq 3: B	−10,519	1,147.2	$120.4	$146	$159	$−232	$6	$329	$3.1	.268
(se)		(158.0)	(11.2)	(21)	(29)	(149)	(13)	(158)	(.31)	
Beta		.19	.26	.17	.13	−.04	.01	.04	.18	
Blacks (N=912)										
Eq 1: B	6,069	860.2								.080
(se)		(96.8)								
Beta		.28								
Eq 3: B	−5,273	641.1	78.4	100	30	410	−26	−135	2.9	.376
(se)		(119)	(8.9)	(14)	(22)	(125)	(10)	(103)	(.24)	
Beta		.21	.30	.24	.04	.11	−.08	−.04	.33	
White workers (N=984)										
Eq 1: B	7,657	802.6								.055
(se)		(105.9)								
Beta		.235								
Eq 3: B	−6,639	656.4	64.8	128	136	238	−39	340	3.2	.359
(se)		(125.7)	(9.3)	(15)	(25)	(118)	(10)	(120)	(.26)	
Beta		.19	.24	.28	.17	.07	−.12	.08	.32	

(continued)

TABLE 8.2 (*continued*)

	Unadjusted Constant	Education	Occupational Status	Age	Seniority	Father's Education	Father's Occupational Status	Parents' Economic Condition	Annual Hours Worked	R^2
Black workers (N=657)										
Eq 1: B	6,246	610.4								.052
(se)		(101.7)								
Beta		.23								
Eq 3: B	−4,048	649.0	76.9	83	64	122	−62	113	2.8	.359
(se)		(136.7)	(11.0)	(15)	(24)	(139)	(12)	(103)	(.26)	
Beta		.24	.29	.25	.11	.03	−.19	.04	.36	
White supervisors (N=397)										
Eq 1: B	8,827	734.3								.045
(se)		(170.3)								
Beta		.21								
Eq 3: B	−2,613	751.2	56.4	73	174	−189	30	−570	2.7	.343
(se)		(192.3)	(13.5)	(24)	(37)	(200)	(16)	(197)	(.44)	
Beta		.22	.22	.16	.23	−.05	.10	−.14	.26	
Black supervisors (N=123)										
Eq 1: B	6,334	641.5								.083
(se)		(194.1)								
Beta		.29								
Eq 3: B	−2,782	966.9	10.0	84	95	279	16	−405	1.7	.230
(se)		(309.6)	(21.5)	(49)	(57)	(275)	(25)	(267)	(.63)	
Beta		.43	.05	.21	.17	.12	.07	−.14	.24	

	Constant									R^2
White managers (N=405)										
Eq 1: B	6,429	2,107.4								.153
(se)		(247.0)								
Beta		.39								
Eq 3: B	−7,794	1,480.7	118.1	189	109	−400	28.9	−285	1.5	.350
(se)		(281.0)	(21.5)	(39)	(52)	(231.5)	(19.5)	(264.5)	(.68)	
Beta		.27	.27	.24	.10	−.08	.07	−.05	.09	
Black managers (N=72)										
Eq 1: B	7,628	1,168.5								.134
(se)		(354.2)								
Beta		.37								
Eq 3: B	−1,005	−510.5	57.4	135.4	−235.8	550.1	104.4	−167	2.96	.517
(se)		(475)	(27.6)	(75.6)	(89.9)	(436.5)	(35.5)	(591.3)	(.89)	
Beta		−.16	.27	.26	−.36	.16	.40	−.03	.41	

Source: First published in Wright, 1978d. Copyright © by the University of Chicago Press. Reproduced by permission.
B = Raw coefficient
(se) = Standard error
Beta = Standardized coefficient
Independent variables: Eq 1 = education only
Eq 3 = education, age, seniority, background, occupational status, and annual hours worked

Hypothesis 9.1 predicts that the difference in returns to education between whites and blacks will be substantially reduced when we control for class position. In chapter 6 we have already shown that workers get much lower returns than do either managers or small employers. And in Table 8.1 above, we observed that blacks are more concentrated within the working class than are whites. This would suggest that a substantial part of the overall difference in returns to education among blacks and whites might be a consequence of the class distribution within the two race categories.

Table 8.2 presents the returns to education for black and white males in various class positions, using PSID data. Table 8.3 presents the formal statistical tests of the significance of the differences in Table

TABLE 8.3
Returns to Education for Black and White Males Within Class Positions

	Racial Differences in Returns to Education[a] in	
Class Position	Eq 1	Eq 3
All black and white males		
Slope difference	$959	$ 533
t-value	6.0***	2.7**
Workers		
Slope difference	192	7
t-value	1.3	ns
Managers and supervisors		
Slope difference	464	593
t-value	1.9*	1.9*
Managers		
Slope difference	938	1,991
t-value	2.2*	3.6***
Supervisors		
Slope difference	93	−216
t-value	ns	ns

Source: Data from Panel Study of Income Dynamics.
Independent variables: Eq 1 = education only
                      Eq 3 = education, age, seniority, background, occupational status, and annual hours worked
Significance levels on a one-tailed test:
*** .001
** .01
* .05
ns $t < 1$
[a]Total annual income is the dependent variable.

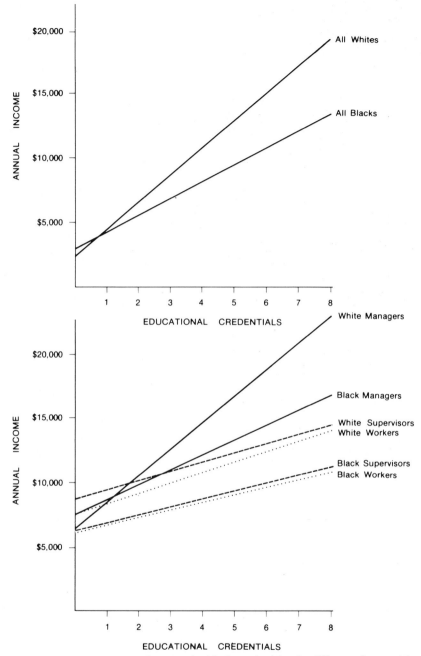

Figure 8.1. Returns to education for blacks and whites in different class positions. Note: Educational credentials are defined as follows: 0 = no education; 1 = some elementary; 2 = elementary; 3 = some high school; 4 = high school; 5 = high school + nonacademic; 6 = some college; 7 = college; 8 = graduate training. (*Source: Data from Panel Study of Income Dynamics. Figure courtesy of the UW Cartographic Laboratory.*)

8.2.[6] The results are given for equations (1) and (3) specified in chapter 6. Figure 8.1 graphically presents the returns to education for the simple regression of income on education. (The income gaps between races will be discussed below.)

As in the findings of the studies reported above, the Panel Study also indicates that black males as a whole get lower returns to education than white males. In the simple regression of income on education, black males get an average of $860 for each educational credential compared to $1819 for white males (significant at the .001 level). For equation (3) (i.e., controlling for family background, age, seniority, occupational status, and annual hours worked) the returns for whites are $1147 and for blacks $614. These results are quite consistent with the usual findings about racial differences in returns to education.

When we look separately at the working class, the racial differences in returns to education are considerably reduced. In neither of the equations do black and white workers differ significantly in returns to education. In the simple regression of annual income on education, the returns to education for all blacks were only 47% of the returns for all whites; within the working class, the returns for blacks in this same equation are 76% of the returns for whites. When all of the controls in equation (3) are added, the returns for black workers become virtually identical with the returns for white workers (they differ by only 1%), whereas the returns for all blacks remain about 50% the returns for all whites. This strongly suggests that class structure mediates the effects of race on the income determination process.

The comparison of blacks and whites within the manager/ supervisor category poses a somewhat different problem from the comparison within the working class. Managers/supervisors do not constitute a class position in the same sense as workers or capitalists. As explained in chapter 2, the manager/supervisor category represents a contradictory location within class relations, and as such managers/ supervisors are spread out in a series of positions between the working class and the bourgeoisie. It was precisely for this reason that in chapter 7 we examined the returns to education within specific levels of the managerial hierarchy.

[6]Comparable results using the SWC data can be found in Wright and Perrone (1977), and in Wright (1976b, pp. 354, 366).

Most of these results have also been reported in Wright (1978d). The formal statistical tests used in Table 8.2 are more conservative than those used in Wright (1978d), where the conventional dummy variable interaction model was used to calculate the t-tests, necessarily yielding a larger t-value for any given difference in coefficients between two populations. See appendix C for a discussion of this issue.

In chapters 6 and 7 we found that the returns to education for all managers/supervisors were considerably greater than for managers/supervisors at the bottom levels of the managerial hierarchy (mere supervisors). Thus, if blacks tend to be concentrated at the bottom of the managerial hierarchy while whites are spread out throughout the hierarchy, then a comparison of black to white managers/supervisors would in effect become a comparison of bottom positions to the overall hierarchy. In such a situation, it would be expected that black managers/supervisors would have lower returns to education than their white counterparts.

Furthermore, it would also be expected that this difference in returns to education between blacks and whites within the managerial category should be especially large when occupational status is controlled for in the regression. Among managers/supervisors, education influences income primarily through two routes. First, as we have stressed throughout this study, education serves as a selective filter which influences how high in the managerial hierarchy an individual is likely to rise. Secondly, education influences the market situation of the labor power of managers and supervisors (as it does for any other wage laborer). This latter route is tapped in the regression equations by occupational status. In the simple regression of income on education, equation (1), the education coefficient embodies both of these mechanisms for translating education into income. When we control for occupational status in equation (3), however, we are in effect holding constant the market channel through which education influences income, and thus the coefficient of the education variable can be viewed as a rough indicator of the strength of the direct hierarchical route alone. Again, if black managers/supervisors are confined to the bottom rungs of the managerial ladder, the education coefficient in the equations which include occupational status should be especially small.

Finally, if this line of reasoning about the differences between black and white managers/supervisors is correct, then we would also expect that within the supervisor category examined separately, the returns to education for blacks and whites should be roughly equal. The supervisor level is the one position within the manager category as a whole which we can isolate in the PSID data. When we examine supervisors by themselves, the problem of the different dispersions of blacks and whites throughout the managerial hierarchy ceases to matter, and thus the returns to education for blacks and whites should be reasonably similar. Among managers proper, on the other hand, we would expect greater returns for whites for the reasons spelled out above for the entire manager/supervisor category.

As is evident in Table 8.3, among all managers/supervisors and among managers taken separately, the returns for blacks are indeed smaller than for whites, especially in the equations containing occupational status. In the comparison between black and white supervisors, on the other hand, the returns to education do not differ significantly in any of the equations. In the simple regression of income on education, the annual income returns for black male supervisors are only 13% less than for whites. When the additional controls are added in equations (2) and (3), the returns for black supervisors actually become slightly greater than for white supervisors (although the differences are not statistically significant).

Although it was anticipated that black managers would have lower returns to education than white managers, it was not expected that the partial returns in equation (3) would be essentially zero. The expectation was merely that the hierarchical promotion mechanisms among blacks would be blunted, but not that such mechanisms would be so weak as to generate no returns to education when occupational status was held constant.

One possible clue to these results might be found if we examine the occupational distribution among white and black managers (Table 8.4).

As would be expected, black managers are considerably more concentrated among unskilled and semiskilled manual occupations than are white managers (38.5% compared to 13%). What is somewhat sur-

TABLE 8.4
Occupational Distribution Among Managers for Black and White Males

Distribution	White Managers	Black Managers
Professional, technical, and kindred	27.6%	22.5%
Professionals	22.3	9.3
Technicians	3.0	0.0
Teachers	2.3	13.2
Managers and administrators	35.2	25.0
Sales	4.7	.8
Clerks	1.9	1.7
Craftsmen and kindred	20.5	11.5
Operatives, laborers, and misc.	13.1	38.5
Total	100.0[a]	100.0

Source: First published in Wright, 1978d. Copyright © by the University of Chicago Press. Reproduced by permission.
[a]Percentages do not add to 100% because of rounding.

prising is the much higher proportion of black than white managers who are teachers (13% compared to 2%). To express this in a different way: nearly 60% of the black managers in professional or technical occupations are teachers, whereas this is the case for fewer than 10% of white professional-technical managers. Remember, these are real managers, people who state that they have some say in the pay and promotions of their subordinates, rather than simple supervisors. This implies that these teacher-managers either occupy administrative positions within their educational institutions or direct research projects in which they have say in the pay and promotions of research assistants (all but one of the black teacher-managers were college or university teachers).

If the regressions in Table 8.2 are rerun excluding teachers from the managerial category, the results are much more as expected (Table 8.5). The returns for black and white supervisors are essentially the same as in Table 8.2. Black male managers still generally have lower

TABLE 8.5
Returns to Education[a] for Blacks and Whites Within the Manager/Supervisor Category, Excluding Teachers

Class Category	Eq 1	Eq 3
Supervisors		
White males	$732	$761
(se)	(182)	(208)
Black males	506	934
(se)	(217)	(350)
Difference	226	−173
t-value[b]	ns	ns
Managers		
White males	2,154	1,570
(se)	(256)	(293)
Black males	1,582	880
(se)	(476)	(473)
Difference	572	690
t-value	ns	1.2

Source: First published in Wright, 1978d. Copyright © by the University of Chicago Press. Reproduced by permission.

[a]Total annual income is the dependent variable.

[b]The t-values in this table differ slightly from those published in Wright, 1978d, where a somewhat different technique was used to calculate the standard error (se) of the difference in coefficients.

returns than white male managers (although the differences are not statistically significant), but the returns are not nearly so small as in the regressions including teachers.

I do not have a particularly coherent explanation why the presence of so many teachers among black managers should have such a drastic effect on the education coefficient for black managers in equation (3). Obviously, it has something to do with the interrelationship of education, status, and income among this specific subgroup of managers, but to say this merely describes the problem rather than providing a theoretical explanation.

In any event, the important point for hypothesis 9.1 is that nearly 80% of all black males are in the working class or the supervisory category, and in these class positions blacks and whites receive essentially the same returns to education. Much of the aggregate difference in returns to education among blacks and whites can therefore be reasonably considered a consequence of the class distribution of races.

CLASS DIVISIONS WITHIN RACIAL GROUPS

Hypothesis 9.2. *The differences between black male workers and managers/supervisors will be less than between white male workers and managers.*

We have already implicitly explored this hypothesis in our discussion of black managers above. Table 8.6 presents the income gaps for class comparisons among blacks and whites, and Table 8.7 presents the comparisons of returns to education for different class positions within race categories.

The results only partially confirm this hypothesis. It is clear from Table 8.7 that black workers and managers differ much less than white workers and managers in returns to education, but the income gaps between black workers and managers in Table 8.6 are essentially as large as between white workers and managers. Among whites, the mean income of workers is 62% of the mean income of managers; among blacks the figure is 64%. When the various controls in equation (3) are added, the expected income of white workers becomes 86% of white managers, while for black workers the figure is 83% of black managers. Overall, therefore, it still pays off for a black to become a manager, even if the returns to education are no greater for black managers than for black workers.

One other result in Tables 8.6 and 8.7 is worth noting. All of the class differences among whites taken separately are essentially as strong as among all respondents in the survey. This means that the general conclusions arrived at in chapter 6 cannot be considered artifacts of the race distribution within classes.

CONCLUSION: THE INTERPLAY OF RACISM AND CLASS DOMINATION

It would be a mistake to interpret the results for hypothesis 9 above as indicating that all racial discrimination is really disguised class oppression. Although it is true that the differential returns to education for blacks and whites largely disappear when we control for class, this does not imply that race is an insignificant dimension of inequality in American life. The empirical problem is to sort out the complex interplay of racism and class relations, not to obliterate the former in the latter.

The most obvious way in which racism intersects class relations is in the social processes which distribute people into class positions in the first place. In recent years sociologists have devoted considerable attention to the effects of racial discrimination on *occupational* mobility chances of blacks compared to whites. To my knowledge, there have been no studies which systematically explore the role of racism in the distribution of individuals into different positions within the social relations of production. Of particular importance in such a study would be the social processes which select people into the managerial/supervisory category and the mechanisms which regulate the promotion patterns up managerial hierarchies. Racism would affect the distribution of races within authority structures in two general ways: first, as in the sorting process for occupations, various forms of racial discrimination affect access to the mechanisms which sort people into the managerial hierarchy (educational credentials, connections, and the like). Since, as was argued earlier, people with lower credentials will tend not to be promoted above people with higher credentials, the result will be a higher concentration of blacks at lower levels of the managerial structure and a higher concentration of blacks in the working class. Second, and perhaps more importantly, because of the necessity to legitimate the social relations of domination embodied in managerial hierarchies, racism will directly tend to prevent the promotion of blacks above whites. Of course, this does not mean that blacks will never be promoted above whites. Particularly when strong political struggles against racism occur, corporations and bureaucracies may see the imperatives of legitimation as requiring the

TABLE 8.6
Average Income Gaps Between Class Positions Within Racial Categories

| | Average Income Gap[a] | | | | | |
| | White Males | | | Black Males | | |
Class Comparisons	Difference in Mean Income	Eq 1	Eq 3	Difference in Mean Income	Eq 1	Eq 3
Workers vs. managers/supervisors	$4,192	$3,273	$1,163	$2,312	$1,839	$470
Workers income as % managers/sup.	73%	78%	92%	79%	82%	95%
% difference in means elim. by controls		22%	72%		20%	80%
t-value of gap		9.8***	3.9***		4.5***	1.2
Workers vs. managers	6,962	5,434	2,083	4,781	3,750	2,175
Workers income as % managers	62%	68%	86%	64%	70%	83%
% difference in means elim. by controls		22%	70%		22%	55%
t-value of gap		11.8***	4.5***		5.2***	2.9**

Workers vs. managers (excl. teachers)	4,695	3,893	1,026
Workers income as % managers	64%	69%	90%
% difference in means elim. by controls		17%	78%
t-value of gap		4.8***	1.7*
Employers vs. workers	14,232	12,397	7,217
Workers income as % employers	44%	52%	66%
% difference in means elim. by controls		13%	49%
t-value of gap		8.7***	4.7***
Employers vs. managers	7,270	7,935	6,790
Managers income as % employers	72%	69%	73%
% difference in means elim. by controls		-9%	7%
t-value of gap		5.5***	4.9***

Source: Data for whites, blacks, from Panel Study of Income Dynamics.

Independent variables: Eq 1 = education only

Eq 3 = education, age, seniority, background, occupational status, and annual hours worked

Significance levels on a one-tailed test:

*** .001
** .01
* .05

[a]Average income gaps represent the difference in expected incomes for two groups evaluated at a level of the independent variables in the regression equal to the average of their respective means on the independent variables.

TABLE 8.7
Returns to Education for Different Class Positions Within Racial Categories

	Differences in Returns to Education[a]					
	White Males			Black Males		
Class Comparisons	Eq 1	Eq 2	Eq 3	Eq 1	Eq 2	Eq 3
Workers vs. managers/supervisors						
Slope difference	$840	$534	$504	$568	$-213	$-82
t-value	4.5***	2.4**	2.3**	2.7**	ns	ns
Workers vs. managers						
Slope difference	1,305	894	825	559	-931	-1,159
t-value	4.9***	2.9**	2.7**	1.5	1.8*	2.3**
Workers vs. managers (excl. teachers)						
Slope difference	1,352	975	914	972	-215	231
t-value	4.9***	3.0**	2.9**	2.0*	ns	ns
Employers vs. workers						
Slope difference	2,866	1,438	1,424			
t-value	3.9***	1.7*	1.6*			
Employers vs. managers						
Slope difference	1,561	544	599			
t-value	2.0*	ns	ns			

Source: Panel Study of Income Dynamics.
Independent variables: Eq 1 = education only
 Eq 2 = education, age, seniority, background, occupational status
 Eq 3 = Eq 2 + annual hours worked

Significance levels on a one-tailed test:
 *** .001
 ** .01
 * .05
 ns = t < 1
[a]Total annual income is dependent variable.

acceptance of some blacks into token positions of authority within managerial structures. But in the absence of such struggles, it would be expected that the logic of hierarchical domination within capitalist production relations and the necessity of legitimating that domination would generate racist patterns of recruitment into and promotion up managerial hierarchies.

The above argument about recruitment and promotion presupposes the existence of racism. Given the presence of intense racist beliefs, it is easy to explain why blacks will not be promoted above whites within hierarchies; but this begs the question about the existence of racism in the first place. It is beyond the scope of this chapter to attempt a systematic account of the origins of racism and the social processes which reproduce it in contemporary American society. What I will do is very briefly indicate the essential thrust of a class analysis of the role of racism in American capitalism, and show how the present study relates to that analysis.

A common mistake made by Marxists in analyzing racism is to assume that all forms of racial discrimination are unequivocally functional for the capitalist class. This is similar to analyses of the capitalist state which argue that every policy by the state is orchestrated by the capitalist class to serve its interests. Such "instrumentalist" views of the state and ideology minimize the intensely contradictory character of capitalist society.[7] Capitalism *simultaneously* undermines and reproduces racism, and it is essential to disentangle these two tendencies if one is genuinely to understand the relationship between class and race in contemporary capitalism.

One of the basic dynamics of capitalist development stressed by Marx as well as many non-Marxist theorists is the tendency for capitalism to transform all labor into the commodity labor power, and to obliterate all qualitative distinctions between different categories of labor. From the point of view of capital accumulation, the more labor power becomes a pure commodity regulated by pure market principles unfettered by personal ties and ascriptive barriers, the more rapidly can capitalism expand. In terms of the logic of accumulation developed by Marx in *Capital*, therefore, there will be systemic tendencies within capitalism to reduce racial discrimination in the labor market, and to treat black labor power as identical with any other labor power.

There may seem, in this respect, to be little fundamental difference between Marxist theory and neoclassical economics. Both recognize

---

[7]For a critique of instrumentalist views in Marxist theory, see Gold et al. (1975) and Esping-Anderson et al. (1976).

that the inherent economic logic of capitalism is progressively to reduce economic divisions between races. But this is only one side of the
story. Capitalism is not, as neoclassical economists see it, solely an
economic system of capital accumulation. It is also a class system in
which workers struggle against capitalists, over both their condition as
sellers of labor power and, potentially, the existence of the capitalist
system itself. Whereas the essential dynamics of accumulation may
lead to an undermining of racial differences in the labor market, the
dynamics of class struggle tend to intensify racism. To the extent that
the working class is divided along racial and ethnic lines, the collective
power of the working class is reduced, and the capacity of workers to
win demands against capital will decrease. The result will be an increase in the rate of exploitation of *both* white and black workers,
although the effects may well be more intense for blacks and other
minorities than for whites.[8]

The analysis of racism as a divide and conquer strategy has perhaps been the central theme in Marxist treatments of the subject. There
are passages in Marx, for instance, that give the impression that racism
can be reduced to a conspiracy among capitalists.[9] Of course, at times
capitalists do collectively adopt strategies which are intended to increase racial and ethnic divisions, as in cases where black and immi-
grant labor is used in strike-breaking. More commonly, however,
capitalists simply exploit existing racial divisions as a way of obtaining
cheaper labor for certain kinds of jobs. Such individual strategies will
tend to reproduce racism even in the absence of secretive collusion
among capitalists.

We thus have a basic contradiction: capitalism tends to undermine all qualitative distinctions between categories of labor, but the
capitalist class needs those qualitative divisions for its own reproduc-

[8]Marxists have often claimed that racism hurt white as well as black workers, but
systematic empirical investigations of this proposition in the United States have been
lacking until recently. Reich (1971, 1973) has shown that in the 50 largest Standard
Metropolitan Statistical Areas, the greater the racial inequality in median family earnings, the greater the inequality of earnings among whites and the weaker the level of
unionization. Szymanski (1976) made similar findings for all 50 U.S. states. Both these
sets of results indicate that racism, in dividing the working class, leads to an increase in
exploitation among all workers, white as well as black.

[9]Marx, writing in 1870 on the Irish question, commented, "In all the big industrial
centers in England there is profound antagonism between the Irish proletariat and the
English proletariat. . . . This . . . is artificially nourished and supported by the bourgeoisie.
It knows that this scission is the true secret of maintaining its power [Marx and Engels,
1972 ed., p. 162]."

tion as the dominant class.[10] Both forces operate. The actual balance between the two depends upon a variety of historical factors. For example, under conditions of extreme shortages of labor, obstacles to labor mobility in the labor market are likely to be rather costly to individual capitalists, and thus it would be expected that racial barriers would be more rapidly eroded by imperatives of accumulation. On the other hand, when there are relatively abundant supplies of labor and when individual differences between laborers make little difference to productivity (because of routinization, automation, etc.), then those strictly economic imperatives are likely to be weaker. The extent to which racial or ethnic divisions within the working class are being deepened or eroded in a given capitalist society cannot, however, be derived directly from the abstract theory of capitalist economic development. It is only when such abstract theory is linked to specific political and ideological developments that it becomes possible to assess the real dynamics of racism in a given society.

The present study does not deal with this historical process; nevertheless, its data can be related both to the perpetuation of important racial divisions within the working class and to the common situation of all workers as workers, regardless of race.

The data presented in Figure 8.1 and Table 8.2 clearly indicate that although black and white workers receive similar returns to education, black male income is less than white male income at every level of education. Table 8.8 presents the average income gaps between blacks and whites within classes. It will be recalled that these gaps indicate what the expected difference in income between a black and a white male within a given class would be if they both had the same value on the independent variables in the equation. In this analysis, the gap is calculated at levels of the independent variables halfway between the means for each group in the comparison being made. As can be seen from this table, the income gaps between races are large and statistically significant for both regression equations within each class category. Furthermore, the addition of the various controls in the multiple regression equations reduces the total difference in mean incomes between races within classes by no more than 50%, indicating that a substantial part of the difference in mean incomes between races

[10]Instead of seeing the relationship of capitalism to racism as an intrinsically contradictory process with political and ideological dimensions, neoclassical economics typically treats racism as a problem of arbitrary individual "tastes" for discrimination on the part of employers and workers (see Becker, 1971, pp. 13–18).

TABLE 8.8
Average Income Gaps Between Races Within Class Categories

	Difference in Mean Income	Average Income Gap[a]	
		Eq 1	Eq 3
All respondents	$5,308	$3,698	$1,868
Black income as % of white	64%	73%	85%
% of difference in means eliminated by controls		30%	65%
t-value		12.2***	6.8***
Workers	2,870	2,203	1,428
Black income as % of white	75%	80%	86%
% of difference in means eliminated by controls		23%	49%
t-value		8.5***	6.3***
Managers and supervisors	4,750	3,100	3,560
Black income as % of white	69%	79%	77%
% of gap eliminated		35%	25%
t-value		6.5***	6.0***
Supervisors	3,872	2,896	2,140
Black income as % of white	69%	76%	82%
% of gap eliminated		25%	45%
t-value		5.8***	4.3***
Managers	5,051	3,707	3,011
Black income as % of white	72%	79%	83%
% of gap eliminated		27%	40%
t-value		4.6***	4.1***

Source: Data from Panel Study of Income Dynamics.
Independent variables: Eq 1 = education only
                        Eq 3 = education, age, seniority, background, occupational
                        status, and annual hours worked
Significance levels on a one-tailed test:
    *** = .001

[a]Average income gaps represent the difference in expected income for two groups evaluated at a level of the independent variables in the regression equal to the average of their respective means on the independent variables.

within classes should probably be directly attributed to racial discrimination.

In terms of our analysis of the components of income within the working class, these results suggest that the wage of black workers typically falls below the value of their labor power. That is, blacks have a sizable income discrimination component in their income, and as a result will generally be exploited at a higher rate than white workers.[11]

Ultimately, the political thrust of the Marxist theory of racism hinges on the other side of the contradiction: in spite of the divisive character of racism and the material differences between black and white workers that racism generates, workers of all races share a fundamental class situation, and thus share fundamental class interests.[12] The central finding of this study—that black and white workers have very similar returns to education—reflects this common class situation. Table 8.2 also indicates that black and white workers have very similar income returns to occupational status (whereas whites taken as a whole have significantly greater returns than blacks taken as a whole); this again reflects the commonality of their class position.

Furthermore, it is easy to show that the income gaps between black and white workers, while significant, are much smaller than the gap

[11]In order so to interpret these results in terms of rates of exploitation it is necessary to assume that two workers who have the same values on all of the variables in equation (3) will have essentially similar complexities of labor (i.e., embodied labor in their own labor power) and intensities of labor (i.e., pace of work within the labor process). Equation (3) contains annual hours worked, and if we accept the above two assumptions, then two workers who have the same values on all the independent variables will produce the same amount of total value in a year. Any difference in their incomes would then reflect differences in the costs of reproduction of their labor power, and thus differences in rates of exploitation. Two factors could undermine this conclusion. First of all, the reproductive costs of labor power are not represented simply by wages, but by fringe benefits, state subsidies for education, and other services, etc. To the extent that such additional elements of the costs of reproducing labor power are themselves correlated with earnings, then if anything we are underestimating the differences in rates of exploitation by looking exclusively at direct income. Secondly, if black workers as a whole are *overqualified* for the jobs which they hold, wage differences could in part reflect social *waste* of potential surplus value rather than superexploitation of black labor in the technical sense of the concept. If a college graduate works on an assembly line, he or she produces no more surplus value and is no more exploited than a high school dropout in the same production process. The complexity of the college graduate's labor is being socially wasted in such a situation. In the strategy used to compare black and white exploitation above, however, this situation would appear as a greater rate of exploitation of the college graduate. There is no way in the present data to differentiate between underemployment and more intense exploitation. For a much fuller discussion of the relationship between econometric models of income determination and the Marxist concept of exploitation, see Wright (1976b, pp. 120–31).

[12]"Fundamental" class interests, it will be recalled from chapter 2, refer to interests defined across modes of production (i.e., interests in capitalism vs. socialism), whereas "immediate" interests refer to interests defined within a given mode of production. Black and white workers may well have conflicting immediate interests under certain circumstances (as do many other categories of labor within the working class), and still share fundamental class interests.

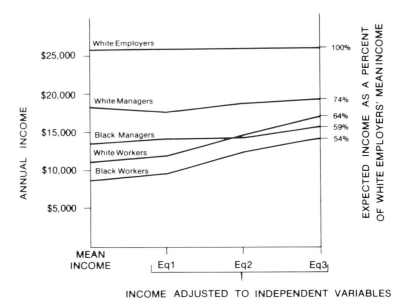

Figure 8.2. Income differences between races and classes. Note: Income is adjusted to white employers' means. Independent variables: Eq 1 = education only; Eq 2 = education, age, seniority, background, and occupational status; Eq 3 = Eq 2 + hours worked. (Source: Data from Panel Study of Income Dynamics. Figure courtesy of the UW Cartographic Laboratory.)

between either and small employers. Figure 8.2 indicates the expected incomes of each race and class category assessed at the level of the independent variables of white employers.[13] The unadjusted mean income of white workers is less than one half that of white employers; the mean income of black workers, on the other hand, is 75% of white workers' mean income. In absolute dollar amounts, the mean white workers' income is over $14,000 below the mean white employers' income, whereas the mean black workers' income is only $2900 below the mean white workers' income. When the various controls in equations (2) and (3) are added, the expected incomes of both black and white workers (evaluated at the white employers' means on the independent variables) increase considerably. Yet the difference between workers and employers is still considerably greater than the differences between workers of different races. These results indicate that compared with even small employers—let alone proper capitalists—the

[13]This procedure is basically similar to the familiar cross-substitution technique employed by Duncan (1969) and others. This was referred to as the "standardized" income gap in chapter 6.

common position of black and white workers within the social relations of production generates a basic unity of economic situation.

In general, the results in this chapter strongly support the central
thesis of this study: that class relations mediate the process of income
determination. Although the data suggest that there are crucial racial
effects on income in American society, and that these racial effects exist
within classes as well as between classes, our findings also demonstrate
that these racial effects are themselves structured by class relations.

9

Class and Sex

The analysis of the interplay of class relations and sexual divisions raises a number of conceptual problems which have been largely ignored throughout this study. Two of these are particularly important: the relationship between individuals and families as incumbents of positions ("empty places") within class relations; and the relationship of the domestic labor of housewives to capitalist relations of production. In order to define adequately the class position of women, both of these problems need resolution.

Many Marxists (as well as non-Marxists) have argued that the family rather than the individual is the appropriate constituent element of class (see Szymanski, 1972, 1973; Stodder, 1973). When this stance is adopted, the class position of the family is usually identified as that of the "head of household," which is generally assumed to be the man in a married couple. These conventions in effect define the class position of married women by the class position of their husbands.

Whether individuals or families are the appropriate elements of class is in part an historical question, not simply an a priori theoretical one. There are certain circumstances in which families rather than individuals fill the "empty places" within the social relations of production, and in such situations the family becomes the appropriate incumbent of class positions. Such is often the case, for example, for the traditional petty bourgeoisie, especially in agriculture. Within the capitalist mode of production itself, kinship groups (rather than nuclear families per se) may occupy the empty places of finance capital. But in general, especially in advanced capitalism, it is more appropriate to view individuals as occupying class positions.[1]

A related conceptual issue concerns the interpretation of domestic labor. Many women do not directly participate in capitalist production, and thus in order to define their class position at all it is necessary to understand the relationship of household production to capitalist production. Some Marxists have argued that household production should be viewed as a subsidiary mode of production within capitalist society. To be sure, like all subsidiary modes of production, domestic production is dominated by capitalism, but nevertheless it maintains a certain autonomy (see Harrison, 1974). Other Marxists have argued that domestic production represents a final, privatized stage within capitalist production itself in which commodities are transformed into consumable use-values (see Secombe, 1974; Benston, 1969). And yet other Marxists have stressed that the interpenetration between the role of women as wage laborers and their role as household producers is critical for understanding the nature of domestic labor itself (see Hartsock, 1975; Coulson et al., 1975). While at times these debates take on a rather scholastic character, the issues they raise are essential for understanding the class position of housewives.

[1]This does not imply that family units are irrelevant in a class analysis. While individuals may generally fill the empty places within social relations of production, families fill the empty places within social relations of reproduction.

In these terms, the working-class position within the social relations of reproduction is filled by families engaged in the reproduction of workers' labor power; the capitalist class position is filled by families engaged in the reproduction of capitalists. This suggests that the notion of "contradictory locations within class relations" can be extended to families: a family occupies a contradictory location within the social relations of reproduction when it reproduces the labor power of individuals in different class positions (i.e., when the members of the family occupy different positions within the social relations of production).

I have not reached a satisfactory solution to the problem of understanding household labor.[2] Given the empirical focus of this study on income inequality, however, it is possible to leave this issue in abeyance, since in any event we will limit the analysis to women in the labor force. Nevertheless, because the direct participation of women within capitalist relations of production is bound up with their role in the household, the absence of a theory of domestic labor unquestionably limits the analysis which follows.

In effect, therefore, I will treat the problem of sex and class in an exactly analogous way to the analysis of race and class in the previous chapter. Women will be treated as individuals inserted into the empty places within capitalist social relations of production rather than as members of family units within social relations of reproduction. We will thus investigate only one dimension of the complex interrelationship of class and sex: the ways in which class and sex interact once women actively enter the labor force.

RETURNS TO EDUCATION FOR SEXES WITHIN CLASS CATEGORIES

Hypothesis 10.1. *The returns to education of men and women will be much closer within class positions than across class categories.*

As in the research on racial differences in returns to education, one of the most consistent findings in studies of sex and income is that women tend to get lower income returns to education than men. Suter and Miller (1973) found that controlling for occupational status, full-time employment, and lifetime work experience, women received less than half the wage and salary returns to education of men (and less than half the income returns to occupational status as well). Even when

[2]One line of reasoning which I find attractive, but not without problems, is to define household labor primarily in terms of social relations of reproduction. As discussed in note 1 above, families rather than individuals are the appropriate units within social relations of reproduction. A housewife in a family which occupies the working-class position within social relations of reproduction (because it reproduces workers' labor power) would thus be in the working class because of her position within the family and the family's position within the relations of reproduction. The difficulty with this approach is understanding rigorously the distinction between "production" and "reproduction." Much of the actual activity of housewives involves the production of use-values, even if the function of this production is reproduction of labor power. Since most concrete social activity involves simultaneously productive and reproductive dimensions, it seems somewhat arbitrary to understand families narrowly in terms of the latter. This line of thought is explored in an extremely interesting way by Bertaux (1977).

career women (defined as women who have worked at least three quarters of the time since leaving school) were analyzed separately, the returns to education were much less than for men. Hudis (1974, p. 104) found that the returns to education for women were lower than for men for both hourly earnings and total annual earnings, controlling for race, weeks worked, hours worked, and occupational status. Iams (1973, p. 142), in an elaborate study of the effect of sex on hourly wages, found that the returns to education were lower for women within specific age cohorts for the simple regression of income on education, as well as for a complex regression equation controlling for tenure, occupational prestige, unionization, public employment, region of the country, and several other variables. He further found that the returns to education for women were significantly smaller than for men in 9 of the 14 industrial sectors, and absolutely smaller in all but one. Finally, Treiman and Terrell (1975) found that controlling for number of children under age 6, number of children 6 to 18, percentage of years worked, hours worked per year, and occupational prestige, the returns to education for wives were less than a quarter of the returns for husbands.

On the basis of these findings it would seem fairly safe to conclude that women get fewer dollars out of their education than men. But as in the studies on racial differences, class position has not been examined in these comparisons of men and women. Hypothesis 10.1 argues that if we look at returns to education for men and women within class positions, the differences will be considerably reduced.

We will examine the returns to education for men and women within class positions using two regression equations:

$$\text{Income} = a + b_1 \text{ Education} \tag{1}$$

$$\text{Income} = a + b_1 \text{ Education} + b_2 \text{ Decile Occupational Status} \\ + b_3 \text{ Age} + b_4 \text{ Job Tenure} \tag{7}$$

Since the Panel Study of Income Dynamics contained questions on class position only for heads of household (see appendix A), we will analyze sex differences in returns to education using only the data from the 1969 Survey of Working Conditions. We will also restrict this analysis of sexual differences in returns to education to full-time participants in the labor force, defining full-time employees as people who work 30 hours a week or more, in order to avoid the special problems involved in part-time labor.

Table 9.1 presents the basic regression coefficients for the SWC data, and Figure 9.1 indicates the mean incomes for each level of education for workers and managers in different race-sex categories. As in the studies cited above, men and women differ significantly in returns

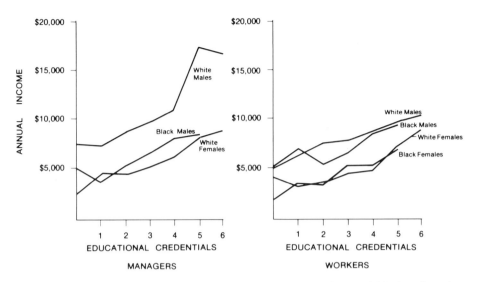

Figure 9.1. Mean income for each education level for white and black male and female workers and managers. Note: Educational credentials are defined as follows: 0 = no education; 1 = some elementary; 2 = elementary; 3 = some high school; 4 = high school; 5 = high school + nonacademic; 6 = some college. (*Source: Data from Michigan Survey of Working Conditions. Figure courtesy of the UW Cartographic Laboratory.*)

to education in the simple regression of income on education: men receive nearly $1450 for each increment in education, whereas women receive only $950. In the expanded regression equation the difference in returns falls just below the 5% level of significance, but the difference is still relatively large in absolute magnitude. Furthermore, the sexes differ substantially in the income returns to occupational status in this equation: men receive over three times as much income from a decile increase in occupational status as do women.

When we look within the working class alone, the greater returns to education for men than for women disappear entirely. In the simple regression of income on education, white women actually receive nearly $100 more for each increment in education than do white men, although the difference is far from significant statistically. In the expanded equation, the returns to education for white men and women differ by only $15, out of total returns of about $700 for each group. Furthermore, white men and women also do not differ significantly in returns to occupational status within the working class.

Among black workers the results are slightly more complex. In the simple regression, black women receive considerably larger returns to education than black men, although because of the small sample size for blacks in the Survey, the difference is not statistically significant. In

TABLE 9.1
Returns to Education and Other Variables for Men and Women Within Class Positions

Class Comparisons	Eq 1	Income Returns in Eq 7				
		Education	Decile Status	Age	Tenure	N
All						
Males	$1,442	$1,147	$491	$46	$89	867
Females	952	810	133	9	26	395
Diff. in coefficients	490	337	358	37	63	
t-value[a]	2.8**	1.5	2.9**	1.6	1.5	
All whites						
Males	1,403	1,134	488	44	91	783
Females	955	776	155	4	37	342
Diff. in coefficients	448	358	333	40	54	
t-value	2.3**	1.5	2.5**	1.6	1.2	
White managers/supervisors						
Males	1,934	1,546	670	73	4	324
Females	1,042	822	358	28	2	94
Diff. in coefficients	892	724	313[b]	45	2	
t-value	1.5	1.2	ns	ns	ns	

White workers						
Males	764	705	212	35	12	322
Females	862	690	110	-2	72	230
Diff. in coefficients	-98	15	102	102	-60	
t-value	ns	ns	1.1	1.1	1.5	
Black workers						
Males	737	458	336	37	-8	39
Females	1,084	1,440	-108	65	-42	37
Diff. in coefficients	-348	-982	444	-28	33	
t-value	ns	2.1*	1.8*	ns	ns	

Source: Data from 1969 Survey of Working Conditions, for full-time participants in the labor force only.

Independent variables: Eq 1 = education only

Eq 7 = education, decile occupational status, age, and tenure

Significance levels on a one-tailed test:

*** .001

** .01

* .05

ns $t < 1$

[a]Most of the analysis of the 1969 SWC data was completed for an earlier study (Wright and Perrone, 1975, 1977) in which the standard dummy variable interaction method of testing slope differences between groups was used. This method yields a larger t-value than the one adopted throughout most of this book. The first two panels of Table 9.1, however, were generated at a later date, and the more conservative, direct t-test was therefore used. This means that in the first two panels, pairwise deletion of missing data was adopted, whereas in panels 3–5, listwise deletion was used.

[b]The difference in coefficients may differ from the subtracted difference due to rounding.

the expanded regression, black female workers receive significantly greater returns to education, but black male workers receive significantly greater returns to status.[3] In any event, in neither equation do black male workers receive greater returns to education than black female workers.

As in the analysis of race differences in chapter 8, white male managers/supervisors have considerably higher returns to education than white female managers/supervisors (although because of the relatively large standard errors for white women, the difference is not statistically significant). In both the simple regression of income on education and the expanded regression, white female managers/supervisors receive only about 50% of the returns to education of white male managers/supervisors. This is an even greater difference than among all white men and women, where women receive about two thirds of the returns of men. Again, as in our discussion of the differences between black and white male managers, it would be expected that this large difference between male and female managers/supervisors reflects the concentration of female managers at the bottom levels of the managerial hierarchy. Unfortunately, there is no way of distinguishing mere supervisors in the SWC data, as we did in the PSID analysis of race differences among managers.[4]

Overall, these results support hypothesis 10.1. When class position is held constant, the large differences in returns to education between men and women in the labor force that have so often been noted in the literature disappear. Although it remains to be shown whether this will hold for actual positions within the managerial structure, it is certainly true for the working class as a whole; and this covers over two thirds of all women and over 40% of all men.

---

[3] I do not have a specific interpretation for these results. The much higher returns to education for black female workers than for black male workers may well be due to sampling fluctuation. In the 1973 QES replication of the 1969 Survey, black female and black male workers had virtually identical returns to education in the simple regression of income on education, while black male workers had returns for the expanded regression equation that were larger, although not statistically significant.

[4] One suggestive piece of evidence for this expectation comes from the QES study. Respondents with supervisors were asked whether their supervisor was a man or a woman; 40% of the women, and only 2% of the men, in the sample who had supervisors said that they were supervised by women. Although it is not possible from these data to determine the proportion of subordinates of female managers/supervisors who are women, these figures do suggest that female managers/supervisors generally supervise mainly women, whereas male supervisors supervise both men and women. This would tend to support the hypothesis that female managers/supervisors are highly concentrated at the bottom of authority hierarchies relative to male managers.

TABLE 9.2
Income Gaps and Returns to Education and Other Variables for Class Positions Within Sex Categories

Class Comparisons	Difference in Mean Incomes	Income Gap[a] in Eq 1	Income Gap[a] in Eq 7	Regression Coefficients Eq 1 Education	Regression Coefficients Eq 7 Education	Eq 7 Decile Status	Eq 7 Age	Eq 7 Tenure
White males								
Managers/supervisors vs. workers	$3,190	$2,298	$1,371	$1,170	$841	$459	$38	$-9
Workers as % of managers	71%	78%	85%	40%	46%			
% of difference elim. by controls		28%	57%		28%			
t-value		6.0***	3.5***	4.7***	2.7**	2.5**	ns	ns
White females								
Managers/supervisors vs. workers	$880	$527	$57	$180	$131	$247	$30	$-71
Workers as % of managers	84%	90%	99%	83%	84%			
% of difference elim. by controls		40%	94%		27%			
t-value		2.1*	ns	ns	ns	3.2**	1.5	1.4

Source: Data from 1969 Survey of Working Conditions, for full-time participants in the labor force only.

Independent variables: Eq 1 = education only

Eq 7 = education, decile occupational status, age, and tenure

Significance levels on a one-tailed test:

*** .001

** .01

* .05

ns t < 1

[a]Evaluated at the grand means of the independent variables for the entire sample. Education = 3.0; age = 39.6; tenure = 6.4; decile occupational status = 5.8.

CLASS DIVISIONS WITHIN SEX CATEGORIES

Hypothesis 10.2. *The differences between female managers and workers will be less marked than between male managers and workers.*

If in fact women are concentrated at the very bottom of managerial hierarchies, then female workers and managers/supervisors should look much more similar than male workers and managers/supervisors. Table 9.2 presents the income gaps, and the returns to education and other variables, for workers and managers/supervisors within sex categories.[5] White male workers and managers/supervisors differ by $1170 in returns to education in equation (1) and $840 in equation (7); the corresponding figures for white women are $180 and $130. Similarly for income gaps: the mean white male workers' income is only 71% of the mean white male managers/supervisors' income, whereas the mean white female workers' income is 84% of the white female managers/supervisors'. When the various controls in equation (7) are added, the gap in income between white female workers and managers/supervisors is a mere $57, or less than 1% of the expected income for white female managers. The gap between white male workers and white male managers/supervisors in equation (7), on the other hand, is $1371, or 15% of the expected income for white male managers/supervisors in this equation. These results suggest that the class divisions among women are considerably less marked in economic terms than among men.

CONCLUSION

It is important to emphasize that the results discussed above do not show that discrimination on the basis of sex is merely a form of class oppression, any more than the results in the previous chapter showed that racism was inconsequential for the structure of income inequality. All that we have shown is that some of the differences between men and women are clearly mediated by their positions within class relations, not that sexual inequality is a mere epiphenomenon.

As in the analysis of racism, sexual discrimination can be seen as having two basic effects in the context of our empirical investigation. First, it clearly influences the distribution of men and women into class positions. Table 9.3 indicates the class-sex-race distributions for the

---

[5]Income gaps are assessed at the overall sample means for the independent variables. Since for most of these the values for men and women are not so drastically different, the two points at which to assess the income gap are relatively close. The gap in all the comparisons is thus assessed at the same point and it is possible in Table 9.3 to compare the income gaps across comparisons.

TABLE 9.3
Distribution of Classes Within Race-Sex Categories

	Males		Females	
Class Category	White	Black	White	Black
Employers	11.5%	4.9%	2.3%	1.6%
Managers/supervisors	40.2	32.5	26.8	23.3
Workers	43.5	61.4	67.3	72.7
Petty bourgeoisie	4.9	1.2	2.0	2.4
Total	100.0	100.0	100.0	100.0
N (both samples)	2,100	168	1,135	159

Source: Percentages are averages of frequencies from the 1969 Survey of Working Conditions and the 1973 Quality of Employment data for all participants in the labor force. For distributions within each sample, see Wright, 1976a, pp. 353, 365.

SWC and QES data combined. (The figures are for all participants in the labor force, not merely full-time participants.) Two thirds of all white women and nearly three quarters of all black women in the labor force fall into the working class, compared to 44% of all white men and 61% of all black men. In a complementary manner, only 27% of all white women are managers or supervisors, compared to 40% of all white men. If data on the managerial hierarchy proper were available, this disproportion would certainly be even greater. Sexist ideologies and their material embodiment in hiring and promotion practices undoubtedly account for much of this pattern.

Second, sexual discrimination generates substantial income inequality between men and women within classes. This can easily be seen in the analysis of income gaps between sexes in Table 9.4. The income gap between male and female workers is considerably less than between all men and women, but it is still large and highly significant. When the various controls in equation (7) are added, the gap actually increases, indicating that the different incomes of male and female workers are not a consequence of the age-tenure-status-education composition of the sexes.

Furthermore, the data clearly indicate that the income gap between sexes within the working class is considerably greater than the gap between races. In terms of gross mean incomes, the gap between white male and white female workers is almost two and a half times as large as the gap between black and white male workers ($3083 vs. $1236). When the various controls in equation (7) are added, the income gap between black and white male workers (at the grand means of the independent variables) drops to just over $500, while the gap between white male and female workers remains over $3000.

TABLE 9.4

Gaps in Income Between Males and Females Within Class Categories

Class Comparisons	Sex Difference in Mean Income	Income Gap[a] in	
		Eq 1	Eq 7
All classes	$4,914	$5,034	$4,912
Female income as % of male	50%	49%	51%
% of gap elim. by controls		−2%	0%
t-value[b]		***	***
All whites	5,189	5,265	4,957
Female income as % of male	49%	48%	50%
% of gap elim. by controls		−1%	4%
t-value[b]		***	***
White managers/supervisors	5,393	5,092	4,677
Female income as % of male	51%	50%	51%
% of gap elim. by controls		6%	13%
t-value		7.4***	6.3***
White workers	3,083	3,320	3,363
Female income as % of male	61%	58%	59%
% of gap elim. by controls		−8%	−9%
t-value		15.7***	15.5***
Black workers	1,641	2,189	2,505
Female income as % of male	75%	67%	67%
% of gap elim. by controls		−33%	−53%
t-value		4.6***	4.3***
White male vs. black male workers	1,236	736	532
Black as % of white	84%	91%	94%
% of gap elim. by controls		40%	57%
t-value		1.4	ns

Source: Data from 1969 Survey of Working Conditions for full-time participants in the labor force only.

Independent variables: Eq 1 = education only

Eq 7 = education, decile occupational status, age, and tenure

Significance levels on a one-tailed test:

*** .001

** .01

* .05

ns $t < 1$

[a]The income gaps in these comparisons are all evaluated at the grand means of the independent variables for the entire sample: education = 3.0, age = 39.6, tenure = 6.4, decile occupational status = 5.8.

[b]The t-values for workers were calculated using the standard analysis of covariance technique involving dummy variable covariates. The t-values in the first and second panels were calculated using the procedure employed throughout the rest of this study.

These results indicate some of the difficulties in analyzing class relations simply in terms of individuals rather than families. At the individual level, the results of the comparison of income gaps between races and sexes within the working class suggest that sexual inequality is greater than racial inequality. However, married, white, working-class women generally share in the consumption generated by the wages of white working-class men. Thus the gap in actual *living standards* between men and women (at least married men and women) will generally be much less than the gap in living standards between black and white working-class families, even though the gap in individual earnings is greater between sexes than between races. It may be convenient to abstract away from the complications introduced when class relations are analyzed in terms of families rather than individuals, but such an abstraction unquestionably limits our understanding of the relationship of sexual divisions to class relations.

To go beyond this rather one-dimensional picture of the interactions of sex and class it would be necessary to have data on class position and income of both men and women within family units, as well as concrete data on the sexual division of labor within the household. If such data were available it might be possible to approach the complex problem of analyzing the relationship between inequalities generated within social relations of production and inequalities generated within social relations of reproduction (as defined in notes 1 and 2 to this chapter). Such an investigation is impossible with available data.

In spite of these limitations in the present data, we have shown that in the analysis of sexual differences in income it is essential to include measures of class position. Capitalism certainly did not create inequalities between the sexes, but capitalist class relations shape the way such inequalities function within capitalist society. Thus, in our analysis of returns to education, much of the differential returns for men and women appear to be mediated by their positions within the social relations of production. Although the data presented here include only full-time participants in the labor force, they do suggest that the analysis of sexual inequalities is incomplete if it is detached from a broader class analysis of capitalist society.

10

Conclusions

At the most general level, the results of this study clearly show that class, defined in terms of social relations of production, plays an important role in income determination in American society. Not only are class positions characterized by very different levels of income, but class positions have a strong and consistent impact on the ways in which various other factors, such as education, affect income. In this sense one can say that position within the social relations of production structurally *mediates* income determination in capitalist society.

A number of other, more specific generalizations can be drawn from the results.

1. *The division between property-drawing and non-property-owning classes remains substantial even in advanced capitalism.* It may seem ironic that in a Marxist study of the relationship of income in-

equality to class relations, there has been virtually no empirical analysis of the principal class antagonism within capitalist society: the capital-labor relationship. Although we have been able to analyze in some detail the contradictory class position between the petty bourgeoisie and the capitalist class (small employers), we have not been able to analyze proper capitalists. And we certainly have not touched on anything that could legitimately be called the "ruling class" within advanced capitalist society. Ultimately it is important to investigate income determination in the capitalist class itself, but this is simply impossible using survey data.

Nevertheless, in spite of the partial nature of the analysis of property relations, the results clearly demonstrate that even small property ownership is consequential. The mean income of small employers is over twice that of workers and remains large even when we control for education, age, background, seniority, status, and annual hours worked. Furthermore, the income gap between employers and workers is much greater than between workers and managers, or between race and sex categories within the working class.

Income, of course, is only one of the ways of empirically demonstrating the reality of class divisions. If data were available, it would be easy to demonstrate that classes, defined by social relations of production, are even more decisively differentiated in terms of wealth and political power. Real economic control over the means of production—property ownership in the substantive rather than juridical sense—remains the essential basis of distributive relations, and any investigation of inequality needs to take these relations of production into systematic consideration.

For over a generation theorists of the postindustrial society and the managerial revolution have argued that authority and/or knowledge stratification has superseded property stratification as the organizing principle of inequality in contemporary society. Our results indicate that even when a simple juridical criterion is used to define property relations (self-employed employers), and even when the sample necessarily excludes the wealthiest segments of the capitalist class, the division between those who own property and those who do not is substantial, and that it is considerably greater than the differences between "knowledge classes" or "authority classes."[1]

2. *The impact of class position on income cannot be considered simply an artifact of various characteristics of the individuals who*

---

[1]Even if, by chance, a member of the ruling class fell into the sample and agreed to cooperate with the survey, the truncation of the income variables at $99,999 would grossly understate the income differences between the capitalist class proper and the working class.

occupy class positions. Throughout this study, class positions have been viewed as "empty places" in the social structure. The link between class position and income has thus been conceptualized as a consequence of the structure of class relations as such, rather than of the attributes of the individuals filling the class positions.

The results of the empirical investigation support this view of the relationship between social relations of production and income. Class continues to add to the explained variance in individual-level income equations even when social background, education, age, status, and other characteristics of individuals are already controlled for in a regression equation. And the income gaps between classes, especially between small employers and either workers or managers, do not disappear even when all of these individual attributes are held constant.

Of particular interest in these results is the relationship of class position to occupational status. Occupational status—or some closely related metric of occupational position—has dominated the quantitative sociological research on income inequality. The general argument is that in industrial societies incomes are primarily attached to occupational positions. For those who hold this view, the key social processes to unravel are the mechanisms which determine, first, how people achieve given occupational positions (the status attainment process) and secondly, how such positions are translated into income.

The data in this study do not indicate that occupational position is unimportant for understanding income inequality. Both because occupation reflects positions within the labor market and because occupational status is a basic dimension of ideological relations, occupational position is bound up with income inequality. What the results do indicate is that in strictly empiricist terms, class position is at least as powerful an explanatory variable in predicting income as occupational status. What is more, net of various factors such as education or background, class generally explains about twice as much variance in income as occupational status.[2] Class cannot simply be viewed as a loose proxy for occupational status. It represents one of the basic structural factors in the income determination process.

[2]It must be remembered that in these various empirical comparisons of class and occupational status, a rather crude measure of class is used (three dummy variables, one for workers, one for managers, and one for small employers). No indicator of position within the manager hierarchy was available other than the distinction between mere supervisors and proper managers. Perhaps even more significantly, the contradictory class position between the petty bourgeoisie and the working class (semiautonomous employees) was merged with the working class throughout the empirical investigation. It would be expected that the ability of social relations of production to explain variance in income would be considerably enhanced if data were available containing a more complete set of class criteria.

3. *The concept of contradictory locations within class relations is important for understanding the link between production relations and exchange relations within a class analysis.* Class relations in advanced capitalist society do not correspond to the simple, dichotomous view of classes and class struggle. While it is still true that the fundamental antagonism between the working class and the bourgeoisie determines the contours of the entire class structure, contradictory positions within class relations play an important role in advanced capitalist society.

In the present study we have paid particular attention to managers and supervisors, the contradictory class locations between the working class and the bourgeoisie. The results discussed in chapters 6 and 7 indicate that the character of this contradictory location at the level of *production relations* has specific consequences at the level of *exchange relations*, namely that (a) income increases sharply as you move up the managerial hierarchy; and (b) the income returns to education are much greater among managers than among workers.

These patterns were interpreted as reflecting the special problems of social control of managerial labor. To recapitulate the argument briefly: because of their contradictory location between the working class and the capitalist class at the level of production relations, managers have varying degrees of real responsibility and power within the production process. This does not imply that such power is unconstrained by the bourgeoisie itself (indeed, if it were unconstrained managers would not occupy contradictory locations), but it does mean that it becomes particularly important to the capitalist for managers to behave in responsible ways. Whereas for workers conformity to the rules is the basic behavioral norm, much more than mere conformity is needed from managers. The result is that managerial behavior is controlled more through an elaborate structure of inducements than through repression. In particular, there will tend to be a steep income gradient attached to career ladders among managers, i.e., to levels in the managerial hierarchy. For a variety of other reasons there will also tend to be a steep education-credential gradient attached to the managerial hierarchy (because of the training and socialization associated with education, the use of credentials as a filtering mechanism, and the need to legitimate the hierarchical organization of power within production). The net result of these interrelated education and income gradients within the managerial hierarchy is that managers receive much greater increases in income for each additional increment in education than do workers (i.e., they receive greater returns to education).

"Greater returns to education" has a particular meaning within Marxist theory. If the value of labor power is understood as containing a component reflecting the historical costs of reproducing labor power of average skills, and a second component reflecting the socially necessary costs of reproducing additional skills, then the greater returns to education among managers relative to workers reflect a systematic tendency for their wages to be above the value of their labor power. Managers thus receive an income privilege component in their wage, a component which lowers their rate of exploitation and sets them off from the working class at the level of exchange relations.[3]

In more general theoretical terms, these results indicate the importance of carefully investigating production relations in any analysis of exchange relations (i.e., distribution). This is, of course, obvious for comparisons between the working class and the capitalist class. The traditional Marxist analysis of exploitation is precisely an effort to link production relations to exchange. Our analysis of contradictory locations within class relations suggests that the logic of production relations is important for understanding not only income distribution between capitalists and workers but income inequality among non-property-owning classes as well.

4. *The effects of race and sex on income inequality are clearly mediated by class position.* Few issues have generated more debate within the American Left during the past decade than the question of how racism and sexual discrimination should be understood within American capitalism. And few problems have received more attention by academic sociologists engaged in stratification research than racial discrimination. (Sexual discrimination has only recently become an object of general interest among sociologists.) The results of our analysis of the interactions between class and race and between class and sex have something to say to both of these sets of issues.

For the academic sociologist, the results demonstrate that class position plays an important role in structuring the relationship between racial and sexual discrimination and income inequality. In par-

---

[3]As has been reiterated several times, the argument that managers receive a wage above the value of their labor power—the reproductive costs of managerial skills—has nothing to do with the argument that they are paid (or not paid) a wage above their "marginal productivity." There is a tautological sense in which employers would not pay managers what they pay them unless they felt that it was in some sense "profitable," that is, in some sense the marginal cost to the capitalist of paying such a wage to the manager is at least equal to the benefit the capitalist receives. But this is simply a definition of minimally rational resource allocation; it has nothing to do with exploitation in the Marxist sense and the concept of the value of labor power. The value of labor power is an objective concept referring to the costs of producing a particular kind of commodity,

ticular, the income returns to education for black and white workers and for male and female workers are virtually identical, whereas the returns for all whites are much greater than for all blacks, and the returns for all men are much greater than the returns for all women. This suggests that a large part of racial and sexual discrimination operates by concentrating blacks and women within the working class and the bottom levels of the managerial category.

For Marxists, the results affirm the basic class unity among workers regardless of race and sex. The differences between workers and either managers or employers are much greater than the differences between races or sexes within the working class even on so narrow an issue as income. This is especially dramatic for returns to education. While workers of all race-sex categories have similar returns to education, the returns for workers as a whole are much less than for managers and supervisors or for small employers. This commonality of returns to education within the working class, regardless of race or sex, reflects a common underlying structure of causation which impinges on all workers simply because of their position within the social relations of production. As has been stressed in chapters 8 and 9, this does not imply that racial and sexual discrimination are insignificant social realities, but it does support the view that the starting point for understanding both of them should be an analysis of class relations and the articulation of race and sex with class position.

These diverse results do not in and of themselves prove the superiority of the Marxist view of social inequality over other perspectives. It would undoubtedly be possible, without a great deal of mental gymnastics, to reinterpret most of the results in terms of the logic of human capital theory in economics or the assumptions of status attainment research in sociology. But of course, it would be also possible, after the fact, to construct human capital and status attainment interpretations of the exact opposite results if they had occurred.

Concrete empirical results never decisively prove or disprove paradigms, since any respectable theoretical paradigm is always capable of ad hoc amendment to accommodate virtually any unexpected findings. What we can say, however, is that the various hypotheses explored in this study flow naturally from our analysis of social rela-

---

labor power. It is not a subjective concept referring to how "valuable" such labor power is to the individual capitalist. Obviously there is an indirect relationship between these two concepts, for if labor power were not valuable to the capitalist, he would refuse to pay a price equal to the value of that labor power for its use. But this does not imply that the valuableness and the value of labor power are equivalent concepts.

tions of production in advanced capitalism, and that most of the results were anticipated by the logic of that analysis. Conventional sociological and economic studies of income determination have been totally silent on the relationship between social relations of production and social relations of exchange. Their preoccupation with the individual level of analysis would suggest that even if they were to treat social relations of production seriously, it would be as an additional variable in the lives of individuals, not as dimensions of class structures worthy of study in their own right. Marxist theory provides a basis for the systematic theoretical examination of levels of determination beyond the motivations and actions of individuals, for questions about classes and social structures. The empirical results of this study have, I hope, also demonstrated that Marxist theory provides a powerful framework for answering those questions.

All empirical studies are ultimately preliminary investigations for future research. This study of class mediations of income inequality certainly warrants such a designation. Several lines of future research are suggested by the investigations of the present study.

1. *The development of more refined indicators of class relations.* This entire study of class and income was based on extremely crude measures of class location. The contradictory location between the proletariat and the bourgeoisie was defined by two questions, both of which were exclusively focused on the authority dimension of class relations: Do you supervise anyone on the job, and do you have any say in their pay or promotions? The contradictory location between the proletariat and the petty bourgeoisie, on the other hand, was impossible to operationalize at all, and thus had to be merged with the working class throughout the research.

If the study of class mediations is to advance, it is essential to develop more sophisticated measures of class. The manager and supervisor class location should be defined primarily in terms of the real capacity to make decisions over investments and accumulation, the use of the productive apparatus, and the control of labor within production. And within each of these dimensions of control, it is essential to define more precisely the interlocking domains and levels of control. This would make it possible to define more substantively the actual position of managers within the broad contradictory location within class relations, and to specify managerial positions which properly belong within the bourgeoisie itself.

The semiautonomous employee category is in even more need of specification and operationalization. This is a difficult problem and will require considerable theoretical discussion as well as empirical investigation. Exactly what does it mean to have some degree of real control over one's immediate labor process? How can real and nominal control be distinguished? Does the meaning of "autonomy" vary from one production process to another? If the analysis of proletarianization is to go beyond global statements about the destruction of the traditional petty bourgeoisie and the dequalification of labor power, then these and other questions need to be rigorously examined, and answered.

2. *The historical investigation of contradictory class locations.* One of the most serious limitations of the present research was the essentially static character of the data employed. In chapter 3 we argued that one of the critical thrusts of Marxist theory is the investigation of the historical processes through which social structures are transformed, especially through class struggles. Although the analysis of more or less static relations of reproduction plays a part in such an historical investigation of transformation, the heart of Marxist theory is the investigation of transformation itself.

In order to study such transformations empirically it is essential to have meaningful data on class relations over time. This is a difficult problem, since the most plentiful sources of historical data—census reports—are usually inadequate for estimating class distributions. Census data are typically gathered in terms of occupational categories rather than social relations of production, and thus can provide only the crudest basis for studying the transformations of class structures. Of course, we can easily determine how the formal, juridical categories of class have changed (percentage of people self-employed, engaged in wage labor, or working for the state, for example), but it is much more difficult to see how positions within the social relations of production have actually changed. Perhaps the most effective approach would be to gather extremely detailed work histories from people in different age cohorts in which questions on class relations were carefully asked. These data, when combined with census occupational data to correct for differential mortality rates of people within different classes, could then be used to reconstruct the structure of empty places within the social relations of production at different points of time in the past.

3. *The comparative study of class structures and class relations.* The present research is not only limited in time, it is limited in space. The income determination process discussed in this book is not simply mediated by positions within the class structure; the entire process is also mediated by the class structure itself. Being a worker or being a manager will have different consequences for the income determina-

tion process, depending upon the shape of the class structure within which that working-class position is located. A fully elaborated Marxist theory of income determination would involve an account of the ways in which social structures mediate the very mediations of classes within that structure. This higher-order mediation is illustrated in Figure 10.1.

Such mediations of mediations can be studied on a comparative basis. It is necessary to isolate distinctively different types of class structures within capitalist societies, and investigate how the income determination processes differ across such structures. The most obvious lines of demarcation within such a typology of overall class structures would be between the imperialist centers and the dependent periphery of the capitalist world system. The income determination process will obviously work in very different ways in these different kinds of capitalist societies. To mention just one issue, peripheral societies still have large precapitalist sectors, and many workers retain real links to various forms of subsistence production (i.e., production for direct consumption rather than for the market). The income determination process for workers in such a situation is conditioned not only by their relation to capital, but by their relation to these non-capitalist forms of production. In contrast, very few workers in central capitalist societies are tied to such noncapitalist forms of production.

It would also be anticipated that the income determination process would operate in very different ways in those advanced capitalist societies in which there is a fully developed welfare state apparatus than it does in those with a more restricted state. The fact that income distribution varies so substantially across advanced capitalist countries would support this expectation. Wiles (1974), in an extremely interesting study, has shown that if we examine posttax, posttransfer income—i.e., the net real income available to individuals—there is an

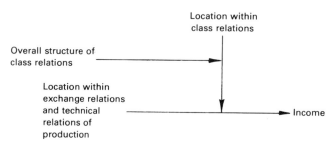

Figure 10.1. Model of determination of macro- and micromediations within the income determination process.

enormous range in the degree of inequality in advanced capitalist societies. For example, the "semidecile ratio" (the ratio of the net income of people at the top 5% of the income distribution with the net income of people at the bottom 5%) for the United States in 1968 was about 13:1. That is, the net real income of people at the 95th centile was 13 times greater than the net real income of people at the 5th centile. In Britain, in 1969, the figure was 6:1 and in Sweden, 3:1 (Wiles, 1974, pp. 48; xiv). These distributions, of course, are for the entire population. There is no discussion of the income distribution between or within classes defined by the social relations of production. Nevertheless, such data strongly suggest that the class mediations of the income determination process are likely to vary significantly across these societies. The critical next step in developing the Marxist theory of income determination is to elaborate an explicit theory of these societal-level mediations of the class mediations within the income determination process.

4. *The analysis of how people are sorted into class locations.* Although the analysis of empty places in the social structure has priority over the analysis of the people within those positions, nevertheless it is important to understand the mechanisms by which people are distributed into class locations. Bertaux (1977) has suggested that such an investigation be termed "anthroponomy," the process of the production and distribution of people. The theoretical and empirical problem, then, is to understand the anthroponomic practices which are specific to given classes. Just as class location mediates the income determination process, it would be expected that class location would decisively mediate the anthroponomic practices by which people are distributed into classes.

Of particular interest in the study of the processes by which people are sorted into classes would be the investigation of the movement of people back and forth across various class boundaries, especially across the boundary between the working class and the traditional petty bourgeoisie. Too often Marxists portray the fate of the petty bourgeoisie as a one-way process of proletarianization. While it is undoubtedly true that there has been a progressive reduction of petty bourgeois places within the social relations of production, it is much less true that the movement of individuals is strictly in one direction. On the contrary, there is much anecdotal evidence that many working-class people at some point in their work lives at least attempt to set themselves up as independent, self-employed petty bourgeois (typically as small retail store owners). While such attempts generally fail, this movement in and out of petty bourgeois class locations (or what might be termed the "circulation of the petty bourgeoisie") has extremely important ramifications at the political and ideological levels, especially for legitimating the "free enterprise" system.

5. *The analysis of the relationship between class structure and the forms of organization of capitalist production.* Throughout most of this study we have treated the social organization of capitalist production as a single, homogeneous reality, but in fact, it displays decisive variations. In part these are rooted in different phases or stages of capitalist development (competitive capital vs. monopoly capitalism, for example), but in part they also reflect persistent differences in the forms of capitalism within advanced capitalism. In contemporary American capitalism, it would be important to distinguish at least among the following forms of organization of production: individually run competitive capital; franchise capital (and other forms of competitive enterprises which are directly dependent on monopoly capital); monopoly capital; and state-organized production. Although the fundamental social relations of production may remain the same in all of these, there are clearly important differences, especially in terms of the contradictory class locations we have emphasized. A top manager in a monopoly corporation, for example, is clearly in a different empty place within class relations from a top manager in a small competitive firm. To be a semiautonomous employee in a state bureaucracy may represent a quite different position from a semiautonomous class location within a small firm. A fully developed class analysis of income determination would look at the interactions between class location and the specific organization of production within which those positions were embedded, rather than simply at the direct ways in which class mediates income determination.

6. *The analysis of the family and class relations.* As briefly suggested in chapter 9, families can be thought of as occupying locations within the social relations of reproduction. The present study has been mainly concerned with exploring the relationship between social relations of production and social relations of exchange. It is also clearly important to investigate the relationship between social relations of production and reproduction and between social relations of reproduction and exchange. Such an investigation would necessarily revolve around the analysis of families and their role in income determination. This would be particularly important for the analysis of interactions between sex and class, but it is important for the general analysis of class relations as well.

The investigation of the role of the family in income determination would involve questions such as: What is the relationship between use-value production within the family and income determination through exchange relations? In what ways does this relationship between use-value and exchange-value sources of consumption vary across classes, across capitalist societies, across stages of the development of capitalism? What is the relationship between use-value production within the family and the role of women in the market, and how does this vary with class location and stage of capitalist development? How do the social relations of production structure the social relations of reproduction? If a Marxist analysis is to adequately comprehend the specificities of the relationship between sexual oppression and class relations, these and other questions need to be addressed.

7. *The extension of the analysis of structural mediations beyond the study of income determination.* The general strategy of analysis advanced in this study can be applied to a much broader range of questions than simply income. Class does not merely mediate the income determination process, it also mediates the processes of consciousness formation and political action. A very simple model of determination of class consciousness, for example, could be represented as in Figure 10.2. In this model, an attempt is made to link the micro and macro processes of determination. At the microlevel, the class location of individuals is seen as mediating the relationship between various individual characteristics and that individual's consciousness as well as establishing the basic limits within which that consciousness can vary. This entire microprocess, however, is mediated by the overall class structure. Being a worker in a class structure with few workers has decisively different consequences for consciousness than being a worker in a class structure with many workers.

The ways in which the macro class structure mediates these microprocesses, however, is itself structured by the historically specific forms of class struggle that occur within that class structure. These forms of class struggle occur within limits established by the underlying class structure, but within those limits the specific forms of struggle are shaped (selected) by the microprocesses of consciousness formation. Finally—and ultimately this is why the model of determination is a dialectical, dynamic model—the forms of class struggle contribute to the transformation of the class structure itself. It is for this reason that the system can never be in purely static equilibrium; the very conditions for the overall structure of determination are themselves transformed in the process of that determination.

The model in Figure 10.2 is not meant to be comprehensive. Many other structural elements and processes would need to be added in a fully developed theory of consciousness (for instance, the forms of the state and politics; the structure of ideological relations; the relationship

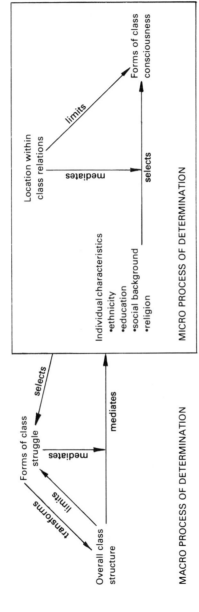

Figure 10.2. Model of determination of class consciousness.

between class struggles and nonclass struggles). The essential point in the present context is that such processes can be represented in this kind of formal model, and such formal models can facilitate systematic empirical investigation.

After a long period of systematic exclusion from American social science, Marxism is reemerging as a serious theoretical force. In the 1960s this resurgence of Marxist perspectives largely took the form of radical critiques of the accepted wisdom in various academic disciplines. Increasingly in the course of the 1970s these critiques have been transformed into the elaboration of a positive alternative. New questions are being asked, new answers are being formulated, and new research agendas are being generated.

This book is an initial result of that process. It has attempted to take the theoretical challenge and insights of the emerging Marxist social science onto an empirical terrain familiar to non-Marxist social scientists. If nothing else, I hope that this effort has established the empirical significance of various issues raised within contemporary Marxist theory.

Regression equations, of course, cannot establish the general validity of a conceptual paradigm. Especially where disagreements over theoretical issues are reinforced by powerful ideological commitments, empirical results alone can never be decisive. Nevertheless, the kind of empirical investigation pursued in this study may help to demonstrate the scientific side of Marxism, and in so doing expand the possibilities for sustained theoretical debate.

APPENDIX A

Data Sources

Four different data sources will be used to investigate the various hypotheses discussed in chapter 4.

THE PANEL STUDY OF INCOME DYNAMICS (PSID)

Since 1968, the University of Michigan Institute for Social Research (ISR) has been conducting a panel study of households across the United States. Each year the heads of these households have been reinterviewed on a wide variety of topics concerned with income, standards of living, work, and similar issues. When individuals leave a family and begin a new household, or when families split apart, both old and new households are included in the study. As a result, the original sample of 5000 households has grown to nearly 6000 households, in spite of a certain amount of attrition due to deaths and non-responses.

The original sample was stratified in order to oversample blacks and poor people. As a result, an elaborate system of weights has been developed to make the sample approximately a national random sample. These weights were readjusted after the fifth wave of the study (1972) in order to compensate for differential nonresponses during the first five years of the study. In every year since 1970 the response rate has been well over 95%, and thus no additional changes in weights were felt to be necessary (see IRS, 1972, pp. 9–46, for a further discussion of the sample and weights).[1]

Until the 1975 interview year, the study did not contain the necessary questions to allow for a class analysis of the data. In the 1975 questionnaire, several items which I had submitted to the project director were included (along with a number of others) which make at least a rough class typology possible. The data we will use, therefore, come primarily from this single year of the study.

Since most of the questions in the Panel Study are asked only of heads of households, whom the researchers in the project generally assumed to be the husband in married families, the PSID data can really only be used to investigate the relations of class and income among men. Nevertheless, because of the large sample size and the richness of the questions asked on the survey, we will use the Panel Study as the central data source for most of the hypotheses.

THE SURVEY OF WORKING CONDITIONS, 1969 (SWC)

A second source of data is the ISR Survey of Working Conditions. This survey consists of a national random sample of some 1500 adults

---

[1]A word needs to be said about the randomness of the sample in the Panel Study. Although the response rates have been very high in the third through eighth years of the study, they were not terribly high during the first two years (76% and 90%, respectively). By the eighth wave of the survey, then, when the questions on class position were added, the net response rate was only slightly above 50%. Even with the elaborate system of weightings used to compensate for differential nonresponses, the sample we are using cannot really be considered a true random sample of the American population.

If we were especially interested in studying frequencies, this nonrandomness would pose a serious problem. For example, 19.3% of the men in the weighted sample who are active in the labor force are professionals, compared to only 14% in the population as a whole; only 8.7% of the men in the sample are laborers or service workers, compared to some 18% of the total population. Given this departure from expected frequencies for the active in the labor force. The major focus of the study was job satisfaction and working conditions, but enough questions were asked about employment status, position within authority hierarchies, income, and other variables relevant to our concerns to enable us to use the data to test a number of our hypotheses. Since the Survey includes women, these data will be especially relevant for hypotheses 10.1 and 10.2 about the interactions of class and sex.

THE QUALITY OF EMPLOYMENT SURVEY, 1973 (QES)

This survey is basically a replication of the 1969 Survey of Working Conditions. A number of questions on the earlier survey were dropped, however, and this made the 1973 replication somewhat less useful for our purposes. In particular, self-employed respondents were not asked whether or not they had employees in the 1973 survey, and thus it is difficult for us to distinguish the petty bourgeoisie from small employers. We will therefore rely more heavily on the 1969 Survey in the hypotheses concerning sex differences.

THE HIERARCHY IN ORGANIZATIONS STUDY

These data were gathered by Arnold Tannenbaum and associates (Tannenbaum et al., 1974) as part of a cross-national comparison of hierarchical structures within economic organizations in five countries: the United States, Austria, Italy, Yugoslavia, and Israel. In each country five large and five small plants were selected for study, and within each plant an assortment of people from different levels of the authority structure was interviewed. While the data do not represent random samples within each country, they have the advantage of containing extremely detailed information about each respondent's position within the authority hierarchy of the plant. We will, therefore, use these data to explore the various hypotheses which concern divisions within the managerial hierarchy.

---

occupational distribution, we cannot have a great deal of confidence in the frequencies for class distribution in the Panel Study. Our main statistical technique, however, will be linear regression analysis, which is much less sensitive to nonrandomness. As long as nonresponses are more or less random with respect to the residuals in a regression equation, the estimated coefficients will remain unbiased estimates of the true population coefficients. We will assume that this is the case throughout this analysis.

APPENDIX B

Variables

The discussion of variables in this appendix will focus primarily on the definitions and operationalizations in the PSID data. The variables in the SWC and QES data will be mentioned only when they differ in significant ways from the PSID data. The variables used in the Hierarchy study are discussed in chapter 7.

OPERATIONALIZATION OF CLASS

None of the surveys available for this study enables us to operationalize precisely the class typology presented in Table 2.3. In particular, none of them contains any information on the extent to which individuals actually control their own labor process. Thus it is impossible to define the contradictory class position between the petty bourgeoisie and the proletariat (semiautonomous employees), and as a result throughout the present research such positions will be merged with the working class itself. Since most "semiautonomous employees" are probably located fairly close to the working class anyway, this should not seriously distort the results.

All of the surveys also lacked any information on the relations of real economic ownership (i.e., actual control over investments and accumulation) as discussed in chapter 2. In defining capitalists, therefore, we must rely on the formal legal criterion of being self-employed and employing others. This means that a top executive in a monopoly corporation would not be placed in the bourgeoisie. Since it is unlikely that any such individuals appear in these surveys, this is unlikely to affect the analysis significantly. Because of these limitations, the operationalization of class which will be used throughout this research should be viewed as a first approximation, clearly in need of further refinement.

Table B.1 presents the basic operationalization of class we will use with the PSID data. The questionnaire items used to construct this typology appear in Table B.2. Several comments on the typology are necessary.

First, approximately 2.8% of the respondents stated that they were both self-employed and worked for others. Of these ambiguous cases, nearly two thirds (1.7% of the sample) said that they had employees. Since it seemed reasonable to assume in such cases that the individual was probably mainly an employer, these individuals have been included in the employer category. The most important results of the study were run separately for employers who said that they were self-

TABLE B.1
Criteria for Class Position in the Panel Study of Income Dynamics

Class Category	Self-employed (D5)[a]	Employ Others (D12,D8)	Supervise Others (D14)	Say in Pay or Promotions (D16)	Employed (D5)
Employers	Yes	Yes	Yes[b]	Yes	No
Managers	No	No	Yes	Yes	Yes
Supervisors	No	No	Yes	No	Yes
Workers	No	No	No	No	Yes
Petty bourgeoisie	Yes	No	No	No	No

[a]These numbers represent the question number in the questionnaire administered; see Table B.2.

[b]Self-employed people did not actually answer questions D14 and D16, but these responses are implicit in their response to question D12.

TABLE B.2
Items in the PSID Questionnaire Used to Operationalize Class Position

SECTION D: EMPLOYMENT

D1. We would like to know about your (HEAD'S) present job—are you (HEAD) working now, looking for work, retired, a housewife, or what?

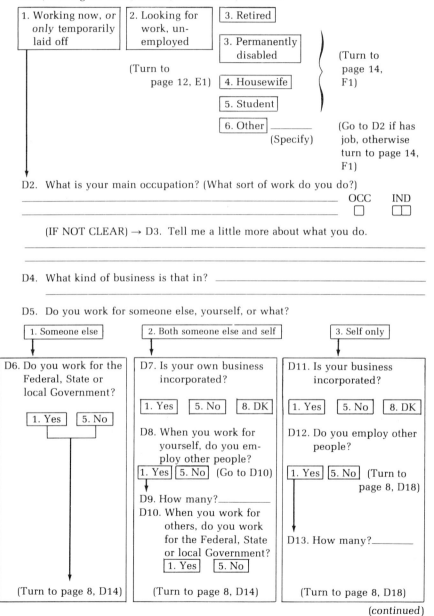

D2. What is your main occupation? (What sort of work do you do?)

_____ OCC   IND
_____   ☐   ☐☐

(IF NOT CLEAR) → D3. Tell me a little more about what you do.

_____
_____

D4. What kind of business is that in? _____
_____

D5. Do you work for someone else, yourself, or what?

(Turn to page 8, D14)   (Turn to page 8, D14)   (Turn to page 8, D18)

(continued)

TABLE B.2 (*continued*)

D14. Do you supervise the work of others, or tell other employees what work to do?

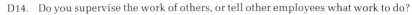

☐ 1. Yes   ☐ 5. No   (Go to D17)

D15. About how many people are you responsible for? _____
D16. Do you have any say about their pay or promotion?

☐ 1. Yes   ☐ 5. No

(Go to D17)

D17. Does your boss have a supervisor over him?
☐ 1. Yes   ☐ 5. No

D18. How long have you had this job? _____

(If *one year or more*, turn to page 9, D24)
(If *less than one year*)

D19. What month did you start this job? _____
D20. What happened to the job you had before—did the company fold, were
        you laid off, or what? _____
D21. Does your present job pay more than the one you had before?

☐ 1. Yes, more   ☐ 5. No, same or less

D22. On the whole, would you say your present job is better or worse than the
        one you had before?

☐ 1. Better   ☐ 5. Worse   ☐ 3. Same ──→ (Turn to page 9, D24)

D23. Why is that?_____
        _____
        _____

        (Turn to page 9, D24)

employed only, and in all instances the results were essentially identical to those of the enlarged employer category. In the case of respondents who stated that they were both self-employed and worked for others but did not employ anyone, it seemed unreasonable to assume that the individual was either mainly petty bourgeois or mainly a worker. These respondents, 1.1% of the sample, have thus been excluded from the analysis.

Second, the designation "employer" is being used rather than "capitalist" since the large majority of individuals in this category are small businesspeople: 77% of the employers employed fewer than ten workers, and only 7% employed 50 workers or more. The distribution of number of employees of the employers in the sample is given in Table B.3.

Third, many of the people classified as "supervisors" probably belong in the working class proper. To be classified as a supervisor one need only say "yes" to the question: "Do you supervise the work of others or tell other employees what work to do?" The head of a work team who really has no capacity to invoke sanctions on other workers would probably be classified as a supervisor by this criterion. The "manager" category, on the other hand, is unambiguously in the contradictory position between the working class and the bourgeoisie since to be in this category one must have some say in the pay or promotions of subordinates. Throughout our analysis of the manager/supervisor class position, therefore, we will examine the results both for the combined category (managers and supervisors) and for managers taken separately.

The operationalization of class in the 1969 Survey of Working Conditions is essentially the same as in the Panel Study. Only two differences are worth mentioning. First, the question about having a say in pay and promotions of subordinates was not asked in the Survey, and thus it is impossible to make the distinction between supervisors and managers. Secondly, the supervision question itself was posed in a somewhat ambiguous fashion in the Survey: "Do you supervise people on your job?" In the Panel Study the question explicitly mentions supervision of other *employees* on the job. The result is that in the

TABLE B.3
Number of Employees and Expected Income

Number of Employees	Mean Annual Taxable Income	Employers in Each Category	
		N	%
1–2	$18,811	90	36.3
3–5	29,752	72	29.0
6–9	21,598	28	11.3
10–19	26,247	24	9.7
20–49	36,694	16	6.5
50–99	43,106	10	4.0
100 or more	36,092	8	3.2
All employers	$25,898	248	100%

TABLE B.4
Characteristics of the Data Sets for Basic Class Operationalizations

Questions Available for Operationalizing Class	Panel Study of Income Dynamics	1969 Survey of Working Conditions	1973 Quality of Employment Survey
Do you supervise anyone on the job?	No	Yes	Yes
Do you supervise other employees?	Yes	No	No
Do you have say in pay and promotions of subordinates?	Yes	No	No
Are you self-employed?	Yes	Yes	Yes
Do you employ others?	Yes	Yes	No
Special assumptions used in operationalizing class	People who say they are both employers and work for others are probably mainly employers.	Teachers are generally nonsupervisors even if they say they supervise people on their jobs.	
Restrictions on the sample used in this study	Males only	Active participants in labor force only (work 20 hours a week or more)	
Effective N for this study	3,205	1,533	1,496

Survey well over half of all elementary and secondary school teachers reported that they "supervise" people on the job. In the Panel Study less than a quarter of all teachers said that they were supervisors. Presumably the difference is that the SWC teachers assumed that supervision of students counted as supervision. In the SWC data, therefore, teachers have all been classified as workers rather than managers/supervisors. While this undoubtedly results in a misclassification of some of the teachers, this is a less serious error than classifying most teachers as managers.

The 1973 QES lacked the question on having employees. When we use this survey we will assume that all self-employed people who say that they supervise people on the job are employers. In other respects the operationalization of class is the same as in the 1969 Survey.

The operationalization of class in the Hierarchy study is discussed in chapter 7.

Table B.4 summarizes the questions available for the operationalization of class in the Panel Study and two surveys, along with other characteristics of the samples.

INCOME

The Panel Study provides an extraordinarily rich source of data on income. Each year the heads of the households in the sample were asked detailed questions on wages, asset income, transfer income, business income, and much more. Unfortunately, in a number of instances the data on the computer tape were bracketed into ranges rather than presented in raw form. It was necessary in such cases to estimate the actual dollar amount of income by interpolating between categories and extrapolating in the open-ended category. The method for this estimation procedure is presented in Wright (1976b, pp. 162–64).

On the basis of these diverse income data, five income variables were constructed: total annual taxable income in 1974, "permanent" income, nonwage income in 1974, wage income in 1974 (earnings), and imputed hourly wage. In each case these variables refer to the head of household's income before taxes. Since the results using these alternative income measures were virtually identical in nearly all cases, the analysis reported in this study is limited to the first income variable. Formal definitions of the other measures and the regression results using them can be found in Wright (1976b).

Oddly enough, the PSID data tape did not actually contain a variable for the head's total annual income. It was necessary, therefore, to construct this variable from several others—total family taxable income (FI), head's labor income (HLI), wife's labor income (WLI), and wife's asset income (WAI). No composite head's asset income variable was available. "Labor income" represents wage and salary earnings plus a part of business income.[1] Of these, only WAI had to be estimated from a bracketed variable. Since in general the wife's asset income only amounted to a few thousand dollars at most, the error introduced by this estimation should not be terribly significant. In principle, the head's total annual income is equal to: FI − WLI − WAI. The difficulty is that the raw score variables are truncated at $99,999. As a result it is possible for the actual total annual income of the head to be much higher than $99,999 and yet for the expression FI − WLI − WAI to be much less than this. Thus, the following convention was adopted: if the head's labor income is greater than FI − WLI − WAI, then the head's total income is set equal to the head's labor income; otherwise it is set equal to FI − WLI − WAI. Since in fact very few individuals in the survey have incomes in excess of $99,999, little distortion is introduced by this procedure.[2]

Total annual taxable income thus includes the head's income from rents, interest, assets, wages, salaries, bonuses, businesses, and most other taxable sources. Taxable income does not include transfer payments such as social security, welfare, or scholarships, which are not taxed. The result is that the total income of the poor will be somewhat understated. In terms of our analysis this will probably tend to *increase* the returns to education among workers, and thus, if anything, would tend to reduce the hypothesized differences between classes.[3]

[1]The Panel Study apportioned business income into an imputed-earnings component and a return-on-investment component in the following way. The total number of hours worked in a year by the businessman was calculated; he/she was then arbitrarily "credited" with $1 for each of these hours. This figure was then subtracted from total business income. The remainder was then divided in two parts: half was added to the $1 × number-of-hours-worked to produce a total "labor part of business income," and the other half was considered the asset part of business income. Similar procedures were used to apportion rent, farm income, income from roomers, and other "mixed" incomes (see ISR, 1972, pp. 307–8 for a more detailed discussion). As far as I am aware, there is no real theoretical rationale for any of these procedures.

[2]The alternative to this procedure for estimating the head's total income would have been to add income from rent, interest, bonuses, businesses, etc., to the head's labor income. Since each of these variables except for HLI was bracketed, this would have involved considerably more error than the procedure adopted.

[3]The omission of untaxed transfer income from the income variable will probably increase the income returns to education among workers since it would be expected that such transfer income would be most significant among less educated sections of the working class.

The total taxable income variable also does not systematically include realized capital gains. A question was included in the study on windfall income ("Did you get any other money in 1974—like a big settlement from an insurance company or an inheritance?") and people were asked more generally if they had income from any unspecified source in 1974. Although some realized that capital gains may have been included in the responses to these questions, it is unlikely that such income is generally included in the taxable income variable. Unrealized capital gains are totally excluded. As a result, the income of employers and perhaps managers will be somewhat understated by this variable.

Income in the SWC and QES Data

Neither of these data sets contained as elaborate data on income as the Panel Study. The income variable is simply measured as total personal income of the respondent in raw dollars.

A Note on the Form of the Income Variable

Throughout this study, the income variables will be used in raw, unlogged dollars. The coefficients in equations using unlogged dollars are much more easily interpretable than in equations using logarithmic transformations of income. In the unlogged equation, the coefficient for the education variables tells you how much additional income would be expected for an increase of one unit of education. In the logged equation, the coefficient tells you approximately what the percentage increase would be. Unless the theory on which the equations are based is couched in terms of proportional increases (i.e., rates of return rather than absolute returns), the unlogged equations are more immediately understandable. Since the hypotheses developed in chapter 4 are all based on an analysis of absolute returns to education, the unlogged form of the equation is more appropriate for the task at hand.[4]

[4]Within a human capital framework, where education is viewed as an "investment" in human capital quite analogous to investment in physical capital, it makes some sense to estimate a parameter which can be viewed as the human capital analogue to interest rates (i.e., rates of return to education). In our analysis, however, the education coefficients using unlogged income are much more immediately interpretable in terms of the hypotheses we are testing, and thus raw income will be used.

It should be noted that in a number of cases, the use of natural logarithms does make a difference in our results. For example, in the comparisons of blacks and whites, when unlogged income is used, white males as a whole have significantly larger education coefficients than black males. When logged income is used, white males have signifi-

If the relationship between education and income were in fact highly nonlinear, then this use of unlogged income could indeed generate some serious distortions in the results. The linear approximation of a nonlinear relationship could seriously underestimate the returns to education for more highly educated individuals, and since there is a relationship between education and class, this could distort some of our class comparisons. As is indicated in chapter 6, however, the relationship between the education variable and unlogged income is quite linear, and thus this should not be a serious problem.

EDUCATION

Education is measured by a quasi-credential scale rather than by years of education, in the following manner:

0 = no schooling or illiterate
1 = some elementary school
2 = completed elementary school
3 = some high school
4 = high school
5 = high school plus nonacademic training
6 = some college
7 = college degree
8 = graduate training

Each step in this scale represents a socially recognized level of education. In practice, it is highly unlikely that any of the results of this study would have been different if years of education had been used instead, but sociologically a credential is a more meaningful unit of education than a year.[5]

---

cantly smaller coefficients than black males. Given that black males have lower absolute incomes than white males at every level of education, this difference in results is hardly surprising. Since the education coefficient in an equation predicting logged income roughly indicates the proportional increase in income for a unit increase in education, a smaller absolute increase among blacks in the raw income equation can easily produce a greater *rate* of increase in the logged income equation. The choice of which form of the income variable to use should therefore be based on the substantive theoretical problems being investigated. Again, since the hypotheses in chapter 3 are structured around raw income, we will use this form of the variable throughout our analysis.

[5]There is no general consensus in research on income inequality whether years or quasi-credentials of education constitute a more appropriate variable. In fact, the question is almost never even raised. From a theoretical point of view, if one adopts a human capital perspective on the relationship of education to income, in which income is seen

Education will be used in regression equations in two forms, first as the single, nine-level scale presented above, and second, as a series of six dummy variables. When the dummy variables are used, the left-out category will be levels 0–2 in the above scale, i.e., elementary school or less education.

The QES and SWC data use essentially the same scale, except that no distinction is made between high school and high school with additional nonacademic training.

STATUS

Occupational status is measured by the standard Duncan status scale adjusted for the 1970 census occupational categories (see Featherman et al., 1975, appendix B). In the Panel Study, the three-digit occupation codes were recorded only for the 1974 interview year. Since this is the year during which the income reported in the 1975 interview was earned, there is no particular disadvantage in not having the three-digit codes for the 1975 interview year. In effect, we have the occupational status for each individual at the beginning of the year in which we have income data, and the class position at the end of the year (i.e., beginning of the following year).

Approximately 8% of the sample were split-offs in the 1975 interview year (i.e., heads of new households), and thus three-digit occupation codes from 1974 were unavailable. In these cases, only one-digit occupational codes were available for the 1975 interview year. For these individuals the mean status scores for the one-digit occupational code were used. In the SWC data, only decile status scores were available.

JOB SENIORITY

Job seniority or job tenure is a simple measure of the number of years worked on the current job. For employed people, this is the number of years working for current employer; for self-employed people, it is the number of years in the present business.

---

as a return to real increments of skill level, expertise, etc., then years of education is probably the better variable. If, on the other hand, one views education primarily as a certification process used in job recruitment screening, then the quasi-credential version of the variable is more appropriate. At any rate, both versions have been extensively used in the literature.

This variable has a very different theoretical meaning in the perspective underlying our analysis than in standard economic treatments of job tenure. Specifically, in human capital theory, seniority would be viewed as a proxy for the experience gained within a particular job setting, and thus as a measure of productivity. In our analysis, on the other hand, job tenure is more central to the social control logic of income, since seniority pay increases constitute one of the basic devices for structuring inducements into jobs.

AGE

The variable "age" has a double meaning in income determination models. On the one hand, age is a fairly good measure of labor market experience, especially for the analysis of income among men (in the PSID data, the correlation between age and actual number of years worked is .94). Within the general human capital framework such experience would be considered another ingredient in productivity. But age is also a proxy for history, for the specific historical conditions that have shaped the economic lives of successive cohorts. When sociologists control for age in studies of income inequality and status attainment, the rationale is usually a concern for cohort effects rather than a desire to control for labor market experience as such.

In the present research, it does not particularly matter which of these interpretations of age is used. We are less interested in studying age effects in their own right than in showing that the class effects are not simply artifacts of age distributions within classes.

FAMILY BACKGROUND

The Panel Study contained three family background questions which we will use: father's education, father's occupation, and "average" parental economic situation. The first of these is measured on the same scale as respondent's education. Father's occupation appears only as a one-digit occupation code. This code was converted to a status score by attributing the mean occupational status to each occupational category. This is clearly a mediocre measure of occupational status, but it is the best available in the present data. Finally, average parental economic situation during the respondent's childhood consists of a three-point scale:

1 = parents were generally poor
2 = parents were generally about average
3 = parents were generally well off

As in the case of age and status, we will not be particularly concerned with class differences in these background variables, but will mainly use them as controls.

Neither the QES nor the SWC data contained any background information at all.

ANNUAL HOURS WORKED

When total annual income is a dependent variable one obvious source of variation is the total number of hours worked during the year. This variable was calculated by asking respondents how many weeks they worked in the previous year and how many hours, on the average, they worked per week. Although this variable undoubtedly is subject to considerable measurement error, it will enable us to see whether or not any of the class differences are simply consequences of the amount of time spent earning the income.

NUMBER OF EMPLOYEES

Small employers were asked how many people they employed. This variable was scaled:

0 = none
1 = 1–2 employees
2 = 3–5 employees
3 = 6–9 employees
4 = 10–19 employees
5 = 20–49 employees
6 = 50–99 employees
7 = 100–499 employees
8 = 500 or more

No subject in the study had 500 or more employees, so the practical maximum of the scale is level 7.

APPENDIX C

Statistical Procedures

STATISTICAL TESTS

Most of the hypotheses presented in chapter 3 constitute hypotheses about interactions between class and various other variables. The standard statistical approach for dealing with such problems is the analysis of covariance. I compared the various class categories and the sex and race categories within classes in terms of a series of regression equations to see: (a) if they differed significantly in the slopes of the independent variables in the equations, especially education; and (b) if a significant "gap" in income existed between the compared groups when the independent variables were held constant. Figure C.1 illustrates these two kinds of comparisons for the simple regression of income on education for managers and workers.

The test for the significance of slope differences simply involves testing whether the slope of the manager minus worker education coefficient is significantly different from zero. The conventional procedure for such a test is to pool the groups being compared into a single sample, construct a dummy variable that is equal to 1 for one of the groups and zero for the other, and then estimate a regression equation which contains as independent variables all of the original independent variables, all of the original independent variables multiplied by the dummy variable, and the dummy variable itself. It is quite simple to show that in such an equation the coefficients of the dummy variable interaction terms constitute the difference between the coefficients of the independent variable for the two groups (see Kmenta, 1971, pp. 419–23). Thus a simple t-test on these dummy variable interaction terms constitutes a test of the slope differences between the groups in question.

This is a rather cumbersome procedure, since it involves constructing large correlation matrices consisting of all the independent variables and dummy interactions. Furthermore, separate matrices must be calculated for every comparison being made. A much simpler procedure is simply to treat the coefficients of the independent variables in the regressions for the two groups being compared as normally distributed variables with expected values equal to the coefficient, and then to perform a direct t-test of their difference. Suppose we estimate the simple regression of income on education for two groups:

Group 1: Income $= a_1 + b_1$ Education;
Group 2: Income $= a_2 + b_2$ Education.

The direct t-test is then

$$t = \frac{b_1 - b_2}{(se_{b_1}^2 + se_{b_2}^2)^{1/2}}$$

where se_{b1} and se_{b2} are the standard errors of the coefficients b_1 and b_2, respectively. The conventional dummy-variable interaction strategy uses the following t-test:

$$t = \frac{b_1 - b_2}{[(v_1 se_{b_1}^2 + v_2 se_{b_2}^2)/(v_1 + v_2)]^{1/2}}$$

where v_1 and v_2 are the degrees of freedom for groups 1 and 2, respectively. This t-value is always greater than or equal to the simpler way of calculating t, and thus if anything the simpler t-test is a more conservative procedure.[1] We will use the simpler t-test throughout the analysis of the PSID data.

[1] A discussion of the relationship between the t-test we will use and the t-test proposed by Mallinvaud (1966, pp. 304–6), can be found in Wright (1976b, pp. 165–67).

The analysis of the QES and SWC data was completed before I was aware of the advantages of this simpler t-test. Since in general the two tests produce the same results, and the dummy variable interaction approach is the usual method anyway, it did not seem necessary to redo the entire analysis using the direct t-test.

The analysis of "gaps" in income, controlling for values on the independent variables, poses rather different problems from the analysis of slope differences. The difficulty is that the magnitude of this gap is strictly dependent upon the level of the independent variables at which it is evaluated. Thus, in Figure C.1, if managers and workers were compared at zero education (the usual constant term in regression equations), the gap would be slightly negative; if they were compared at the workers' mean education ($\bar{E}_w$), the gap would be positive but relatively small; if they were compared at the managers' mean education ($\bar{E}_m$), the gap would be positive and large.

Probably the most common convention in such exercises is to evaluate the gap at the level of the independent variables equal to the means for the hypothesized privileged group. Thus, when Duncan (1969) examines how much of the total difference in mean income between blacks and whites can be attributed to differences in the values of the independent variables for the two races, he substitutes the white mean values into the black equation and examines what the expected income would be. This procedure serves the polemical point of showing what the incomes of a disadvantaged group would be if they were not disadvantaged in their personal characteristics (education, age, experience, IQ, etc.) but were still disadvantaged in their ability to transform those personal characteristics into outcomes (money, occupations, etc.).

We are less interested in revealing what a worker's income would be if he or she had all the personal characteristics of a manager than in examining the differences between the working class and the managerial category as structural positions within class relations. This means that the income gap should be evaluated at an average level of the independent variables rather than at the means of the privileged category. This will be accomplished by assessing the gap in incomes at the average of the means of the two groups being compared. The income gap at this point represents the expected difference in income between a worker and a manager with identical education equal to the average of the mean worker and mean manager education. We will refer to the comparison of expected incomes at this point as the analysis of the "average gap" in income between the groups being compared.

If the constant term in the regression equations is shifted to the point at which we want to assess the income gap, then the statistical

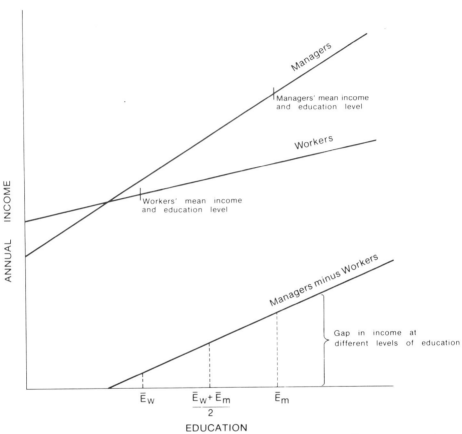

Figure C.1. Illustration of method of structural comparisons. $\bar{E}w$ = mean worker education; $\bar{E}m$ = mean manager education; $(\bar{E}_w + \bar{E}_m)/2$ = level of education at which the gap in income will be evaluated.

test for the significance of the income gap is simply a t-test of the difference in constant terms for the groups being compared. This t-test can be calculated in the same manner as in the slope comparisons.[2]

Since the average income gap is assessed at a different level of the

___

[2]In computer packages like SPSS where the correlation matrix and the accompanying means and standard deviations of the variables can easily be output on cards, it becomes very simple to perform a large number of different comparisons among a series of groups. All that is necessary is to change the means on the independent variables from their true values to an adjusted value corresponding to the point at which one wants to assess the income gap. When this is done, the constant term in regression equations calculated from the correlation matrix using these adjusted means becomes the adjusted constant discussed above.

independent variables in each comparison, it is not possible to directly compare average income gaps across different comparisons. This is particularly a problem when different groups have very different slopes (e.g., workers and managers), since in this case the income gap increases as you evaluate it at higher levels of the independent variables. In order to compare gaps across comparisons it is thus necessary to assess the gap at the same point on all comparisons. We will, therefore, also calculate a "standardized income gap" by assessing the gap at the level of the independent variables of employers, the most "privileged" category in our analysis.

In the original analysis of the QES and SWC data in a paper by Wright and Perrone (1975), the income gaps were assessed at the overall sample means for each of the independent variables rather than at the average of the means for the groups being compared. Since, in practice, it makes little difference which of these two conventions is adopted, the income gaps for the SWC data will not be recalculated using the procedure described above.

Since all of the hypotheses spelled out in chapter 4 posit a specific direction for the differences being tested, one-tailed t-tests will be used throughout the analysis. In general the differences being examined are large, and few if any of the conclusions would have been different if a more conservative two-tailed test had been adopted.

A NOTE ON WEIGHTING AND MISSING DATA

All of the regression equations in the Panel Study will be estimated using the weighted sample. In order to avoid inflating the sample size in a given regression (and thus decreasing the standard errors of the regression coefficients), the weights for the subjects included in a particular regression will be divided by the mean weight for those subjects. The N for a regression equation will thus be very close to the true number of cases included in the regression.

Missing data in the regressions were handled through pairwise rather than casewise deletion (i.e., the correlation coefficients on which the regressions were based were each calculated for all cases for which data were available on both variables in the correlation). The usual procedure when using pairwise deletion is to take the lowest N in any of the correlations as the N for the regression equation as a whole. However, since we are substantively interested mainly in the coefficient for the education variable and in the adjusted constant term, the N in the correlation of education and income will be used.

POSSIBLE BIASES DUE TO RESTRICTIONS
OF THE SAMPLES

All of the data used in this study are restricted to active, working participants in the labor force. This undoubtedly introduces certain biases. Most obviously, since most unemployed people belong in the working class, our estimates of the class distribution will somewhat understate the size of the working class.

This restriction of the sample may also tend to bias some of the results for returns to education. Under most circumstances, the rate of unemployment is especially high among less educated people. The exclusion of the unemployed from the analysis will thus tend to bias the returns to education *downward* (if the unemployed had been included, the expected income of poorly educated individuals would be less, and thus the returns to education greater). Conceivably, this might affect some of our class comparisons, since this bias is undoubtedly greater in the working class than in other classes. On the other hand, as already indicated in the discussion of the income variables, the exclusion of transfer income probably tends to increase the returns to education among workers. While there is no reason to assume that these two biases in fact cancel each other out, it does seem unlikely that the net bias in returns to education is terribly large because of the restrictions on the sample.

PRESENTATION OF RESULTS

Rather than encumber the text with endless tables and figures, I have presented only data that are directly discussed in the analysis, and have, therefore, excluded the tables of correlation matrices upon which the regression equations are based. These matrices, along with complete results for all the different income-dependent variables and complete results for the SWC and QES data, can be found in Wright (1976b, pp. 289–375).

References

Alexander, K. L., Eckland, B. K., and Griffin, L. J. 1975. The Wisconsin model of socioeconomic achievement: A replication. *American Journal of Sociology*, 81(2), 324–342.

Althusser, L. 1970a. *For Marx*. Trans. by B. Brewster. New York: Vintage Press.

———. 1970b. From "Capital" to Marx's Philosophy. In Althusser and Balibar, 1970. Pp. 11–70.

———, and Balibar, E. 1970. *Reading Capital*. Trans. by B. Brewster. London: New Left Books.

Balibar, E. 1970. The basic concepts of historical materialism. In Althusser and Balibar, 1970. Pp. 199–308.

Barber, B. 1957. *Social stratification*. New York: Harcourt, Brace and World.

Baudelot, C., Establet, R., and Malemort, J. 1974. *La petite bourgeoisie en France*. Paris: Maspero.

Becker, G. S. 1971. *The economics of discrimination*. 2nd ed. Chicago: University of Chicago Press.

_____. 1975. *Human capital*. New York: National Bureau of Economic Research.

Bell, D. 1973. *The coming of post-industrial society*. New York: Basic Books.

Benston, M. 1969. The political economy of women's liberation. *Monthly Review*, *21*(4), 13–27.

Bertaux, D. 1977. *Destins personnels et structure de classe*. Paris: Presses Universitaires de France.

Bettelheim, C. 1975. *Economic calculation and forms of property*. Trans. by J. Taylor. New York: Monthly Review Press.

Bhaskar, R. 1975. *A realist theory of science*. Leeds: Leeds Books.

Bielby, W. T., and Kalleberg, A. L. 1975. The differentiation of occupations. Paper presented at American Sociological Association Annual Meeting, August.

Blau, P., and Duncan, O. D. 1967. *The American occupational structure*. New York: Wiley.

Bluestone, B. A. 1974. *The personal earnings distribution: Individual and institutional determinants*. Social Welfare Regional Research Institute, Boston College, Publication 20.

Bourdieu, P. 1977. *Reproduction in education, society, and culture*. Trans. R. Nice. Beverly Hills, Cal.: Sage Publications.

Bowles, S., and Gintis, H. 1976. *Schooling in capitalist America*. New York: Basic Books.

Braverman, H. 1974. *Labor and monopoly capital: The degradation of work in the twentieth century*. New York: Monthly Review Press.

Browning, H., and Singelmann, J. 1978. The transformation of the U.S. labor force: The interaction of industry and occupation. *Politics and Society*, *8*(3–4).

Bukharin, N. 1921. *Historical materialism*. (Authorized English translation.) Ann Arbor: Ann Arbor Paperbacks, 1969.

Burawoy, M. 1978. Toward a Marxist theory of the labor process: Braverman and beyond, *Politics and Society*, *8*(3–4).

_____. 1979. *Manufacturing consent: Changes in the labor process under monopoly capitalism*. Chicago: University of Chicago Press. Forthcoming.

Cain, G. G. 1976. The challenge of segmented labor market theories to orthodox theory. *Journal of Economic Literature*, Dec. 1976, pp. 1215–1257.

Carchedi, G. 1977. *On the economic identification of social classes*. London: Routledge and Kegan Paul.

Carter, M. J. 1977. To abstain or not to abstain (Is that the question?): A critique of the human capital concept. In J. Schwart, ed., *The subtle anatomy of capitalism*. Santa Monica, Cal.: Goodyear Publishing Co.

Coleman, J. S., Campbell, E. O., Hobson, C. J., et al. 1966. *Equality of educational opportunity*. Washington: U.S. Office of Education.

Coulson, M., Magaś, B., and Wainwright, H. 1975. The housewife and her labor under capitalism—a critique. *New Left Review*, *89*, 59–71.

Cutler, A., Hindess, B., Hirst, P., and Hussain, A. 1977. *Marx's Capital and capitalism today*. London: Routledge and Kegan Paul.

Dahrendorf, R. 1959. *Class and class conflict in industrial society*. Palo Alto, Cal.: Stanford University Press.

Davis, K., and Moore, W. E. 1945. Some principles of stratification. *American Sociological Review*, *10*, 242–249.

De Vroey, M. 1975. The separation of ownership and control in large corporations. *The Review of Radical Political Economics*, *7*(2), 1–10.

Doeringer, P., and Piore, M. 1972. *Internal labor markets and manpower analysis*. Lexington: D. C. Heath.

Dos Santos, T. T. 1970. On the concept of social class. *Science and Society*, 34(2), 166–193.

Duncan, O. D. 1969. Inheritance of poverty or inheritance of race? In D. P. Moynihan, ed., *Understanding poverty*. New York: Basic Books. Pp. 85–109.

————, Featherman, D., and Duncan, D. 1972. *Socioeconomic background and achievement*. New York: Seminar Press.

Dunkerley, D. 1975. *The foreman*. London: Routledge & Kegan Paul.

Edwards, R. C. 1972. Alienation and inequality: Capitalist relations of production in bureaucratic enterprises. Ph.D. diss., Harvard University. Publ. as Edwards (1979).

————. 1979. *Contested terrain*. New York: Basic Books. Forthcoming.

————, Reich, M., and Gordon, D. 1975. *Segmented labor markets*. Lexington: D. C. Heath.

Esping-Anderson, D., Friedland, R., and Wright, E. O. 1976. Modes of class struggle and the capitalist state. *Kapitalistate*, no. 3–4, pp. 186–220.

Featherman, D., Sobel, M., and Dickens, D. 1975. A manual for coding occupations and industries into detailed 1970 categories and a listing of 1970-based Duncan socioeconomic and NORC prestige scores. Center for Demography and Ecology, University of Wisconsin-Madison, Working Paper 75-1.

Giddens, A. 1973. *The class structure of the advanced societies*. New York: Harper and Row.

Gold, D., Lo, C. Y. H., and Wright, E. O. 1975. Recent developments in Marxist theories of the capitalist state. *Monthly Review*, 27, 36–51.

Harrison, J. 1974. The political economy of housework. *Bulletin of the Conference of Socialist Economists*, Spring.

Hartsock, N. 1975. Women and economics. Unpublished ms., Department of Political Science, Johns Hopkins University.

Hodson, R. 1978. Labor in the monopoly, competitive, and state sectors of production. *Politics and Society*, 8(3–4).

Hope, K. 1975. Models of status inconsistency and social mobility effects. *American Sociological Review*, 40(3), 322–343.

Hudis, P. M. 1974. The determinants of earnings of men and women in the United States. Unpublished Ph.D. dissertation, University of Michigan.

Iams, H. M. 1973. The effect of sex on hourly wages. Unpublished Ph.D. dissertation, University of Michigan.

Institute for Social Research. 1972. *A panel study of income dynamics: Study design, procedures, available data, 1968–1972 interviewing years*. Vol. 1. Ann Arbor: ISR.

Jencks, C., Smith, M., Acland, H., et al. 1973. *Inequality*. New York: Harper and Row.

Keat, R., and Urry, J. 1976. *Social theory as science*. London: Routledge and Kegan Paul.

Kmenta, J. 1971. *Elements of econometrics*. New York: The Macmillan Co.

Kuhn, T. 1970. *The structure of scientific revolutions*. Chicago: University of Chicago Press.

Landecker, W. S. 1960. Class boundaries. *American Sociological Review*, 25, 868–877.

Lasswell, T. 1965. *Class and stratum: An introduction to concepts and research*. Boston: Houghton Mifflin.

Lenin, V. I. 1914. A great beginning. In *The essentials of Lenin*. London: Lawrence and Wishart, 1947.

Lenski, G. 1966. *Power and privilege: A theory of social stratification*. New York: McGraw-Hill.

Lipset, S. M. 1968. Social stratification: Social class. *International Encyclopedia of the Social Sciences*.

Mallinvaud, E. 1966. *Statistical methods of econometrics*. Chicago: Rand McNally.

Marglin, S. 1974. What do bosses do? The origins and function of hierarchy in capitalist production. *Review of Radical Political Economics*, 6(2), 60–112.

Marx, K. 1859. *Preface to a contribution to the critique of political economy*. In K. Marx and F. Engels, *Selected works*. New York: International Publishing, 1972. Pp. 181–185.

———. 1867. *Capital*, vol. 1. New York: Modern Library, 1906; New York; New World Paperbacks, 1967.

———, and Engels, F. 1972. *Ireland and the Irish question*. New York: International Publishers.

Masters, S. 1975. *Black-white income differentials*. New York: Academic Press.

Mayer, K., and Buckley, W. B. 1970. *Class and society*. 3rd ed. New York: Random House.

Mincer, J. 1970. The distribution of labor incomes: A survey. *Journal of Economic Literature*, 8(1), 1–26.

Mok, A. L. 1978. Occupations and class in advanced industrial societies. Paper presented at American Sociological Association Annual Meeting, September.

Noble, D. 1978. The social choice in machine design, the case of automatically-controlled machine tools, and a challenge for labor. *Politics and Society*, 8(3–4).

Ossowski, S. 1963. *Class structure in the social consciousness*. London: Routledge and Kegan Paul.

Parkin, F. 1971. *Class inequality and political order*. New York: Praeger.

Parsons, T. 1970. Equality and inequality in modern society, or social stratification revisited. In E. O. Lauman, ed., *Social stratification: Research and theory for the 1970s*. Indianapolis: Bobbs-Merrill.

Plant, R. 1978. Community: Concept, conception, and ideology. *Politics and Society*, 8(1), 79–107.

Poulantzas, N. 1973a. On social classes. *New Left Review*, 78, 27–54.

———. 1973b. *Political power and social class*. London: New Left Books.

———. 1975. *Classes in contemporary capitalism*. London: New Left Books.

Przeworski, A. 1977. Proletariat into a class: The process of class formation from Karl Kautsky's *The class struggle* to recent controversies. *Politics and Society*, 7(4), 343–401.

Reich, M. 1971. The economics of racism. In D. M. Gordon, ed., *Problems of political economy*. Lexington: D. C. Heath. Pp. 107–113.

———. 1973. Racial discrimination and the white income distribution. Unpub. Ph.D. dissertation, Harvard University.

Roach, J. M. 1973. *Worker participation: New voices in management*. Report no. 594. New York: The Conference Board.

Rush, H. M. F. 1971. *Job design for motivation: Experiments in job enlargement and job enrichment*. Report no. 515. New York: The Conference Board.

Secombe, W. 1974. The housewife and her labour under capitalism. *New Left Review*, 83, 3–24.

Sewell, W. H., and Hauser, R. M. 1975. *Education, occupation and earnings: Achievement in the early career*. New York: Academic Press.

Siegel, P. 1965. On the costs of being a negro. *Sociological Inquiry*, 35, 41–57.

Stodder, J. 1973. Old and new working class. *Socialist Revolution*, 17, 99–110.

Stolzenberg, R. H. 1973. Occupational differences in wage discrimination against black men: The structure of racial differences in men's wage returns to schooling, 1960. Unpublished Ph.D. dissertation, University of Michigan.

————. 1975a. Education, occupation and wage differences between white and black men. *American Journal of Sociology*, 81(2), 299–323.

————. 1975b. Occupations, labor markets and the process of wage attainment. *American Sociological Review*, 40(5), 645–665.

Stone, K. 1974. The origins of job structure in the steel industry. *Review of Radical Political Economics*, 6(2), 113–173.

Suter, L. E., and Miller, H. P. 1973. Income differences between men and career women. *American Journal of Sociology*, 48(4), 962–974.

Sweezy, P. 1942. *The theory of capitalist development*. New York: Monthly Review Press.

————. 1974. Some problems in the theory of capital accumulation. *Monthly Review*, 26(1), 38–55.

Szymanski, A. 1972. Trends in the American class structure. *Socialist Revolution*, 10, 101–122.

————. 1973. Response to Stodder. *Socialist Revolution*, 17, 110–118.

————. 1976. Racial discrimination and white gain. *American Sociological Review*, 41(3), 403–14.

Tannenbaum, A. S., Kavčič, B., Rosner, M., et al. 1974. *Hierarchy in organizations*. San Francisco: Jossey-Bass.

Thurow, L. C. 1967. Causes of poverty. *Quarterly Journal of Economics*, 81, 323–42.

————. 1975. *Generating inequality*. New York: Basic Books.

Touraine, A. 1971. The post-industrial society. Trans. by L. F. X. Mayhew. New York: Random House.

Treiman, D. J. 1977. *Occupational prestige in comparative perspective*. New York: Academic Press.

————, and Terrell, K. 1975. Sex and the process of status attainment: A comparison of working women and men. *American Sociological Review*, 40(2), 174–200.

Warner, W. L. 1949. Social class in America. New York: Harper and Row.

Weber, M. 1922. *Economy and society*, ed. Gunther Roth. New York: Bedminster Press, 1968.

Weiss, R. 1970. The effect of education on the earnings of blacks and whites. *Review of Economics and Statistics*, 52(2), 150–159.

Wiles, P. J. 1974. *Distribution of income, east and west*. Amsterdam: North-Holland.

Wiley, N. 1967. America's unique class politics. *American Sociological Review*, 32(4), 529–541.

Williams, R. M., Jr. 1960. *American society: A sociological interpretation*. 2nd ed. New York: Alfred A. Knopf.

Woodward, J. 1965. *Industrial organization*. Oxford: Oxford University Press.

Wright, E. O. 1975. Alternative perspectives in the Marxist theory of accumulation and crisis. *The Insurgent Sociologist*, 6(1), 5–39.

————. 1976a. Class boundaries in advanced capitalism. *New Left Review*, 98, 3–41.

————. 1976b. Class structure and income inequality. Unpub. Ph.D. dissertation, University of California, Berkeley. (An earlier version of this book.)

————. 1978a. *Class, crisis and the state*. London: New Left Books.

————. 1978b. Class, occupation, and organization. Paper presented at American Sociological Association Annual Meeting, September.

————. 1978c. Intellectuals and the working class. *The Insurgent Sociologist*, 8(1), 5–18.

————. 1978d. Race, class, and income inequality. *American Journal of Sociology*, 83(6), 1368–1397.

————. 1978e. Varieties of Marxist conceptions of class structure. Institute for Research on Poverty Discussion Paper 524–78.

————, and Perrone, L. 1975. Classi sociale, scuola, occupazione e reddito in U.S.A.: Una analisi quantitativa sulla disequaglianze sociale in una societa post-industriale. *Quaderni di Sociologia*, 24(1–2), 55–91.

————, and Perrone, L. 1977. Marxist class categories and income inequality. *American Sociological Review*, 42(1), 32–55.

————. and Singelmann, J. 1978. Proletarianization in advanced capitalist societies: An empirical intervention into the debate between Marxist and post-industrial theories. Institute for Research on Poverty Discussion Paper 519–78.

Zeitlin, M. 1974. Corporate ownership and control: The large corporation and the capitalist class. *American Journal of Sociology*, 79(5), 1073–1119.

Zimbalist, A. 1975. The limits of work humanization. *Review of Radical Political Economics*, 7(2), 50–59.

Index

Institute for Research on Poverty
Monograph Series

Erik Olin Wright, *Class Structure and Income Determination*. 1979

Joel F. Handler, *Social Movements and the Legal System: A Theory of Law Reform and Social Change*. 1979

Duane E. Leigh, *An Analysis of the Determinants of Occupational Upgrading*. 1978

Stanley H. Masters and Irwin Garfinkel, *Estimating the Labor Supply Effects of Income Maintenance Alternatives*. 1978

Irwin Garfinkel and Robert H. Haveman, with the assistance of David Betson, *Earnings Capacity, Poverty, and Inequality*. 1977

Harold W. Watts and Albert Rees, Editors, *The New Jersey Income—Maintenance Experiment, Volume III: Expenditures, Health, and Social Behavior; and the Quality of the Evidence*. 1977

Murray Edelman, *Political Language: Words That Succeed and Policies That Fail*. 1977

Marilyn Moon and Eugene Smolensky, Editors, *Improving Measures of Economic Well-Being*. 1977

Harold W. Watts and Albert Rees, Editors, *The New Jersey Income—Maintenance Experiment, Volume II: Labor-Supply Responses*. 1977

Marilyn Moon, *The Measurement of Economic Welfare: Its Application to the Aged Poor*. 1977

Morgan Reynolds and Eugene Smolensky, *Public Expenditures, Taxes, and the Distribution of Income: The United States, 1950, 1961, 1970*. 1977

Fredrick L. Golladay and Robert H. Haveman, with the assistance of Kevin Hollenbeck, *The Economic Impacts of Tax—Transfer Policy: Regional and Distributional Effects*. 1977

David Kershaw and Jerilyn Fair, *The New Jersey Income-Maintenance Experiment, Volume I: Operations, Surveys, and Administration*. 1976

Peter K. Eisinger, *Patterns of Interracial Politics: Conflict and Cooperation in the City*. 1976

Irene Lurie, Editor, *Integrating Income Maintenance Programs*. 1975

Stanley H. Masters, *Black–White Income Differentials: Empirical Studies and Policy Implications.* 1975

Larry L. Orr, *Income, Employment, and Urban Residential Location.* 1975

Joel F. Handler, *The Coercive Social Worker: British Lessons for American Social Services.* 1973

Glen G. Cain and Harold W. Watts, Editors, *Income Maintenance and Labor Supply: Econometric Studies.* 1973

Charles E. Metcalf, *An Econometric Model of Income Distribution.* 1972

Larry L. Orr, Robinson G. Hollister, and Myron J. Lefcowitz, Editors, with the assistance of Karen Hester, *Income Maintenance: Interdisciplinary Approaches to Research.* 1971

Robert J. Lampman, *Ends and Means of Reducing Income Poverty.* 1971

Joel F. Handler and Ellen Jane Hollingsworth, *"The Deserving Poor": A Study of Welfare Administration.* 1971

Murray Edelman, *Politics as Symbolic Action: Mass Arousal and Quiescence.* 1971

Frederick Williams, Editor, *Language and Poverty: Perspectives on a Theme.* 1970

Vernon L. Allen, Editor, *Psychological Factors in Poverty.* 1970

Institute for Research on Poverty
Poverty Policy Analysis Series

Timothy Bates and William Bradford, *Financing Black Economic Development.* 1979

Joel F. Handler, *Protecting The Social Service Client: Legal and Structural Controls on Official Discretion.* 1979

Joel F. Handler, Ellen Jane Hollingsworth, and Howard S. Erlanger, *Lawyers and the Pursuit of Legal Rights* 1978

Maurice MacDonald, *Food, Stamps, and Income Maintenance.* 1978

Robert H. Haveman, Editor, *A Decade of Federal Antipoverty Programs: Achievements, Failures, and Lessons.* 1977

Robert D. Plotnick and Felicity Skidmore, *Progress Against Poverty: A Review of the 1964–1974 Decade.* 1975